Business Transformation Essentials

Business Transformation Essentials

Case Studies and Articles

Edited by

AXEL UHL *and* LARS ALEXANDER GOLLENIA

GOWER

Gower Applied Business Research
Our programme provides leaders, practitioners, scholars and researchers with thought provoking, cutting edge books that combine conceptual insights, interdisciplinary rigour and practical relevance in key areas of business and management.

Published by
Gower Publishing Limited
Wey Court East
Union Road
Farnham
Surrey, GU9 7PT
England

Ashgate Publishing Company
110 Cherry Street
Suite 3-1
Burlington, VT 05401-3818
USA

www.gowerpublishing.com

British Library Cataloguing in Publication Data
A catalogue record for this book is available from the British Library

Library of Congress Cataloging-in-Publication Data
(Applied for)

ISBN: 9781472426987 (hbk)
ISBN: 9781472426994 (ebook – PDF)
ISBN: 9781472427007 (ebook – ePUB)

Printed in the United Kingdom by Henry Ling Limited, at the Dorset Press, Dorchester, DT1 1HD

Contents

List of Figures

List of Tables and Boxes

Tables

Boxes

About the Editors

Prof. Dr Axel Uhl is the co-founder and Head of the Business Transformation Academy. He is also a member of the Business Transformation Services Leadership Team within the Services Division of SAP. Dr Uhl is a professor at the University of Applied Sciences and Arts Northwestern Switzerland. Prior to joining SAP, Prof. Uhl worked in senior management positions at Novartis, KPMG, DaimlerChrysler and Allianz. He holds a PhD in economics, and master degrees in business administration, educational sciences and information technology.

Lars Alexander Gollenia is Head of Business Transformation Services at SAP and a member of the SAP Services Delivery Executive team. Business Transformation Services is a global Line of Service with a local presence in all geographies. He is the co-founder and sponsor of the Business Transformation Academy, a global thought leadership network comprising leading academics and selected executives of Fortune 2.000 companies. He has held a number of positions in the management consulting space. Prior to his current role he was responsible for Business Consulting in the EMEA region. Gollenia is a graduate in business administration from the Friedrich-Schiller University of Jena, Germany and studied economics and international management at Harvard University in Boston, USA.

List of Contributors

Prof. Paola Bielli, Bocconi University
Paola Bielli is Professor of Information Systems at Bocconi University in Milan (Italy). She is a faculty member of the Management and Technology Department at Bocconi University and of the Information Systems Unit of the SDA Bocconi School of Management. Her current research and teaching interests include ICT in small businesses, IS governance and ICT financial management, offshoring, and ICT-based innovation. Contact: paola.bielli@unibocconi.it

Beate Brüggemann and Rainer Riehle, Institute for International Social Research
Beate Brüggemann and Rainer Riehle head the Institute for International Social Research (INFIS), whose work includes studies into conditions and requirements for changes in operational structures, from small workshops to large companies, and also into problems of regional, cross-border development potential. Contact: brueggemann@infis.eu

Lilian Corvington, Vodafone
Lilian Corvington is the Global Implementation Lead for EVO and 3TM and has directed several similar large-scale programs world-wide. Previously, she was Director of Global Transformation and Process Management at Alcatel-Lucent. She has been an independent management consultant and a partner at Deloitte & Touche earlier in her career, with a focus in the Telecom and Retail industries. Lilian has two Masters Degrees: MBA/MIS and Manufacturing Production Planning. Contact: lilian.corvington@vodafone.com

Joachim Follmann, Mercedes-Benz
Joachim Follmann started his career with Daimler in 1988. He held several functions in production planning and corporate strategy. In 2000 he took over the planning for Mercedes-Benz C-, E- and S-Class and cost planning. From 2005 until 2009 he headed the manufacturing division of Mercedes-Benz South Africa. Since end of 2009 he is responsible for the Mercedes-Benz production strategy as well as the Mercedes-Benz Production System. Contact: joachim.follmann@daimler.com

Dr Gabriel Giordano, Ohio University
Gabriel Giordano is an Assistant Professor of Management Information Systems in the College of Business at Ohio University. He was formerly an Assistant Professor of Information Systems at IESE Business School. Gabriel's current research looks at virtual work teams, computer-based deception, communication in computer-mediated work settings, and transformational enterprise systems. His work has been published in top academic and practitioner outlets, and it has been reported about by major TV, radio, newspaper, and web news outlets. Contact: giordano@ohio.edu

Annabelle (Lamy) Giordano, Ohio University
Annabelle Giordano is currently Assistant Director of the Centers of Excellence in the College of Business at Ohio University. She was previously a Field Liaison at Reid Consulting Group, and a Research Assistant at IESE Business School. She has also held numerous positions in marketing administration and development. Contact: giordana@ohio.edu

Lars Alexander Gollenia, SAP
Lars Alexander Gollenia is head of Business Transformation Services (BTS), the global management consultancy organization of SAP. Previously, Lars held various management positions in the management consulting sector. Prior to his current role he was responsible for Business Consulting for EMEA. Lars has a graduate degree in Business Administration from the Friedrich-Schiller University of Jena, Germany, and he studied strategic and international management at the Harvard University, Boston. Contact: lars.gollenia@sap.com

Robert Günther, SAP
Robert Günther is a Managing Principal at SAP and leading the Center of Expertise for Transformation Management with a focus on Organizational Change. Prior to SAP, he was a Manager at IDS Scheer AG in Business and Process Consulting where he overlooked numerous IT Transformation projects in the Automotive, Consumer Products and Manufacturing industry. He has considerable international experience from working with major clients in the US, Middle East and Japan. Contact: robert.guenther@sap.com

Oliver Hanslik, former SAP
Dipl. Kfm. Oliver Hanslik is a former researcher and an associate of the Business Transformation Academy at SAP. He studied business administration in Mannheim (Germany), Leuven (Belgium), and Seoul (South Korea).

Former to SAP, Oliver Hanslik worked for Audi, TRW, and AFS GmbH. His areas of interest are sustainability, mobility, quality and marketing management.

Prof. Dominic Houlder, London Business School
Prof. Dominic Houlder researches and advises major B2B service firms on developing C suite client relationships and more effective collaboration across lines of service, geographical boundaries and external partner organizations. He is currently working with PriceWaterhouse Coopers, G4S, Eversheds, SAP and Saatchi & Saatchi. He designed and led London Business School's new executive workout program for B2B service businesses, "Unlocking Your Client's Strategy". Contact: dhoulder@london.edu

Tomasz Janasz, SAP
Tomasz Janasz is a business administration graduate from the University of Hamburg. In 2008, he joined SAP as a business consultant with a main focus on project management, software implementation process, and quality assurance in major transformation initiatives. Since 2010, he has been a research associate at the Business Transformation Academy, where he has been given the responsibility for industry research and communication. He also co-developed the BTM². Currently, Tomasz is pursuing his PhD at the University of Wuppertal (Germany) conducting research on the innovative concepts for urban mobility. Contact: t.janasz@sap.com

Tammy Johnson, SAP
Tammy Johnson is the North Central Practice Head within Business Transformation Services in North America, leading a team of Business Transformation Principals focusing on transformation roadmaps, innovation, business architecture, and value management. She has over twenty years of consulting experience developing enterprise application strategies for global organizations requiring significant value adoption, organizational redesign and process improvement. Contact: tammy.johnson@sap.com

Lisa Kouch, SAP
Lisa Kouch is a Senior Project Manager at SAP. She is a graduate of Villanova University and is a registered Project Management Professional (PMP) with PMI. Previous to joining SAP, Lisa worked for The Amber Group and Accenture specializing in the Financials, Controlling, and Project Management areas. Contact: lisa.kouch@sap.com

Michaela Kresak[t], SAP

Michaela Kresak was SAP's Global Program Director for Vodafone, with more than 15 years of experience in the telecommunications industry, working for operators, start-up companies and large consultancies around the world. Michaela held a Master's degree from the University of Vienna and the University College Dublin, and an Executive MBA from the University of Fribourg and the Cambridge Judge Business School.

Sebastian Laack, Mercedes-Benz

Sebastian Laack is Senior Manager of Lean Administration in HR at Mercedes-Benz.

Nils Labusch, University of St. Gallen

Nils Labusch is a research assistant and PhD student at the University of St. Gallen (HSG). After graduate studies and work in Münster and New Jersey, he joined the group of Prof. Dr Winter at the Institute of Information Management in 2011. His current research topics are related to the support of business transformations and the related decisions. Contact: nils.labusch@unisg.ch

Dr Gerrit Lahrmann, BMW Group

Dr Gerrit Lahrmann is currently working at the department of Enterprise Architecture Management of BMW Group. He is a former research assistant at the Institute of Information Management at the University of St. Gallen.

Kim MacGillavry, DHL Freight

Kim MacGillavry is head of Transformation at DHL Freight and member of its management board. During the last 20 years Kim was responsible for product and service innovation in various multinational companies. By designing, developing, and launching a multitude of products and services, he gained a lot of experience in dealing with the complexities of innovation in large enterprises. Kim has a Master in Applied Economics from the University Faculty Saint-Ignatius Antwerp in Belgium. Contact: kim.macgillavry@dhl.com

Dr Matthias Messmer, Titoni Ltd.

Matthias Messmer is International PR Director of Titoni Ltd. Messmer holds an M.A. from HSG and a PhD from University of Konstanz. Before joining Titoni Ltd., he was a consultant for the Department of Foreign Affairs and a Senior Research Fellow at the University of Fribourg. He is the author of the following books: *China – West-Eastern Encounters* (2007), *Jewish Wayfarers in*

Modern China – Tragedy and Splendor (2012), and *China's Vanishing Worlds – Countryside, Traditions and Cultural Spaces*. Contact: mmessmer@titoni.ch

Uli Muench, IBM

Uli Muench is a Partner, SAP Practice in the Industrial Sector at IBM Global Business Services. Former to that, he was Vice President of Business Transformation Services at SAP America. He has held a number of leadership positions in strategy consulting, including aligning business and IT strategies, value management, value road mapping and business process optimization. He and his teams have developed global implementation and deployment strategies, and have managed programs for global clients.

Dr Oliver Müller, University of Liechtenstein

Dr Oliver Müller is Assistant Professor at the Hilti Chair of Business Process Management (BPM) at the University of Liechtenstein. Prior to his academic career, he gained industry experience as a professional consultant for supply chain management and as a visiting researcher at SAP Research. Oliver's current research interests include business process management, service research, and change and innovation management. Contact: oliver.mueller@uni.li

Jan Musil, SAP

Jan Musil has over 20 years of consulting, general management and operations experience in the IT industry. He is currently leading the Global Project Management Practice in the SAP Services organization. Jan is passionate about project management excellence; he works closely with SAP customers advising how to improve time to value through efficient use of acceleration techniques proven in SAP implementations. Since starting in SAP in 1996, Jan has held various roles in product development, quality management, customer support, consulting organization and operations in the United States, Germany and Czech Republic. Contact: jan.musil@sap.com

Joerg Noack, SAP

Joerg Noack is SAP Chief Solution Architect at SAP America Inc., with over 18 years of experience in the IT industry. He is certified as SAP Global Business Transformation Manager and engages as trusted advisor for international enterprises to master implementation of SAP Business Suite components on a global scale. Contact: joerg.noack@sap.com

Dr Martin Petry, Hilti AG
Dr Martin Petry became Hilti's CIO in 2005. He is responsible for a global team of 400 IT employees. Since 2009, he is also in charge of Hilti's Business Excellence initiatives. Martin came to Hilti in 1993 and has held various leadership roles in Liechtenstein, Switzerland, Japan, Great Britain and on a global scale since then. Martin earned his PhD in applied mathematics from Georg-August University in Göttingen.

Till Schauen, Freelance writer
Till Schauen was born in 1961 in Germany. He received Master of Arts in English and American Studies in 1992 in Frankfurt. Till has worked in various positions in the theatre for almost two decades – from 1978 till 1997. Since 1997, he has been a free-lance writer with an emphasis on automobile history. Contact: schauen@tillschauen.de

Alexander Schmid, SAP
Alexander Schmid is a junior researcher and PhD student at the SAP Business Transformation Academy. He studied management, informatics, and biology and holds a Master of Arts in Business Administration from University of Zurich, Switzerland. Prior to his work at the BTA, Alexander worked for over five years as a Business Intelligence and IT consultant. Contact: alexander.schmid01@sap.com

Dr Theresa Schmiedel, University of Liechtenstein
Dr Theresa Schmiedel is a Research Assistant at the Institute of Information Systems at the University of Liechtenstein. She holds a PhD in Business Economics from the University of Liechtenstein and a Diploma in Economics from the University of Hohenheim, Stuttgart, Germany, which she conducted partially at York University, Toronto, Canada. Her research interests focus on the role of social factors in the Information Systems discipline, particularly on the interconnection of culture and BPM. Contact: theresa.schmiedel@uni.li

Andreas Schönherr, Zurich Insurance Group Ltd.
Andreas Schönherr is the Head of Group Planning and Performance Management at Zurich Insurance Group Ltd. Prior to that, he was the Head of Global Finance Solutions and his responsibilities included the development, implementation, and support of a Global Finance Landscape. Additionally, his team was responsible for major Finance Transformation Projects and Initiatives globally. He is a graduate of Business Economics and holds Professional certifications in Project and Portfolio Management as well as Auditing. Contact: andreas.schoenherr@zurich.com

Werner Schultheis, Randstad Deutschland GmbH & Co. KG
Werner Schultheis is Director IT and Processes at Randstad Deutschland GmbH & Co. KG. Before he changed to IT and Processes, he was Director Business Development and District Manager in the sales organisation. He holds an engineering degree of the TU Darmstadt, Germany. Contact: werner. schultheis@de.randstad.com

Helmut Schütt, Mercedes-Benz
Helmut Schütt is Vice President and CIO at Mercedes-Benz Cars and Vans.

Paul Stratil, SAS Automotive Systems GmbH
Paul Stratil is Head of Corporate IT at SAS Automotive Systems GmbH. Prior to that, he worked for various affiliations of Mercedes, Daimler, Chrysler, and Smart Car in Europe, Asia, and the Americas. With his more than 25 years of experience in the field, and speaking four languages fluently, his core expertise is the optimization and re-shaping of business by using IT, innovations, process optimization, and organizational development to create business value in international contexts. Contact: paul.stratil@sas-automotive.com

Prof. Dr Stephanie Teufel, University of Fribourg
Prof. Dr Stephanie Teufel is the Director of the IIMT (International Institute of Management in Technology) at University of Fribourg, Switzerland and holds a full professorship in ICT Management at the faculty of Economics and Social Sciences. Dr Teufel has published numerous international publications in the fields of information security management, innovation and technology management as well as mobile business. Contact: stephanie.teufel@unifr.ch

Simon Townson, SAP
Simon Townson is a Chief Enterprise Architect, and Business Transformation Principal at SAP. For the last 18 years, he has worked as a lead IT consultant with a variety of industry sectors to help transform their organizations. Simon was one of the contributors to SAP's Enterprise Architecture Framework that was incorporated into TOGAF. He works as a trusted client advisor with the CTO and strategy functions of large SAP enterprise customers. Contact: simon. townson@sap.com

Prof. Dr Axel Uhl, SAP
Prof. Dr Axel Uhl is head of the Business Transformation Academy at SAP. He has been a professor at the University of Applied Sciences and Arts Northwestern Switzerland (FHNW) since 2009. Axel Uhl received his doctorate

in economics and his master in business information systems. He started his career at Allianz and worked for DaimlerChrysler IT Services, KPMG, and Novartis. His main areas of research are sustainability and IT, leadership, and business transformation management. Contact: a.uhl@sap.com

Prof. Dr Jan vom Brocke, University of Liechtenstein
Prof. Dr Jan vom Brocke holds the Hilti Chair of Business Process Management (BPM) and is Director of the Institute of Information Systems at the University of Liechtenstein. Jan has more than 15 years of experience in BPM projects and has published more than 170 peer-reviewed papers in the proceedings of internationally perceived conferences and renowned academic journals, including *Management Information Systems Quarterly (MISQ)*. He is author and editor of 15 books including *Springer's International Handbook on Business Process Management*. Contact: jan.vom.brocke@uni.li

Thomas von Alm, SAP
Thomas von Alm is head of Services Transformation Management at SAP. In this role he focuses on providing a platform to plan, execute and monitor the business transformation within SAP Services. He started his work with SAP in 2002 as consultant and holds a master degree (FH) in Business Informatics. Contact: thomas.von.alm@sap.com

Prof. John Ward, Cranfield University
Prof. John Ward is Emeritus Professor at Cranfield University, School of Management. John was Professor of Strategic Information Systems from 1992 to 2010 at Cranfield and Director of the IS Research Center from 1993–2005. He has a degree in Natural Sciences from Cambridge, is a Fellow of the Chartered Institute of Management Accountants and is a past-President of the UK Academy for Information Systems. Contact: j.m.ward@cranfield.ac.uk

Frits Wiegel, Vodafone
Frits Wiegel is the Global Head of Process Governance in EVO. He joined Vodafone in 2007. His responsibilities include the development and implementation of Vodafone's Business Process Management strategy, maintaining global process integrity and supporting EVO transformation implementation. Prior to joining Vodafone, he held the position of Corporate Process architect in Alcatel. Frits holds a Master's degree in Business Administration from Bradford University. Contact: frits.wiegel@vodafone.com

Prof. Peter Williamson, University of Cambridge

Peter Williamson is Professor of International Management and Fellow Commoner of Jesus College at the University of Cambridge. He holds a PhD from the Harvard University. He is also Non-Executive Chairman of the Board of Directors of the macro hedge fund manager Tactical Global Management. Contact: p.williamson@jbs.cam.ac.uk

Prof. Dr Robert Winter, University of St. Gallen

Prof. Dr Robert Winter is a fulltime professor of business and information systems engineering at the University of St. Gallen (HSG) and director of the Institute of Information Management. In addition to research in situational method engineering, he is responsible for projects and publications (over 150 journal articles and books) in areas such as enterprise architecture and transformation management. Contact: robert.winter@unisg.ch

Dr Guido Wokurka, SAP

Dr Guido Wokurka is Director at SAP and heading Business Transformation Services in Western Europe. His industry focus is on telecommunications and the energy sector, with customers in the United Kingdom, Scandinavia, the Netherlands, Switzerland, Spain, and Germany. Prior to joining SAP, he was senior manager at Alcatel (now Alcatel-Lucent). Guido holds an executive MBA degree and a PhD in natural sciences. He completed the Advanced Leadership Program at the University of Cambridge last year. Contact: guido.wokurka@sap.com

Dr Stefanie Zeitz, SAP

Dr Stefanie Zeitz is Skill Development Manager within SAP Business Transformation Consulting. Her responsibilities consist of the development of holistic skill maps, sponsorship, management, and training programs for complex business and technology areas, as well as the definition of Global Job Profiles and Career guideline standards. In the last 15 years she has completed numerous projects in the area of Business Transformation Management, Consulting Sales, and Business Development. Contact: stefanie.zeitz@sap.com

Robert Zimmermann, Berlin Phil Media GmbH

Robert Zimmermann, a management consultant and film producer with a long track record within the media industry, is the CEO of Berlin Phil Media GmbH. As manager and consultant, Mr. Zimmermann has worked on a wide variety of projects for prestigious clients such as Lufthansa, the World Bank Group and various international banks. He has held several posts as restructuring manager and is managing partner of eins54 Film GmbH.

1

Introduction

Axel Uhl (SAP) and Lars Alexander Gollenia (SAP)

The interest in managing complex transformation projects has risen significantly, since we published the *Business Transformation Management Methodology* book in 2012. This is reflected in the increasing number of publications in this field and in a more frequent application of the methodology at international companies in numerous countries throughout the world, such as SAP, DHL, and Samsung.

This interest is due, in particular, to the still low rate of success of transformation projects. Only about 30% of IT projects are completely successful (cf. Ward and Daniel 2012; Uhl and Schmid 2013) and an unusually large number of IT projects even end in total disaster (so-called black swans).

Our study results and those of other research teams show that the reasons for failure are usually very similar, and that companies have different competencies for the management of these projects. However, competencies evolve from learning processes, and learning can occur in a variety of ways. The most arduous, and painful, and also most expensive form is learning from one's own experience. If, for example, the Tollgate or Berlin Airport projects were carried out a second time, many of the mistakes that had been made the first time could be avoided.

Another form of learning is based on sharing one's experience and expert knowledge. This form of learning, which has been practiced for thousands of years, is easier, more cost effective, and helps to avoid making the same mistakes all over again.

When we – an interdisciplinary team of experts comprising practitioners, academics, and consultants – first came together six years ago, we set ourselves the target of generating more knowledge about these recurring problems in complex projects and of developing a framework that aims at helping project managers improve their project management.

A great deal has happened since this first meeting. Using dozens of in-depth case studies, our network of experts, which now consists of more than a hundred researchers, company representatives, and consultants, has developed a holistic Business Transformation Management Methodology (BTM²). This methodology is not some kind of recipe for successful transformations, but rather a methodological toolbox that takes into account the interdependence of the most important parameters and contains a variety of tools for holistic management.

Both empirical studies and case studies provided the basis for this methodology. The case studies in particular have proven to be a real treasure trove of practical knowledge. Interestingly, not only have they helped us to develop the BTM², but they have also inspired us to develop the Business Transformation Assessment. This means that we are now in a position where we can evaluate many different transformation projects at varying stages of the transformation process, make predictions about their chances of success, and make important suggestions for improvement.

The use of case studies has proven invaluable in conveying the BTM² know-how, whether in MBA courses or in the training of customers or consultants. A single case study of course does not represent scientific evidence – and this is not even our claim – but it does encourage discussion and analysis and it motivates people to take an intense look at the BTM² and explore it. This prompted the BTM² trainers, who are actively involved in teaching or in practical application to express their desire to have the case studies published in addition to the methodology book.

Besides the case studies, this book also features the results of a Transformation Management Survey conducted together with the University of St. Gallen (Switzerland) showcasing the current state of development of transformation management in practice. Additionally, we also included several articles which explain how expectations with regard to the role of IT management in transformation processes are changing and why the future CIO has to take transformation and innovation aspects into consideration. The readers of this book will also learn what about the potentials of the BTM² and how this holistic business transformation management approach corresponds with other typical methods such as Enterprise Architecture Management, TOGAF (The Open Group Architecture Framework), or ASAP (AcceleratedSAP).

The contributions presented in this book were all developed by the network of the Business Transformation Academy and represent a particularly interesting selection of case studies and articles that were published in our *360° – the Business Transformation Journal.*

We would like to take this opportunity to express our sincere gratitude to all of our authors, customers and partners and, in particular, to SAP AG and the University of Applied Sciences and Arts Northwestern Switzerland, who have given us such loyal and lasting support for so many years. Special thanks go to the entire team of the Business Transformation Academy: Tomasz Janasz, Rita Strasser, Dr Michael von Kutzschenbach, Christine Lorgé, Alexander Schmid, and Janina Berga.

Visit Business Transformation Academy at: www.bta-online.com.
More articles and case studies can be found at: www.360-bt.com.

Prof. Dr Axel Uhl and Lars Alexander Gollenia

2

Transformation Management Survey:
Current State of Development and Potential of Transformation Management in Practice

Gerrit Lahrmann (BMW Group), Robert Winter (University of St. Gallen), Axel Uhl (SAP)

A lot of global companies are currently carrying out major change projects with high strategic relevance. These transformation programs combine business and technical content where information systems and management come together. The following article explains what characterizes current transformation programs and the potential that can be leveraged by applying a holistic transformation management approach. Companies that rate themselves as mature in regard to transformation management assess certain transformation aspects differently than less mature companies.

Transformation describes the fundamental change of a company and is an effective answer to an unstable, permanently changing economic environment.[1] In light of the current economic crisis, many companies have initiated extensive transformation programs e.g. to improve profitability or better control risks. These programs often combine business and technical content by using IT investments as a basis for enabling or facilitating organizational changes.

Examples of such transformation programs that we analyzed include:

- Introduction of a new banking platform for all member companies of a banking group – program duration of two years, budget of 60 million euros
- Global standardization of corporate processes based on an integrative Enterprise Resource Planning (ERP) platform in a high-tech company – program duration of four years, budget in excess of 1 billion dollars

When a company decides that it wants or needs to initiate a transformation program, numerous questions arise. What exactly should the program achieve? What drives a successful transformation program and what prevents it from being carried out? What basic approaches are there for ensuring that a transformation program is successful?

Business practice is a good starting point for answering these and similar questions. That is why the following pages present the results of an empirical study designed to describe the current state of transformation management and point to areas in which further development can be realized.

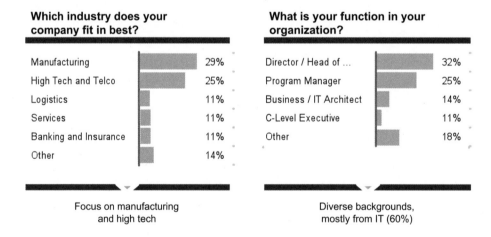

Which industry does your company fit in best?

Manufacturing	29%
High Tech and Telco	25%
Logistics	11%
Services	11%
Banking and Insurance	11%
Other	14%

Focus on manufacturing and high tech

What is your function in your organization?

Director / Head of ...	32%
Program Manager	25%
Business / IT Architect	14%
C-Level Executive	11%
Other	18%

Diverse backgrounds, mostly from IT (60%)

Figure 2.1   Characteristics of Data: Participants

Empirical Study

The study was conducted using a questionnaire. Part I involved collecting demographic information about the company representative and the company in general. In part II, details about the company's transformation program were gathered. Part III introduced a holistic transformation management approach, and the participants had to evaluate its potential. A self-assessment comprised part IV, whereby participants were asked to characterize the maturity of their company with respect to the individual components of the holistic transformation approach and specify to what extent they value each component. Additional questions targeted the completeness of the approach. Finally, in part V, open questions were asked about the aspects of transformation management not covered by the previous questions.

Representatives from 28 companies in the high-tech (25%), manufacturing (29%), banking and insurance (11%), logistics (11%) and service (11%) industries participated in the study. The questionnaire addressed managers such as program leaders, directors, and regional CIOs, in particular at large, international companies. Specialist departments and IT representatives also participated. 72% of the 28 companies in the survey are located in EMEA (Europe, Middle East and Africa), 14% in the Americas and 14% in the Asian Pacific region. More than 70% of the companies have more than 10,000 employees. Figure 2.1 summarizes the key participant characteristics.

Transformation Programs in Practice

The transformation programs analyzed in the study have a typical duration of two to four years and a budget of between ten and 100 million euros (see Figure 2.2). Smaller companies (< 10,000 staff members) have an average of 52 full-time employees committed to the respective program. For larger companies (> 10,000 staff members), this number is 126. Most transformation programs are rooted in business transformation or combine elements of this and IT transformation. The programs strive to reduce costs, increase sales, and improve agility (defined as the ability of a company to respond to changes more quickly). Surprisingly, mitigating risks was not viewed as being very important, despite the recent economic crisis. Figure 2.3 shows how many times one particular goal was mentioned (frequency) and the priority it was associated with. The classification of Baumöl[2] was used and expanded for this purpose.

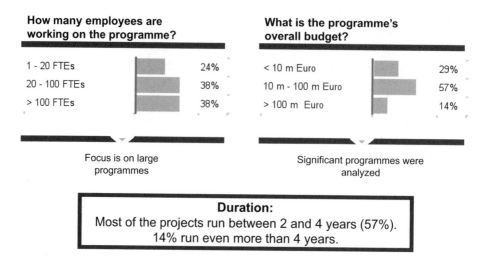

Figure 2.2   Characteristics of Data: Projects

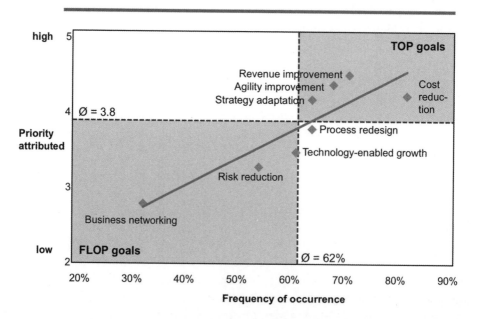

Figure 2.3   Objectives of Transformation Programs

Key Deliverables

Business optimisation (23)

Operating model (9)

Standardized processes and platform (6)

Roadmap (5)

Key Enablers

Top management support (16)

Stakeholder management (8)

Clear responsibilities (5)

Key Inhibitors

Resistance to change (12)

Organisational barriers (8)

Ressource constraints (8)

Figure 2.4   Deliverables, Enablers and Inhibitors of Transformation Programs

Business optimization, business models (operating models), roadmaps, standardized processes and platforms – all functional topics – were mentioned as desired key outcomes ("deliverables") of transformation programs. The enablers of successful transformations are: support from top management, stakeholder management, and clearly communicated responsibilities. Resistance to changes, organizational obstacles, and limited resources prevent successful transformations. Figure 2.4 summarizes those deliverables, enablers, and inhibitors of successful transformation programs.

Holistic Transformation Management

Possible components of a holistic management approach were derived from technical literature to gain an optimal overview of transformation management. The approach is based on the established business engineering framework[3] and breaks down into the following levels:

- strategic level
- structural and process organization level
- IT implementation level.

It comprises thirteen components. Questions about additional required components led to the approach being regarded as complete.

What Potential Does a Holistic Approach Have?

To determine whether transformation programs are more successful when a holistic transformation management approach is used, company representatives were asked to assess the effects of such a program implementation. A transformation program from the respective company or a sample program was used as a basis for the evaluation.

Figure 2.5 summarizes the conclusions of the representatives with respect to program quality, budget, duration, and risk. Program quality refers to the extent to which all objectives were reached and the sustainability of the transformation.

All participants in the study predicted higher program quality if all six proposed components are implemented. Three out of four managers expect a positive effect on the duration and the budget of the program, i.e. a shorter time for implementation and lower overall costs (presuming that the additional time and effort associated with a holistic approach at the beginning will be compensated by the improved program quality). The other 25% of participants associated a holistic approach with a larger program budget and a longer duration. Program risk was generally seen as being lowered by a holistic approach.

What Components do Mature Companies Regard as Being Particularly Important?

One part of the analysis involved determining the maturity of the company in relation to individual transformation management components and the importance placed on these components. To this end, company representatives were asked several questions and responded using a 1-to-5 point scale. Dividing the companies into mature ones (self-assessment of 4 or 5 points) and less

Having all six essential transformation management components in place, what do you think would be their impact?

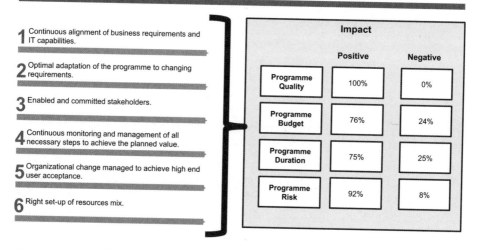

Figure 2.5   Effects on Transformation Programs

mature ones (self-assessment of 1, 2, or 3 points) allows especially noteworthy components to come to the fore. Also, further development opportunities for individual companies could be identified. Companies that regarded themselves as being mature deem the following aspects as more important than less mature companies:

- Active management of transformation in general (as mature companies rated almost all components to be more important than less mature companies)
- Operational and process organization in general (e.g. through a joint Governance Model and Organizational Change Management)
- Specific strategic aspects (e.g. common understanding of business objectives)

What Potential for Further Development Exists?

Components that were viewed as being very important but have a low level of maturity possess more development potential than others. Figure 2.6 shows that the components with potential are the following:

- Identifying and managing interdependencies of projects within and across programs
- Management of program value and
- Business process optimization and innovation services.

It is also these components that tend to exert the most leverage in practice.

Is Holistic Transformation Management already being Practiced in the Real World?

A factor and cluster analysis was performed to identify archetypal transformation management approaches currently pursued in companies.[4] The factor analysis takes into account the maturity of the company with respect to specific components as assessed by company representatives and uses it as input to summarize the effectiveness of these components. The cluster analysis classifies the transformation management approaches in place at the companies based on this information.

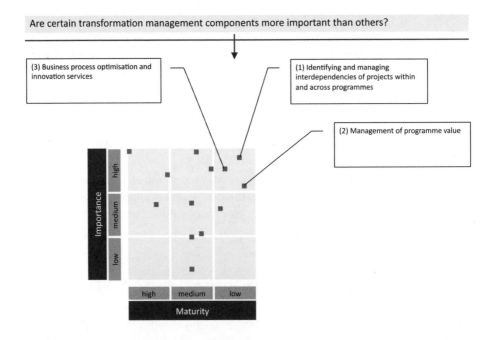

Figure 2.6   Importance vs. Maturity of Components of a Holistic Business Transformation Management

1 Governance model	▪ Joint (customer and partner) governance model ▪ Monitoring of technology trends ▪ High qualified IT people with excellent business understanding
2 Change management	▪ Identifying and managing interdependencies of projects ▪ Organizational change management
3 Holistic planning	▪ Joint (customer and partner) agreement on business objectives ▪ IT architecture services ▪ Mid-term planning and continuous alignment ▪ Professional programme and project management
4 Commitment to transformation	▪ Business process optimization and innovation services ▪ High qualified representative of partner for direct interaction with the top management
5 Benefits management	▪ Transparency on progress, risks, and costs of transformation programme activities ▪ Management of programme value

Figure 2.7   Five Factors Driving Transformation Management (resulting from factor analysis)

Figure 2.7 shows the resulting five factors: Governance model, change management, holistic planning, commitment to transformation, and benefits management.

The cluster analysis identifies three transformation management approaches (see Figure 2.8): the value driven, the un-governed, and the change-driven approach. Those approaches were analysed with regard to the five factors from Figure 2.7.

- The value-driven approach is present in 57% of the examined companies and can be charatericed by a high target driven planning and a high degree of benefit management.
- The change-driven approach (18%) emphasizes the importance of the governance model, change management and management commitment.
- By contrast, the un-governed approach is dominated by little people and technology governance.

All three approaches are similar in that they focus on specific areas but lack a balanced, holistic strategy. Further improvement is therefore possible at all 28 companies, considering the potential of a holistic transformation management approach.

The following three approaches could be identified in the cluster analysis:

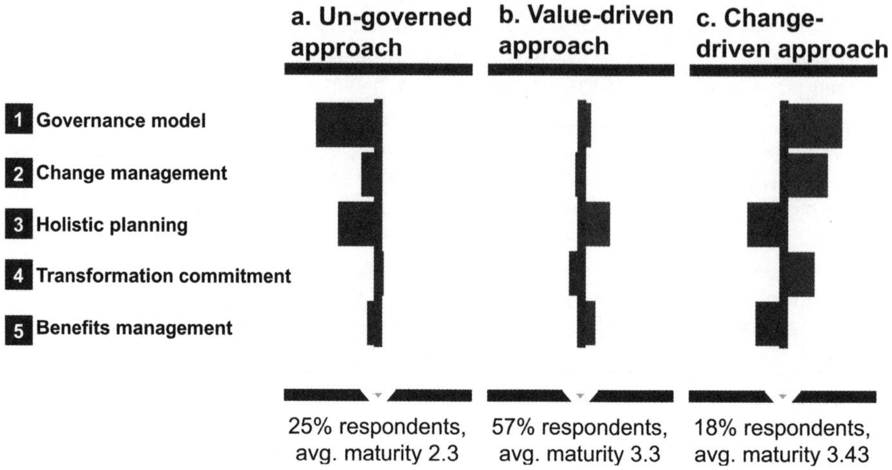

Figure 2.8   Transformation Management Approaches

Summary

Managing transformation programs is an important topic and becomes even more so in large companies. Although different transformation management approaches are in place at the 28 surveyed companies, a holistic approach could not be identified. All participants in the study believed that a holistic transformation management approach would have significant potential for improving quality and thereby achieving and maintaining defined objectives.

The following conclusion can be drawn concerning successful transformation management:

- Companies that consider themselves as experienced in transformation management assess certain components of a holistic approach differently than less experienced companies. This especially applies to active transformation management, structural and process organization, and specific strategic aspects, which are very important to mature companies.
- Reducing costs, increasing sales, and improving agility are the most common objectives of transformation programs. These are all business and not technical objectives. Information systems and technology seem to be regarded by companies as a general prerequisite for successful

transformation management. Surprisingly, reducing risk was not viewed as very important, despite the current economic crisis.

- Drivers and preventers of successful transformation are dominated by "soft" factors. More important is knowing that transformations should be driven by functional and strategic content.

Key Learnings

- Main objectives for transformation programs are cost reduction, revenue improvement and agility improvement. Despite the experience of the financial crisis, risk reduction still has a low priority. Business networking has not arrived at all.
- The main factors driving transformation are the Governance Model, Change Management, Holistic Planning, Commitment to transformation and Benefits management.
- Companies which rate themselves as transformation experienced put either a lot of emphasis on Objective setting and Benefit management (value driven approach) or on Governance, holistic Change Management and Commitment to the transformation initiative (Change driven approach). Companies rating their transformation experiences as low do not put a lot of emphasis on any of those factors (un-governed approach).
- Conclusion: After going through a couple of "painful" transformation initiatives, companies become more sensitive with respect to the benefits or the organizational change aspects of a transformation initiative.
- However, all companies participating in the survey lack a holistic and integrated approach for business transformation management.

Bibliography

1 Moreton, R., 1995. Transforming the organization: The contribution of the information systems function. *Journal of Strategic Information Systems* 4 (2), S. 149–163.

2 Baumöl, U., 2005. Strategic Agility through Situational Method Construction. In: The European Academy of Management Annual Conference (EURAM).

3 Österle, H., Winter, R., 2003. *Business Engineering – Auf dem Weg zum Unternehmen des Informationszeitalters*. Berlin, Heidelberg: Springer.

4 Backhaus, K., Erichson, B., Plinke, W., Weiber, R., 2006. *Multivariate Analysemethoden – Eine anwendungsorientierte Einführung*. Berlin, Heidelberg: Springer.

3

Chief Innovation Officer: A New and Exciting Field of Activity for CIOs

Axel Uhl (SAP), Kim MacGillavry (DHL Freight), Lars Gollenia (SAP)

If you have ever tried to introduce innovation into an established organization, you know how difficult it is. With the increasing pace of change, the challenge will not diminish. Taking up on the topic of "a transformational CIO", and based on a new, yet ancient idea, the authors outline a new approach to organizing transformation and innovation – one in which the CIO may play a major role.

Driven by the technological advances of the last decades, innovation is becoming an increasingly important aspect of business life. In the past, this was a challenge typically bestowed on companies with a high dependency on new products or companies providing technology itself. Nowadays, any company can benefit from the rapidly developing information technology. Technology provides us with greater opportunities to innovate business models, digitalize business processes, increase customer intimacy and enhance customer experience, accelerate product development, and improve the governance of our companies. The most talked about of these technologies include big data management, social media, mobile technology, 3D scanners, and the cloud, while the Internet of services and things and ubiquitous computing also have high potential for innovation.

In the past, it was mainly the Research and Development (R&D) departments who were responsible for innovation, and they focused particularly on product innovation. Whereas innovation for the Chief Information Officer (CIO) usually meant innovation within the area of IT itself ("IT innovates IT") or the digitalization of business processes (process improvements). However, new information technologies promise innovations also at the business model level, thus raising the role of IT to a new, much more strategic level.

Why CIOs Might Be Skeptical

CIOs should be overjoyed in view of these possibilities, but in truth this is seldom the case. Instead, they are often rather skeptical towards the innovation promises of IT companies. The reasons for this are manyfold:

- Organizations that are not driven by innovation usually operate within functional and country silos. The complexity of working, for example, in a matrix structure makes a company inward-directed; then they are less able to tackle the topics and new ideas which require shared cross-functional vision and teams to convert them into value for customers.
- As managers often come from the pre-digital generation, they often fail to understand the new technologies and the associated opportunities and threats for the established business model.
- Another complaint involves the long timespan between developing a functioning application, optimizing the business processes, and realizing the business benefits. This often takes several years and puts the patience of companies to a severe test. Often, past IT investments have not amortized yet, so why should companies invest in new technologies again?
- Specialist departments have inflated expectations concerning the benefits of new technologies – which cannot be met even in the best of circumstances. These expectations are often raised by sophisticated marketing techniques of software manufacturers and IT service providers.
- Many IT departments often operate at full capacity on a daily basis, dealing with their complex IT architectures as well as hundreds of applications, servers, and interfaces. This means neither time nor resources for innovations.
- New technologies could even increase the complexity of the IT infrastructure further, for which neither internal nor external people have the required skills.
- New technologies often come with incalculable risks. Examples are the security aspects of mobile devices, and data privacy in social networks and in the cloud.

While these are all good reasons to observe technological innovations skeptically, the even bigger stumbling blocks probably lie elsewhere.

People Simply Hate Change

Psychological, structural, and cultural problems work against the use of the technological innovation potential in a running company. Human beings simply hate change. We are all creatures of habit, constructed to achieve our goals with as little effort as possible. Not only is this true for individuals, but also for departments and entire organizations: For example, our IT processes are streamlined for efficiency – everything should operate at optimum levels and as error-free as possible. Innovations – in other words, changes – only interfere with those established efficient processes and require a lot of energy.

According to research in the field of cognitive psychology (Kahneman 2013), while people are prone to underestimate the benefits of change, they tend to overestimate risk. The many hierarchy levels of a typical "run the business" organization also hinder innovation because the potential "losers" quickly react with resistance and stifle change or lay out "political pitfalls". Also, the energy level required in organizations that operate in a matrix structure is – due to its complexity – quite high, and this lowers the energy available for driving change across its functional and its country silos.

To summarize, like change in general, IT-driven innovation has a hard time with traditional organizations. However, this should not deny the fact that "IT-enabled" innovation, once implemented successfully, has the potential to result in sustainable, commercial success. Therefore, the question is: how can the psychological and organizational barriers be removed?

Table 3.1   Values of Different Organizational Settings

RUN the business: Stability	CHANGE the business: Agility
Knowledge Protection	Knowledge Sharing
Structures and Processes	Openness
Efficiency	Diversity
Protection of Intellectual Property	Trust
Risk Aversion	Risk Seeking
Manager	Entrepreneurs

Two Systems: Fast and Stable versus Slow and Agile

A successful approach to introduce IT innovations in an organization must provide the following:

1. It must leverage the innovation potential of employees in the company and that of experts from outside.
2. It must establish extensive, fault-tolerant framework conditions for dealing with innovations and protect the new ideas from being confronted with resistance too early.
3. It must accurately present both the benefits as well as the risks of innovations.
4. It must ensure a transfer of knowledge about innovations within the organization.
5. It must prepare the "run the business" organization for subsequent innovations in a structured and coordinated way.

Since implementing innovations in a "run the business" organization is difficult, a logical alternative would be to set up a separate innovation organization (Kotter 2012). This idea is not new but, in fact, as old as mankind – as the human brain is divided into two systems (Kahneman 2013):

*   The "fast system" takes up a large amount of the brain's capacity; it is constantly running automatisms and is associated with low energy requirements. Here decisions are mostly taken automatically, and problems are solved based on past experience ("run").
*   The brain's "slow system" is allocated little capacity but it requires much more energy. Decisions in this system are made based on analysis and creativity ("change").

Like the slow system in the human brain, a "change the business" organization must operate according to rules and values which are completely different from a "run the business" organization – which resembles the fast brain system (see Table 3.1).

What Does a "Change the Business" Organization Look Like?

There may be three pillars to a "change the business" organization. First, it must focus on interdisciplinary networking – that is, exchanging knowledge with specialists from science and practice. Whereas traditional organizations try to find and recruit the best skilled people in order to place them internally and then shield them from outside influences, in a "change the business" organization internal and external experts work closely together to create innovations. This has two advantages which improve the ability to innovate: First, one can access a bigger pool of top experts, since some of them might not be willing to join a company as an employee. Second, external people bringing their external views into the organization help prevent organizational blindness, i.e. distorted perceptions and a company-specific filter for opinions, like, for example, over- or underestimating one's capabilities and/or misjudging competitors.

The main task of the employees who work in such a "change the business" organization should be to coordinate the expert network as well as collecting and sharing knowledge and innovations. This learning experience fosters intrinsic motivation among the network members, which in turn enhances creativity. A high level of trust, a large degree of democracy, and little to no hierarchy are essential aspects for an effective knowledge transfer within the network.

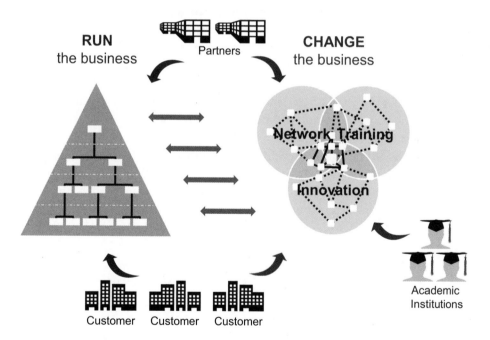

Figure 3.1   The Hierarchical "Run the Business" Organization and the Network-oriented "Change the Business" Organization Work Hand in Hand

Source: BTA.

There are several advantages: The hosting company not only benefits from internal know-how, but also gains access to creative ideas and experiences by interacting with the network. The "run the business" organization profits from the intercultural collaboration of a potentially global network, can examine issues from new perspectives, and question existing approaches in terms of viability without being restricted by internal, political constraints.

Furthermore there are parallels to other approaches: For example, the success principles of "design thinking" are based on a hierarchy-free organization, open discussions, and an interdisciplinary team. There are also parallels with open source communities where highly qualified members contribute voluntarily and without monetary gain – which can bring about surprising developments.

A second pillar of a "change the business" organization could be an innovation lab. Together with technology partners, a laboratory for technologies could be established which is accessible to internal as well as external experts. The goal of the innovation lab would be to collect practical technological experiences, try out creative ideas, or test specific scenarios before implementing them in the "run the business" organization. Agile methods are used to increase the speed and practical use of the prototypes.

The third pillar could be an innovation and transformation academy that supports the implementation of new ideas by providing suitable training. If the ability to innovate and transform is considered to be an essential skill that the company can and must develop, such an innovation and transformation academy performs an important function by contributing to the company's long-term ability to innovate. Its offers could include method training on business transformation, innovation, or lean management. In addition, it would be beneficial to offer management training on how to promote a culture of innovation and change.

Of course, a "change the business" organization does not have to limit itself to these three pillars but could extend to other topics and activities.

Potential Success Factors for Incubators

When a company decides to form an incubator to create new ideas and manage the innovation process outside the "run the business" line organization, the following success factors should be considered:

- To ensure a good internal skill mix in the incubator's teams, expertise from different parts of the organization should be pooled together and enriched with the participation of important external stakeholders, like key suppliers, consultants, or academics.
- Ideally, interested customers are invited to participate in order to ensure that value is created and that there is an immediate commercial adoption at the end of the process.
- Since permanently assigned resources are less likely to be effective for every topic, teams should be purpose-built. This means bringing together the most suitable resources for one specific topic at hand.
- Top managers (ideally from all stakeholders) get involved by sponsoring initiatives and personally reviewing progress.
- The incubator teams predetermine functional alignment in the process so that the line organization can afterwards adopt the innovation into the ordinary running of the business and take charge of rollout and broad-scale dissemination.

Figure 3.1 summarizes the two organizational concepts "run the business" and "change the business".

Essential Partnerships with the "Run the Business" Organization

In all cases, the right organizational anchoring is essential for the success of the "change the business" organization. As mentioned above, a decisive factor is to establish close partnerships with the strategy department of a company as well as with important functional areas, such as human resources, R&D, training and education, marketing, and sales.

On the one hand, a close partnership with the strategy department is essential because important innovations can only be successfully implemented when they are included in the company strategy and actively supported by top management. From the organization's perspective, this would be facilitated if the manager of the "change the business" organization were also a member of the board of the company.

   On the other hand, close partnerships with specialist areas are just as important. They ensure that important know-how carriers are available to work on innovations when needed. At the same time, such cooperation prepares the ground for later change processes in the "run the business" organization thanks to trusted partners who are available in the departments as "allies".

   The reader may wonder now: Is this slow system approach, this "change the business" organization, only a theoretical construct? – On the contrary, it is very realizable. As a matter of fact, there are different types of organizations which have already established concrete examples of "change the business" organizations.

Three Real-Life Examples

Of particular interest is the example of the "Office of Business Transformation" in the United States Army, which was implemented by law in 2009. The office is led by a 3-star general who controls three directorates that focus on army business operations, transformation, and innovation. By co-operating and networking with universities, the United States Army managers are systematically trained and prepared for change processes, innovations are pushed, and the process efficiency and effectiveness were improved with Six Sigma.

   In 2009, SAP initiated its own "change the business" organization called "Business Transformation Academy" (BTA), which started to form a network of experts for innovation and business transformation. Since then, the network has become global, with hubs in North America, Europe, Singapore, and Australia. Over 150 experts from science and practice work together with SAP professionals to generate innovative business ideas, methods of innovation and transformation, and case studies. To ensure the independence of the think tank, the BTA was organizationally affiliated with a university and established as a registered association under Swiss law. The results of the network are available to all interested parties through various channels, one of them being the *360°– the Business Transformation Journal.*

The third example is a global high-tech company that recently started to build up their own Business Transformation Academy in collaboration with SAP. The objective is to drive innovation and transformation and to share knowledge within their expert network. The first 20 IT managers came to SAP Walldorf and were trained in the Business Transformation Management Methodology (BTM²). After completing an exam, they all received their Professional Certification – more than just a souvenir of their trip to Germany.

Conclusions

In the past, CIOs have struggled to drive innovation beyond the scope of their area of responsibility. The reputation of most IT departments suffered from cumbersome and inflexible IT systems and high maintenance costs. The value of IT was not seen and / or not realized to its full extent. The position of a CIO was therefore hardly seen as a big career step or as a main driver for the company's strategy. All this can change. As it has already happened in some companies, the CIO can be promoted to a new role: "Chief Innovation Officer". This makes perfect sense, since technology will be one of the main drivers for future innovation, as we outlined at the beginning.

But to successfully drive innovation, CIOs need to manage and master more than just IT – they need to become change experts and need a new type of organization next to the "run the business" organization: one that is connected to all kinds of experts, internally and externally.

Key Learnings

- The human brain is divided into two parts: A fast, very efficient part and a slow, innovative part.
- Business can imitate this dichotomy for their own end by running an efficient "run the business" organization and a creative "change the business" organization alongside.
- As the success principles and framework conditions of the two organizational forms are quite different, they must run separately, yet work hand in hand.

- The "change the business" organization focuses on innovation and business transformation by exchanging knowledge in an inter- and transdisciplinary network. This network has little to no hierarchies and encompasses key stakeholders, including employees, customers, suppliers, academics, etc.
- The "change the business" organization creates and develops new ideas in a fault-tolerant environment until they are ready to be taken over by the efficiency-oriented environment of the "run the business" organization – where they are further developed into innovations.

Bibliography

Kahneman, D. (2013). Gewohnheitstiere. In: OrganisationsEntwicklung, Nr. 1/2013, S. 4–9.

Kotter, J.P. (2012). Die Kraft der zwei Systeme. In: Harvard Business Manager, 12/2012, S. 22–36.

4

The Transformational CIO

Axel Uhl (SAP), Lars Gollenia (SAP), Uli Muench (IBM)

In today's rapidly changing business environment, there is a mandate for a new breed of Chief Information Officers (CIO) who can bring and support fundamental change to the organization's technical, political, and cultural systems. A transformational CIO helps the management team to develop the vision, gathers support and buy-in from stakeholders, and successfully leads the organization through the transformation.

Abstract

In today's complex, global business world, transformation – despite its original meaning of complete and utter change – has become the norm, both a buzzword and a real, ongoing environment in which change is the only constant. Successful CIOs must not only monitor and react to ongoing change, but also use their skill and knowledge to initiate and support desirable transformation throughout the organization. Whether that transformation takes the shape of mergers and acquisitions, introduction of shared services, business process outsourcing, implementation of enterprise software, or sustainability initiatives, IT will always be involved, and confident leadership is the factor that can spell the difference between success and failure and can help to integrate transformational skills into the DNA of the organization.

The Case for Transformational Change

Business transformation typically takes the shape of highly complex, multifaceted projects that require coordination of interrelated domains such as business and IT. The CIO who is comfortable not only reacting to, but leading, such change – the transformational CIO – must be confident with complexity, able to motivate employees toward a shared goal, and able to implement the processes and governance necessary for true, deep organizational change.

Another crucial skill: being able to identify important drivers and predict their results. Driving forces can take many forms: Technological innovation – which, most recently, has changed how we communicate and share information. Globalization – which increases both supplier and customer bases as much as it does competition. Sustainability – where customer values have forced both business change and industry regulation.

Against this backdrop, business leaders seeking competitive advantage must move beyond tactics that have worked in the past. What's needed is an innovative and coherent strategy, one that addresses opportunities and identifies risks unique to the situation, while remaining aligned with the company's overall goals. Another crucial factor: Any efforts toward transformation must take into account the particular organization's capabilities, resources, and competencies – not just to best effect change, but to ensure that core capabilities and advantages are not undercut by the change itself.

Why Transformations Fail

Unsurprisingly, many transformation projects fail – though perhaps not for the reasons you might guess. Only 25% of unsuccessful projects, it turns out, fail for technical reasons, with the remaining 75% falling apart due to more intangible, but no less important, factors: poorly defined vision or strategy, inadequate stakeholder management, missing skill sets, bad communication, competing programs, or a lack of holistic business transformation management methodology (Isern et al. 2009; Isern and Pung 2007). This underscores the importance of the CIO as more than just the manager of all things technical. Instead, he or she must define strategy, manage the transformation, and lead by example.

Characteristics of the Transformational CIO

To prepare the IT organization for any real change, the transformational CIO must be able to accomplish the three important tasks listed in Figure 4.1.

1 *Envision*: Develop and shape a transformation strategy that fits your organization

2 *Manage* transformation holistically and achieve expected benefits

3 Be a role model for successful transformational *leadership*

Figure 4.1   Characteristics of a Transformational CIO

First, any CIO interested in transformation needs a vision, a view of the future that can excite and convert potential followers. This may be developed by the CIO individually, or emerge from board or management discussions – either way, the CIO must buy into even the most radical vision and be able to convince others of its viability and necessity. This takes energy and commitment, not to mention the ability to inspire trust and dedication.

Next, the CIO must manage the change and achieve the desired results. Some CIOs may inherently know the path forward for a particular project, while others must explore options for achieving the end state. Both must be able to demonstrate progress along the path to the goal.

Finally, the transformational CIO must be a visible leader – one who can motivate and rally employees at all points in the process. Political skills come in handy here: The CIO must inspire, listen, respond, and inform, all the while displaying unswerving commitment in the face of setbacks or doubt. Truly transformational CIOs are at once people-oriented and able to make, and model, deep and sustained commitment to a goal.

1. ENVISION: TRANSFORMATION DRIVERS AND STRATEGY

Any successful transformation starts with vision and strategy. IT can find itself supporting multiple transformation initiatives while running and maintaining traditional IT systems and services. A clearly defined strategy,

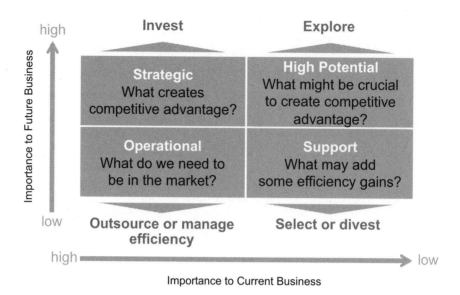

Figure 4.2   Evaluating Transformational IT Strategies
Source: Based on Ward and Daniel 2006.

balancing sometimes conflicting requirements from different business areas and managing the interdependencies between the various programs, is a must-have requirement. To develop a realistic understanding of the business changes and the associated IT requirements, the CIO should address the following questions when defining the IT strategy:

- Drivers: What are the transformation drivers and what impact will they have on the business model?
- Vision and positioning: What are our collaboration options with the business? What is the vision for our future IT model? What is the strategic positioning?
- Value chain: How is the value chain transformed? Which parts must be optimized through IT?
- Competitive advantage: How can we use technology for our competitive advantage, and how can we ensure we realize maximum value through the transformation?
- Ecosystem: What partner organizations might help us reach strategic goals?
- Technology: Which technological concepts are necessary, and what technologies are available?
- Risks: What risks must be considered? How can we address them on a strategic level?

After having a clear understanding of the business transformation initiatives, the CIO needs to plan the investment areas for IT. This requires prioritizing the investment areas and building up new competencies while keeping the operational business running. An applications portfolio (see Figure 4.2) can help to create the appropriate investment strategy. Four different types of initiatives are distinguished:

- Strategic IT initiatives create competitive advantage and serve as the cornerstone of the business transformation strategy.
- High-potential IT areas are initiatives that may be crucial to competitive advantage.
- Operational IT activities are required for the organization to be in the market. These operations must be managed efficiently or outsourced.
- Support initiatives improve efficiency, but are not a priority for the transformation strategy.

The different types of initiatives are linked to specific benefits (see Figure 4.3).

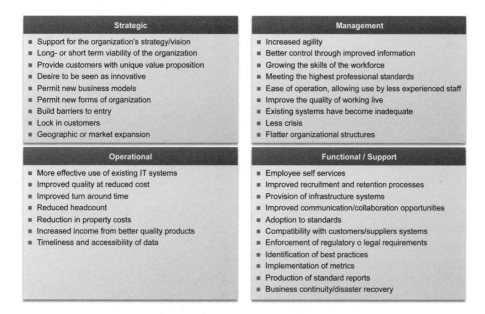

Strategic
- Support for the organization's strategy/vision
- Long- or short term viability of the organization
- Provide customers with unique value proposition
- Desire to be seen as innovative
- Permit new business models
- Permit new forms of organization
- Build barriers to entry
- Lock in customers
- Geographic or market expansion

Management
- Increased agility
- Better control through improved information
- Growing the skills of the workforce
- Meeting the highest professional standards
- Ease of operation, allowing use by less experienced staff
- Improve the quality of working live
- Existing systems have become inadequate
- Less crisis
- Flatter organizational structures

Operational
- More effective use of existing IT systems
- Improved quality at reduced cost
- Improved turn around time
- Reduced headcount
- Reduction in property costs
- Increased income from better quality products
- Timeliness and accessibility of data

Functional / Support
- Employee self services
- Improved recruitment and retention processes
- Provision of infrastructure systems
- Improved communication/collaboration opportunities
- Adoption to standards
- Compatibility with customers/suppliers systems
- Enforcement of regulatory o legal requirements
- Identification of best practices
- Implementation of metrics
- Production of standard reports
- Business continuity/disaster recovery

Figure 4.3   Types of Benefits Associated with the Four Types of Applications / Initiatives
Source: Reproduced with permission from Ward and Daniel 2006.

2. MANAGE: BUSINESS TRANSFORMATION MANAGEMENT

Research indicates that successful transformation starts with a realistic and target-oriented strategy. If the strategy is wrong, the transformation can't be successful. Equally important is the execution of the transformation, as many transformation initiatives fail because they are not properly managed. There is little guidance and few best practices available on how to successfully manage an IT-enabled business transformation. Many programs wind up dominated by IT delivering systems at the expense of the business transformation solutions, while others become highly technical monsters, difficult to manage and harder to modify. To strike the right balance between business and IT requirements, between soft (business change) and hard (technical) factors, a holistic business transformation methodology is required.

A holistic approach to business transformation management includes four phases: envision, engage, transform, and optimize (see Figure 4.4). Together, they involve and integrate discipline-specific technical and methodological expertise from relevant subject areas.

- Envision: Make a case for change and sense of urgency; set the strategy/ vision.
- Engage: Empower people to act on the vision and plan the effort.
- Transform: Change behavior, processes, technology, culture, values.
- Optimize: Internalize, institutionalize, and optimize transformation; create stability.

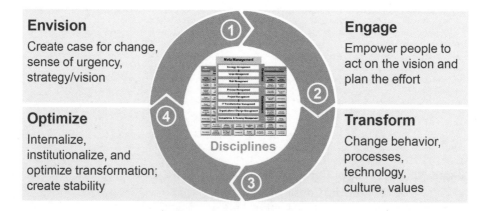

Envision
Create case for change, sense of urgency, strategy/vision

Engage
Empower people to act on the vision and plan the effort

Optimize
Internalize, institutionalize, and optimize transformation; create stability

Transform
Change behavior, processes, technology, culture, values

Disciplines

Figure 4.4   Business Transformation Iterative Cycles

Change happens in cycles rather than in straight lines. The transformation strategy is planned, implemented, stabilized, and optimized before starting the next iterative change cycle required for the organization's ongoing success. In many of the case studies that we analyzed, companies even fail in the first attempt and need to start the transformation again with the learnings taken from the first try.

Using the Business Transformation Management Framework to Drive Transformation

Each transformation project is unique, involving an array of personalities, processes, technologies, and objectives. A framework to manage the financial, social, and technical aspects of a business transformation is key to successful execution. The framework (see Figure 4.5) is based on an iterative, cyclic model that helps define management layers, roles, and disciplines and delivers decision criteria for choosing the right leaders and promoters for key positions. The framework focuses activities using a balanced-scorecard approach for planning and control. It helps create a transformational culture by embedding transformation values and principles within departments, in part through careful and constant communication.

The framework consists of eight individual disciplines that are linked together to create a holistic view on the transformation. Strategy, value, and risk management come together to provide direction for the transformation effort. These disciplines create the case for action, and for the overall vision. Within project enablement, process management helps oversee changes to key business processes, while program management serves as a vehicle for the transformation effort as a whole. IT enables process and technology changes, while people-centered disciplines facilitate the will (via change management) and the skills (via competency management) of key groups.

The Value of Holistic Business Transformation Management

Business transformation management is a process of organizing and managing a project so that benefits outlined in a business case are actually realized.

Transformational CIOs should look to leverage a business transformation management approach, as illustrated in Figure 4.6. While the activities under

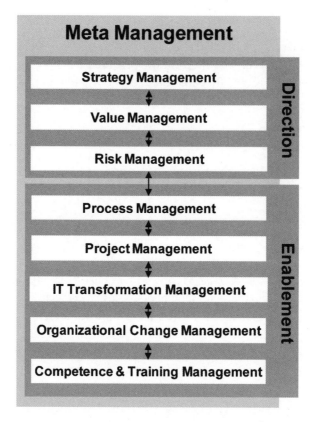

Figure 4.5   Meta Management Framework

the old approach (transactional management) are not wrong or unnecessary, experience shows that, on their own, they are insufficient to deliver the forecasted benefits to the organization.

Central to the business transformation management approach is the identification of, and focus on, the value of the investment. This focus persists throughout the transformation, from initial strategy definition through design and implementation to final review.

3. LEAD: THE QUALITIES OF A TRANSFORMATIONAL LEADER

In today's rapidly changing technology environment, there is a mandate for a new breed of CIO who can help organizations develop a clear vision, gather support and buy-in from stakeholders, successfully guide the organization through transformation, and institutionalize change over time. Whereas a

Old Approach: Managing an IT Project		New Approach: Managing Business Transformation
Technology delivery	▶	Benefits delivery
Value for money – low-level task monitoring	▶	Value for money – benefits tracking
Loose linkage to business needs	▶	Business case with integration with business drivers
IT implementation plan	▶	Change management plan
Business managers as victims	▶	Business managers involved and in control
Large set of unfocused functionality	▶	IT investments that are sufficient to do the job
Stakeholder "subjected to"	▶	Stakeholders "involved in"
Trained in technology	▶	Educated in exploitation of technology – talent harnessed
Carry out technology and project audits	▶	Obtain business benefits, then review with learning – leverage learning

Figure 4.6   The Value of a Benefits-Oriented Approach to Transformation
Source: Reproduced with permission from Ward and Daniel 2006.

transactional CIO might make adjustments to the organizational tripod of mission, structure, and human resources, a transformational leader goes beyond, bringing fundamental change to the organization's technical, political, and cultural systems.

A transformational CIO needs beside functional and technical knowledge a range of competencies and skills:

- Charisma: A transformational leader has a clear vision for the organization, and can easily communicate that vision to group members. For example, he or she can readily detect what is most important to individuals and to the organization as a whole.
- Confidence: A transformational leader has good business sense and is able to see what decisions will positively affect the organization. This gives the leader the ability to act confidently and inspire trust in team members.

- Respect and loyalty: A transformational leader inspires respect and loyalty in individuals by taking the time to listen to their ideas and let them know they are important.
- Expressive praise: A transformational leader praises individuals and teams on a job well done. Letting them know how much they contributed to each success also steels them for future challenges.
- Inspiration: A transformational leader uses praise, inspiration, and confidence to help others do things they weren't sure they could do.

Making Transformational Leadership Part of the Organizational DNA

It is no secret that corporations need to adapt, transform, innovate, and often reinvent themselves if they are to win in today's ever-changing business environment. Leadership is crucial to transformational change. Effective transformational CIOs drive innovation, build a base for financial performance, and cultivate talent through a structured, benefits-oriented approach to change. These gifted leaders help develop the leaders of tomorrow, transform organizations, drive alignment, and grow the business by energizing, empowering, and connecting with people. And it is the businesses that embrace and value transformational skills and build them from within the ranks that will survive and thrive in the coming business environment.

Why is it so difficult to transform an organization? The main issue is that most people find change uncomfortable. Transformation managers are constantly confronted with employees trying to protect the status quo. Effective transformation management should impact the skills of an organization and make transformational skills part of the DNA of an organization. Leaders and top talent play a key role in embedding transformational qualities in the organization.

Takeaways to make transformational skills part of the DNA of an organization:

- Transformational leadership qualities must be valued as career skills.
- Develop transformational leaders from within the organization.
- Make transformation management part of the career paths of top management.

- Never nominate a leader to run the business who has not had experience changing the business.
- Make changing the business (into a permanent, flexible organization) as important as running the business (on a day-to-day basis).

A Unique Position

We live in a world hungry for the skills of the transformational CIO. Technological innovation, global supply chains, economic risks, on-demand applications, and mobility are pushing the need for these skills, and the change they can effect. To succeed, today's CIO must define transformational strategy and visions, use a framework to guide and manage transformation workflow, and position him- or herself as a leader across the organization. A CIO who can do all these things is uniquely positioned to help envision, manage, and lead business transformation that affects the entire organization.

Key Learnings

- A transformational CIO helps to create a vision and strategy for the company's transformation, manages the complex changes through a structured benefits-oriented approach, and serves as a visible transformational leader.
- The CIO must evaluate and prioritize potential business transformation initiatives based on their ability to create a competitive advantage and the availability of resources.
- Business transformation management is a holistic process of organizing and managing complex change initiatives so that benefits outlined in a business case are actually realized and the changes needed are achieved.
- Leadership is crucial to successful transformational change.

Bibliography

Isern, J., Meany, M.C., Wilson, S., 2009. Corporate transformation under pressure. *McKinsey Quarterly*, 24.

Isern, J. and Pung, C., 2007. Driving radical change. *McKinsey Quarterly*, 4, 24.

Ward, J. and Daniel, E., 2006. *Benefits Management: Delivering value from IS and IT investments*. Chichester: John Wiley & Sons.

5

Digital Renewal of 130 Years of World Class Music

Axel Uhl (SAP), Alexander Schmid (SAP), Robert Zimmermann (Berlin Phil Media)

World Class ... Champions League ... for 130 years

Hardly any other organization has been able to remain amongst the international elite for such a long time as the Berlin Philharmonic Orchestra. So what is the secret of success of this unique orchestra?? An orchestra whose 130 concerts a year are always sold out, and whose musicians are celebrated and revered across the globe. But in spite of all those positive aspects and its success, considering the decline of the music business, this orchestra also faces some challenges which could cast doubt over its future.

The Berliner Philharmoniker is a symphony orchestra based in Berlin, the German capital. The orchestra was formed in 1882 under the name Berliner Philharmonisches Orchester. That was when fifty musicians broke away from the chapel directed by Johann Ernst Benjamin Bilse because they were unhappy with the travel arrangements for a concert they were due to perform in Warsaw.

The ensemble gained international recognition particularly from 1954 to 1989, the period when Herbert von Karajan directed the orchestra. The Austrian conductor was renowned all over the world for his perfectionism and virtuosity. Already in the 1970s, he worked together with sound engineers in order to make the perfect digital recording of classical music available to a wider audience.

Today, after nine principal conductors, two world wars, 131 years after its foundation, the Berliner Philharmoniker are made up of 128 musicians. Under the directorship of their principal conductor Sir Simon Rattle and numerous guest conductors, they perform some 130 concerts a year. Ninety of these take place at their home, the Berlin Philharmonic Hall, and 45 are guest appearances on worldwide tours in front of over 300,000 concert-goers. All of the concerts are sold out. Their concerts are broadcasted on television, sold on various media, like CDs and DVDs, and distributed through the Internet via Digital Concert Hall which is the orchestra's virtual concert hall on the Internet. Online since 2008, it provides interested listeners with the possibility to access the sounds and images of the Berliner Philharmoniker through concert videos in outstanding quality. In addition, this platform also provides various documentaries and educational films. Since its inception, Digital Concert Hall has counted over 9.1 million hits, during which a total of over 2.5 million hours of classical music have been streamed. The project integrates seamlessly into social media platforms like Facebook. The Digital Concert Hall is unique throughout the world; no other orchestra has created anything similar to make its music accessible anywhere, anytime.

What drives such a traditional institution as the Berliner Philharmoniker with such a century-old product to adopt the latest Internet technology and take the risk to venture forward into the world of social media? How did the Berliner Philharmoniker in particular manage to emancipate themselves from music labels, producers, distributors, and dealers by taking control of their own value-added chain?

What Traditional Management Theories Cannot Explain

Trying to explain the success of the Berliner Philharmoniker through the lens of traditional management theories would fail across the board. Even the first assumption – that professional management must be in place to provide a strategy for the organization and subsequently control its implementation – does not apply to the Berliner Philharmoniker. There is no traditional management; the Berliner Philharmoniker are democratically organized. They select two orchestra directors and two media directors from within their own ranks to represent the orchestra's interests to the outside world. However, all important decisions are taken by the orchestra itself. This also applies to the choice of the principal conductor as well as to filling vacancies in the orchestra. Meetings are obligatory for each of the 128 musicians, absences are an exception, and decisions are based on majority voting. They build on the experiences of the entire ensemble and ensure that each member can fully identify with the organization. Radical changes are rare because there is always a balance between reformists and traditionalists. Since 2002, the orchestra has been organized as a foundation under public law, which brings together the Berlin Philharmonic Hall – the effective physical concert building – and the orchestra. This plays a major role in providing long-term continuity and security and a solid foundation for the artistic work it performs.

The orchestra itself decides who is to become a provisional orchestra member. On candidate audition days, the orchestra is present and decides together who will be accepted for an initial trial period of one year. Only after a trial year in the orchestra is a definite decision made who is to be given a position for life – again by means of voting. This gives both the candidate and the orchestra sufficient time to find out how well they fit and whether the orchestra is strengthened as a result.

The topic of remuneration is never an issue, as all of the musicians earn the same, irrespective of which instrument they play and how long they have been members. This contradicts another basic assertion of many management theories which postulate that maximum performance can only be achieved through large financial incentives. In contrast to many organizations that rely heavily on material and monetary incentives, the musicians of the Berliner Philharmoniker concentrate solely on their ability and thus ensure that they will continue to be truly world class. Headhunting, which is common practice in almost all the other high-performance organizations, does not exist here.

It is also not necessary to monitor whether the musicians continuously develop in terms of their own performance. There are several explanations for this: In addition to playing constantly in a world-class environment, a lot of musicians have extensive solo and chamber music activities. Each member is challenged and encouraged by the performance of the other musicians. Even though there is no threat of dismissal – these musicians have their job for life – everyone works hard on their own continuous development, partly because it is their calling, but also because there is such intense competition between the musicians. This contradicts another postulation of management theory, which claims that a maximum degree of harmony in teams is necessary to produce maximum performance. It is incredible but true: Although top concert performances rely on the existence of perfect musical harmony between all of the musicians, it is precisely the intense competition that is a prerequisite for continuous development.

This also applies to the relationship between conductor and orchestra. Selected by the orchestra, the principal conductor assumes musical leadership and the most prominent role. It is inevitable that this ambivalent relationship between the orchestra and the conductor can also lead to severe tensions. However, it seems to be precisely this friction that contributes to the achievement of new levels of performance and musical development.

Some management theories also advance the hypothesis that constant high-level performances are only possible if managers or team members are regularly replaced. That only by this measure it is possible to get the input of new ideas and skills that are necessary for continuous development. Many high-performance organizations, including the Berliner Philharmoniker, prove the opposite. The musicians remain in the orchestra for life, and the average tenure of a principal conductor is several decades. Stability in the team and the routine that this entails enable the orchestra to concentrate on the aspects that are essential to perform at the highest level.

Another assumption of management theory is that targets must be easily attainable in order to have a motivational effect. For some time, however, it has been known that, with the same skills and ceteris paribus, people perform better when they set themselves more ambitious targets. This phenomenon can also be observed with the Berlin musicians, whose current aim is to be the best orchestra in the world – nothing more and nothing less. This aspiration, and the pressure to perform that comes with it, unites the orchestra and are the main criteria when selecting the conductor and each individual musician. This target is the benchmark and the criterion against which to evaluate one's own performance. The orchestra sets itself the most ambitious of targets, without which it would not be able to maintain its high level of performance.

These high aspirations have also led to the extensive use of technology by the Berliner Philharmoniker. Herbert von Karajan was obsessed with perfection in sound technology, and one of his main admirers at the time was Akio Morita, the cofounder and chairman of Sony (Connolly 2008). Consequently, Sony and the Berliner Philharmoniker recorded and published the first compact disc of classical music in 1980.

The Challenges of World Class Performance in a Shifting Industry

Although the concerts are always sold out and the orchestra has extremely loyal "customers", a need for change came up, partially due to the aforementioned technological development.

In a book about performing arts, the typical listener of classical music is described as being a middle-aged, senior skilled employee, manager, or office worker with tertiary education and an above-average income (Baumol and Bowen 1966). This profile also rings true for the Berliner Philharmoniker's audience in the established markets. The average age of the concert-goers in Berlin is increasing year on year; that is to say, the same visitors keep coming, but they are rarely joined by new ones. Young visitors, in particular, are rather the exception. This is not only due to different tastes in music. But among the hindrances for the young generation are the relatively high entry prices, the limited availability of tickets, and unfamiliar conventions associated with going to a classical music concert. What should I wear? How should I behave? And so on. The situation is different in emerging countries such as China, Taiwan, Korea, and South America, where people who are interested in culture and music are young and inquisitive, but hardly ever get the chance to visit live concerts performed by major orchestras.

For the Berliner Philharmoniker, in addition to revenues from live concert ticket sales and music marketing via sound recordings for CDs etc., television broadcasts have always played an important role. During the Karajan era, up to twenty CD recordings per year were made. With younger people in particular, however, the consumption of music via the Internet and mobile communication has changed dramatically. This results in dwindling sales of sound storage media and a structural change that is unsettling the well-known major labels. Today, the orchestra publishes between three and five CDs at most annually under difficult economic conditions. The future distribution of music will be largely influenced by Internet companies like Amazon, Apple, Google, and Spotify.

Public television broadcasting organizations have also continuously forced classical music out of the main channels and onto more special interest channels. In the 1980s, for example, the New Year's Concert and the regular Sunday concerts were broadcasted on the main channel and up to six live broadcasts were transmitted to Japan. Today, there are just three live concerts by the Berliner Philharmoniker on television, and their long-term future is in serious doubt.

For years these developments have resulted in reduced income from music sales and marketing returns. Since it was also not possible to play more live concerts, the Berliner Philharmoniker had to think seriously about how they wanted to counteract this development and to sustain their income.

But how could this be achieved?

The Digital Transformation of the Orchestra

In June 1999, the orchestra chose Sir Simon Rattle as the successor to Claudio Abbado, who did not wish to extend his principal conductor contract which was due to expire in 2002. When he assumed office in 2002, Rattle brought with him a number of new ideas. With his Zukunft@BPhil initiative (*Zukunft* is German for future), he started an education program in which orchestra members, teachers, and youth workers through workshops give children and young people an understanding of classical music and dance.

"Zukunft@BPhil should remind us that music is not a luxury but a fundamental human need. Music should be a vital and essential element in the lives of all people," said Rattle about the program (Berliner Philharmoniker 2013). The musicians' awareness of the younger generation as their future audience grew in the process.

Zukunft@BPhil also led to a more in-depth consideration of "new" technologies. The idea was to use new media as distribution channels in order to adapt to the consumption behavior of the new generation.

Step by step, a small group of the Berliner Philharmoniker musicians, led by cellist and media director Olaf Maninger, developed the vision of bringing the live concert experience via a high-quality streaming platform to classic music aficionados. The expectations of these professional musicians regarding the quality of the sound and image broadcasts were uncompromisingly high. They unanimously agreed that the recordings should not just be a standard download of the works, but a live stream of the full concert experience. To do justice to the exclusivity and exceptional quality of the music, it was agreed that the service should not be free of charge. All season's concerts were to be transmitted in a virtual concert hall using an aesthetic imagery all of its own. By making innovative use of the very latest technologies, the aim was to make the essence and works of the

Berlin Philharmonic accessible to a global listening audience that was not regularly able to visit a concert hall in the most authentic way possible. Not least, the orchestra hoped that this would also give itself greater direct and genuine control over its own value-added chain.

To gain the approval of the orchestra's plenary meeting, however, not only technological obstacles had to be overcome. The orchestra musicians were familiar with the additional burden of television broadcasts. Floodlights in the concert hall provided optimal lighting for the cameras but turned playing the instruments into a literally sweat-inducing exercise. Wandering camera teams disrupted the experience for listeners. Not surprisingly, therefore, the idea of creating an infrastructure for a professional stream in the concert hall was not received with eagerness by everyone. But ultimately, the enthusiasm of Olaf Maninger and his supporters was sufficient to convince the orchestra to go along with the experiment. They started to record their works with the help of the latest remote technology without any additional lighting and to make it available to the entire world via the Internet.

In 2008, the company "Berlin Phil Media GmbH" was set up as a subsidiary of the Berliner Philharmoniker Foundation to put it all into practice. With the support of the main sponsor, Deutsche Bank, Berlin Phil Media is responsible for the realization and management services associated with the Digital Concert Hall project. Olaf Maninger and Robert Zimmermann took over the role of the managing directors.

The first version of the Digital Concert Hall went online in December 2008. The first live broadcast – a special concert conducted by Sir Simon Rattle, featuring Johannes Brahms' First Symphony – was transmitted on January 6, 2009. Six remote-controlled, high-resolution cameras had been fitted in the concert hall. For the live broadcast, the pictures and the sound were edited in a new audio-video studio and encoded using two encoders to produce an H.264 stream. Using a content delivery network (CDN), the live streams were made available to fans in Digital Concert Hall via Real Time Messaging Protocol (RTMP).

The stream is provided exclusively by means of online direct distribution, without any sublicensing of the concerts (see Figure 5.1).

The business model of the Digital Concert Hall defines four different price models: annual and monthly subscriptions, as well as 7-day or 30-day access.

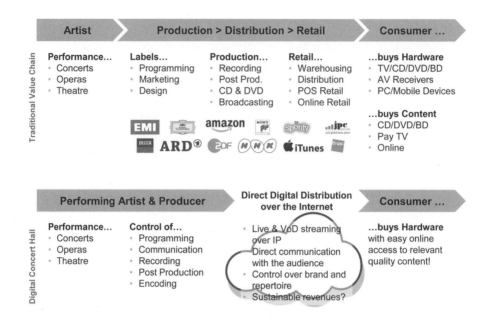

Figure 5.1   Value Chain in the Music Business
Source: Robert Zimmermann.

In addition to the live concert streams, this also includes anywhere, anytime access to the archive, where all of the Berliner Philharmoniker's appearances since the recordings began are available. Also, documentation and information material was produced for the platform and is made available to the subscribers.

To promote the Digital Concert Hall, campaigns were launched on the social media platforms YouTube, Facebook, and Twitter in 2009. This enabled the orchestra to engage for the very first time in a direct dialog with its fans around the world.

Since the launch of Digital Concert Hall in 2008, the overall concept was revised multiple times. In 2012, the Berlin Philharmonic entered a technological partnership with Sony. As part of this partnership, the Digital Concert Hall production facility was equipped like a fully functioning television studio. Seven new HD cameras with the latest remote technology and high-quality HD lenses were installed in the large Berliner Philharmoniker hall to follow the events on stage. Two manned camera systems were also installed, a control center set up, an image mixer fitted, six further recording channels and another streaming encoder added, and audio recording was upgraded from stereo to surround sound. The professional production of the recordings made possible to broadcast live concerts at 120 cinemas simultaneously throughout Europe.

The Web site is now running on HTML5/Flash hybrid technology, and the streaming format complies with the latest HDTV 1080i standard. The server infrastructure was also updated, the signal encoded, and additional channels were made available. So the Berliner Philharmoniker's audio experience is now also available via Sony Internet TVs, apps for the iPhone and iPad, as well as TV apps for Samsung, Google, LG, and Panasonic TVs.

The Digital Concert Hall Today

The Digital Concert Hall proved to be a resounding success. In addition to its existing core audience, the Berliner Philharmoniker was able to attract a total of over 3.8 million visitors with the new streaming platform. The platform media library contains over 200 concert recordings – 175 of which were live broadcasts – 400 hours and around 500 works in the archive, 150 interviews, as well as 20 documentaries and educational projects. The 2.5 million hours of streaming correspond to 600 sold out concerts in the Philharmonic Hall. Fifty percent of the revenue is generated from people who live outside the European Union. Compared to the traditional audience, the age of the average consumer is also lower and, according to statements issued by the operator, it is continuing to fall. By June 2013, over 135,000 users had installed the Berliner Philharmoniker's app on their mobile device.

The social media campaign was very successful and very well received too. Four years after launching it, the Berliner Philharmoniker now boast over 390,000 fans on Facebook, 49,000 followers on Twitter, and 47,000 subscribers on YouTube (as of June 2013). The approximately 400 YouTube clips of concert footage were viewed more than 18 million times across all media so far. For a symphony orchestra, these are astounding figures. If we compare the social media activities of the Berliner Philharmoniker with those of the nine other top orchestras in the world (Gramophone 2008), the Berliner Philharmoniker have more than four times as many Facebook fans as the second-placed orchestra; the Berliner Philharmoniker have the second-largest number of Twitter followers, and almost three times as many YouTube subscribers as any other ensemble. This clearly shows that, of all the orchestras, the Berliner Philharmoniker are reaching the generations in the social media generation the most effectively.

While "liking" someone on social media platforms or "following" their tweets might not prove a particularly strong commitment from a customer relationship perspective, the Digital Concert Hall's success is impressive: It is still the only project of its kind today, with over 300,000 registered users representing a total of 170,000 paid transactions, and 15,000 valid accesses are in circulation at any one time (which equates a growth of over 30% p.a.).

In other words, the Berliner Philharmoniker make a significant contribution to the cultural enrichment of many people throughout the world. And the increasing number of digital distribution channels indicates that the project's success looks set to continue.

Since assuming his role in 2002, the principal conductor Sir Simon Rattle has encouraged the orchestra to address a wider audience and to relax its sometimes rather elitist touch. Who would have then imagined the extent to which the Digital Concert Hall was to achieve this? In this respect, the Digital Concert Hall is a crucial milestone in the continuing digital transformation of one of the world's best orchestras.

A Glance into the Future

With their transformation into the digital age, the Berliner Philharmoniker are well on the way to consolidating their creative and financial independence, but this is not the only challenge they are faced with. In 2018, Sir Simon Rattle will resign from his post as the principal conductor, and discussions have already started about his possible successor, although there is no clear favorite yet. Whoever it will be, he or she will have a very hard time to follow in the footsteps of Sir Rattle, and he or she will have to be a thought leader, both in musical and technological terms. Only in this way will it be possible to maintain the legacy of Karajan and Rattle.

A great deal of trust is placed on the collective wisdom of the orchestra to select the "right" principal conductor and the "right" representatives from within their own ranks. Exciting times lie ahead indeed.

Links

http://www.berliner-philharmoniker.de
http://www.digitalconcerthall.com
http://www.youtube.com/user/BerlinPhil
https://www.facebook.com/BerlinPhil
https://twitter.com/BerlinPhil

Bibliography

Baumol, W.J., Bowen, W.G. (1966). Performing Arts: The Economic Dilemma; a Study of Problems Common to Theater, Opera, Music, and Dance. Twentieth Century Fund.

Berliner Philharmoniker (2013). Orchestergeschichte. Available from: http://www.berliner-philharmoniker.de/orchestergeschichte/sir-simon-rattle [accessed 21.06.2013].

Connolly, K. (2008). The Berlin Phil – live in your own front room. *The Guardian*. Available from: http://www.guardian.co.uk/music/2008/dec/19/berlin-philharmonic-internet [accessed 21.06.2013].

Gramophone (2008). The world's greatest orchestras. Available from: http://www.gramophone.co.uk/editorial/the-world's-greatest-orchestras [accessed 21.06.2013].

Berliner Philharmoniker

A COMMENT BY AXEL UHL

The fascinating thing about the Berliner Philharmoniker is that they actually question many rules of management theory which are generally considered valid.

However, this does not apply to the findings from transformation research. One of the key factors for the success of a transformation is that senior management agrees on the strategy to be adopted. In this respect, the Berliner Philharmoniker go several steps further and ensure the inclusion of the critical mass for change through their democratic decision-making. Also, they do not run the risk of egoistic, individual interests of senior managers setting the strategic and functional course for the organization. They only change what really needs changing – but then it is done with absolute thoroughness and perfection. This often involves lengthy decision-making processes, but ensures a quicker and more successful implementation.

The Berliner Philharmoniker founded a new organization for the transformation and took advice from professional expertise. Clear ideas, which of the processes needed to be changed, which risks were to be taken into account, and which technologies should be used, helped to organize the transformation. Simultaneously, the core value-adding process – the music of the Orchestra – was affected as little as possible. To support the technology, "world-class" partners were engaged. Nevertheless, a step-by-step approach was chosen which reduced the complexity of the change process. It also helped that with Deutsche Bank as the main sponsor there was no need to waste too much energy on the financing of the project, which finally helped to focus on the value realization.

6

The Downturn of a Battleship: How the Proud British Automotive Industry Failed to Transform

Till Schauen, Axel Uhl (SAP)

This is the story of a country which once built nice, good-looking cars, which were in great demand throughout the world. This country still exists, although most of its car manufacturers are no longer around. What can we learn from this?

Abstract

This case study describes how the former proud and strong British automotive industry went through a series of failed transformation until it finally collapsed. It is the first time we apply the BTM² framework not only to a single enterprise but to an entire industry. We then realized that the same principles that cause disasters on a micro-economical level are also true on a macro-economic level.

*****

Today, everyone knows that British car manufacturers in the 1970s built unreliable, technically outdated vehicles that were, therefore, scarcely capable of competing. High costs and numerous strikes did the rest to ensure that their reputation was in tatters. However, this does not explain how and why the industry came to be in such a poor state.

If we want to get to the root of the problems, we have to go back to the time when the British car industry was first established, to a time when it had shut itself off from the rest of the world and, thanks to its protectionist policies, did not have to fear the threat of competition.

Episode 1: Pre-1952

Great Britain was the first region to be properly industrialized, and it was also the first region which had to experience the consequences of a networked economy and the social problems associated with it. In 1912, the Morris car factory, headed by the proud William Morris, was founded. To prepare himself for the increasing competition, William purchased other smaller car manufacturers over the course of the years, including Wolseley, MG, and Riley. By the late 1940s, this had enabled William Morris to become the largest British car manufacturer. However, William Morris – who was later made Lord Nuffield – was not an engineer by nature, and he was not interested in modern production methods. His main interest was rather to make as much money as he possibly could, and he was quite jealous in his driving ambition to be the undisputed leader in his company. Although he was often out of office on business trips, he did not allow anyone else to make decisions. Consequently, the management team changed frequently because directors "were retired" with time, and the company increasingly lost its ability to innovate. Finally, Leonard Lord was brought into the company to safeguard the future of Morris. He did a great job, streamlining the model range and integrating Wolseley and MG in the Nuffield Group. Nevertheless, he left the company several years later after a row with Morris. He swore revenge: "I'm going to take that business at Cowley apart brick by bloody brick!"

The post-war years were particularly tough. The British economy was on its knees, raw materials were rationed, and the government gave clear instructions to the car industry: "Export or die". So Morris exported as much as he could, especially to the USA, where MGB was particularly popular. Even in his own foreclosed market, however, Morris faced increasing competition. The reason for this was Ford's British division, which was producing practical and cheap cars much more efficiently than Morris production plants. This was primarily thanks to the modern Ford plant in Dagenham, where production was standardized and took place in one central location, whereas the Morris production plants were spread over half of England. Each of the four makes had its own assembly plant in a separate location. The bodywork manufacturers, engine suppliers, and other subcontractors were also located in different places. The work carried out at some of these locations was more reminiscent of manufacturing workshops than of modern factories. To a large extent, the employees in these workshops also rejected modern production methods.

The problems at Morris' production plants intensified over time, and he felt that to merge with Austin was the only way of preventing Ford from overtaking him as Britain's largest car producer. Austin was the long-standing number two in the British car market. There, a man had spearheaded the company for several years whom he knew well from former times: Leonard Lord. Lord had a reputation for being rather choleric and had borne a grudge for a long time. It must have given him great pleasure to see Morris now ingratiating himself in the hope of a merger. In any case, he appointed himself as the head of the merged Austin-Morris plant, which was known as the British Motor Corporation (BMC).

However, he did not do much to help BMC to gain new strength. This was due not least to his old grudge against Morris. He began to replace the more modern Morris engines with Austin engines and cited "streamlining" as his justification for doing so. Furthermore, the various BMC brands did not show any signs of affiliation with one another. This continued preventing any knowledge transfer, use of economies of scale in production, or standardized processes. This, together with the associated unfavorable cost structures, led to enormous disadvantages compared to their foreign competitors. "Admiral Leonard Lord" would have loved to oversee a proud fleet of British cars – instead, his consortium of companies resembled rather a collection of "moderately seaworthy, but vehemently independent trawlers, pleasure steamers, and coal barges, which did not even have a common home port".

Episode 2: 1968 – Sir Donald Stokes

The growing quality problems at BMC, caused by outdated production methods, the widespread plants, and poor profitability, even led to a not very quality-conscious behavior of Americans – buying less and less British cars, and so the exports slumped. Jobs were now at risk, so the British government stepped up to the plate. It urged the British car manufacturers to enlarge and to embark on an even more spectacular merger. BMC combined with the British Motor Holding (BMH) to form the British Leyland Motor Corporation (BLMC). BMH brought with it the Leyland truck imperium and, more importantly, Standard Triumph and Jaguar. In doing so, BLMC brought the most important makes and suppliers together under one roof. The British government was delighted to inform the whole world that Britain again had a genuine battleship in the automotive market; behind the chic new façade, however, the same crew as before was mutinying – only now there were twice as many of them…

The captain of this big steamer was Donald Stokes, previously head of BMH. To this day, there are said to be people who still foam at the mouth when they hear this name. Stokes was deemed the epitome of arrogance and incompetence. Of course, in his view, the bureaucracy, the castle mentality in his plants, the miserable productivity, and the chronic shortage of funds were the causes of the current plight.

However, there had been initial signs of innovation, such as the Mini. Since late 1959, it had shaped the future of the small car market. But the levels of sales and service did not stand up to international comparison, and the quality of workmanship fell.

When in 1973, with a 15-year delay, Great Britain opened itself up to the common market of the EEC. Imports flooded the country and left the British cars looking very old. Finally, the state intervened once more – even more drastically than previously – and bought BLMC, the damaged ocean liner, and took it in tow.

Episode 3: Red Robbo

Being concerned for jobs, the government was happy to get involved. A particularly fatal step was taken in 1970. The Conservative Health government wanted to stop British industrial workers' rampant obsession with strikes, and passed a law that was intended to minimize industrial disputes. The result was a huge wave of strikes. The Labor government repealed the law in 1974, but the floodgates had been opened. These strikes had little in common with, for example, strikes in Germany. As there were no general collective agreements in Great Britain, wages were negotiated individually for each plant, sometimes annually. The trade union representatives – called "shop stewards" – were given a disproportionate amount of power: one small supply business was able to paralyze the entire group. "A determined machinist had the navigation bridge in his hand."

One of these determined machinists was Derek Robinson, known as "Red Robbo". He was a shop steward at the Longbridge plant and he got his name because of his communist beliefs. He confronted anybody whom he did not like: the BL management and the government. He was the most high-profile of a series of shop stewards who paid little attention to "trivialities" as falling production figures and atrocious quality. They were not even primarily interested in higher wages; ultimately, it was only about preserving their own power.

BL began to sink, and even the ever-increasing subsidies could do nothing about it. Untethering individual components was of no help either as they sank without trace. In 1979, Red Robbo overshot the mark and was made to walk the plank. The wind had changed, and now Downing Street was home to Margaret Thatcher, the "Iron Lady". Moreover, BL had recently been joined by a small, dynamic speedboat with a rising sun and a letter H on its flag (Honda). The British disease had affected not just BL, but was also rife among other British car manufacturers. Even Ford UK lost greater shares of its independence to Ford in Cologne, and Vauxhall increasingly became a branch of Opel. Lotus struggled through until 1986, when it lost its independence, but then achieved the feat of reinventing itself ten years later and still boasts outstanding vitality to this very day.

Episode 4: The Break-up

The final chapter to date in the British Leyland saga is quickly recounted. With Honda's advanced technology, the newly renamed Rover Group experienced a temporary high, but was then sold to British Aerospace in 1988, which, only six years later, came to the brink of collapse. BMW rushed to the rescue, but they too were unable to resolve half a century of structural chaos and ultimately escaped with just a black eye. Following a failed merger with SAIC, the Indian manufacturer Tata took over the Rover and Jaguar makes after they had briefly been part of the Ford Group. Today, Mini and Rolls-Royce belong to BMW, while Bentley and Bugatti belong to Volkswagen.

What happened to MGB and Triumph? These classic brands are enjoying a new lease on life and are treasured by numerous clubs. Some models currently offer a supply of spare parts that BMLC could only dream about.

What can we learn from this disaster? As a base of our analysis, we will be using the Business Transformation Management Methodology (BTM²) framework (see Uhl and Gollenia 2012) and the experience that we have gained from numerous transformation projects.

1. Meta Management: Culture, Values, Leadership, and Meta Communication

As in almost all failed transformations, the subjectively perceived need for transformation was relatively low, or there was only little commitment at the top level of the BL management to make the necessary changes a business priority. Instead, the pressure from the competition was alleviated by protectionist policies. The arrogance of the senior management, which originated from their previous successes and status mentality, prevented them from fully appreciating their lack of competitiveness. Even when protectionism was removed and the negative consequences of this were clear for all to see, the vanity and egoism of all the stakeholders involved determined their actions, and made them blind to the correct approach. Conflicts were regularly solved by adopting the winner-and-loser principle, and subsequently shifted to a personal level. Most of the communication was indirect via the media and with little consideration for correct procedures. Unrealistic promises prevented an awareness for change in the middle management and at lower levels.

2. Strategy Management

To implement a successful transformation, the top management should have joined forces with the trade unions in an effort to find some common ground and, in an early phase of the transformation, should have repeatedly communicated the benefits of and the need for change. Successful transformations usually have clear CEO sponsorship, which means that the CEO invests a large proportion of his working time in the transformation. However, this was not the case with any of the captains of HMS British Leyland. It was therefore not possible to win over a majority of the organization in favor of change.

Another problem was that those involved thought that the transformation would affect only a part of the company, whereas in reality the entire company with all of its brands and suppliers was affected. This lack of strategic importance made it impossible to implement the necessary changes. The problems that this created could no longer be solved in a later phase of the transformation.

Many mistakes were also made in terms of content. A transformation should begin with a clear vision of the future company in mind and be driven top-down to the middle management level. From there, the transformation should be further operationalized, while making sure that the vision can be implemented. But the vision was not discernible and, for that reason, it could neither be used as a mission statement nor operationalized.

Most successful transformation projects undergo at least two phases. For example, in the first phase, the project usually fails, although crucial skills are developed which usually enable success to be achieved in a second attempt. However, this only applies if a learning process takes place by means of self-reflection which was not the case for the British car industry. The same mistakes were repeated over and over again. Not realizing that mergers without supporting measures tend to weaken competitiveness instead of strengthening it, they were repeated and even increased in terms of their dimensions.

Wrong strategic decisions ("doing the right thing") such as these are extremely difficult to rectify later on.

3. Value Management

Successful transformations always have a clear business case, where both the outlay and the benefits of the transformation are clear. In the case at hand, the outlay that was needed to implement the change was underestimated. Transformations require a great deal of energy and resources. This demand increases exponentially when the organization has only a limited ability to transform, which can be assumed in this case. It was equally unclear what was hoped to be achieved and how to achieve it. There were only very vague ideas about the benefits of the mergers.

Furthermore, the benefits were overestimated and the risks and problems underestimated. There was no detailed business case – as this was considered superfluous. And it was never really assessed how successful the completed takeovers had been.

4. Risk Management

It can be assumed that strategic risk management did not play a major part in the course of the transformation. Nor was there clarity about the strategic risks of mergers or the risks of foreclosing a market. The trade unions were unaware of the risks associated with their labor dispute.

5. Organizational Change Management

Our research shows that a transformation is most likely to succeed when orchestrated, continuous, and incremental changes are initiated at an early stage. In this case, it seems important to first administer to the needs of those who are affected, and only then deal with the actual process and technology issues.

In this regard, a company does need a clear strategy of how to deal with stakeholders' problems. The earlier the problems are addressed, the better. In the case at hand, it would also have been prudent to involve right from the start the representatives of subsidiary companies, trade unions, and politics in the planning of the transformation implementation. This would have enabled them to take the most important stakeholder interests into account when finding a solution. This would then probably have prevented the blocking mentality displayed e.g. by the trade unions.

6. Competence and Training Management

It makes good sense to align the required existing competencies as part of the transformation readiness, because the success of a transformation is always a result of the required work and the competencies that exist for this. The case at hand involved a lack of leadership qualities, but also a lack of specialist know-how, such as process management or engineering expertise. Similar to other examined failed transformations, the people who were in positions of responsibility relied too much on generic knowledge or a third party which they eventually brought into play. In this case, it was the government that ultimately took over the helm and sent the steamer to a watery grave.

7. Program/Project Management

The fact is that transformations cannot be fully planned in advance; and planning must be regularly adapted to changing underlying conditions. In this case, however, it was not possible to identify any form of systematic planning. For this kind of planning, the responsible managers would have had to have experience with implementing transformations – and this was clearly not the case.

8. Process Management and IT Management

From a process management point of view, systematically optimizing processes would have been a crucial factor in regaining the ability to compete. But this would have required collaboration across the various locations and an optimization along the entire value chain. However, there was no willingness to do so. Furthermore, the reductions in labor force caused by efficiency gains were a thorn in the trade unions' side, which is why they were so vehemently against any further automation.

This story has not really reached its conclusion, but we would like to bring our observations in this article to a close with the takeover of Rover and Jaguar by the Indian Tata Group. Significantly, business for them is blooming once again since they have been taken over by the company from the former British colony.

Conclusion

The demise of the British car industry is a prime example of a failed transformation and its consequences. Can we be sure that this kind of thing will not happen today? Of course we cannot. Transformations still fail more frequently than they succeed. The reasons always seem to be the same. If we examine current complex transformations, such as the efforts made by Greece or Spain to bring about reforms, or the energy transition in Germany, we are easily able to identify similar examples to those in the British car industry. In these cases the degree of transformation readiness as well as the subjectively perceived need for transformation seem low – a dangerous combination.

Bibliography

ETH Swiss Center for Automotive Research (2008). Automobilindustrie Schweiz. Branchenanalyse 2008: Aktuelle Bestandsaufnahme von Struktur, Trends, Herausforderungen und Chancen. Available from: http://www.tim. ethz.ch/research/swisscar/topics/automotive_industry/Downloads/Studie_ Deutsch_LV [accessed 14.12.2012].

European Foundation for the Improvement of Living and Working Conditions (2004). Trends and drivers of change in the European automotive industry. Available from: http://www.eurofound.europa.eu/emcc/publications/2004/ ef0427en.pdf [accessed 14.12.2012].

Frankfurter Allgemeine Zeitung (2008). Eine Werkbank für Hersteller aus aller Welt. Available from: http://www.faz.net/aktuell/wirtschaft/britische- autoindustrie-eine-werkbank-fuer-hersteller-aus-aller-welt-1513602.html [accessed 14.12.2012].

Hepburn, Daniel (2011). *Mapping the World's Changing Industrial Landscape*. The Royal Institute of International Affairs.

PricewaterhouseCoopers (2012). Europas Pkw-Markt im Rückwärtsgang – Absatz dürfte 2012 um fünf Prozent sinken. Available from: http://www.pwc. de/de/pressemitteilungen/2012/europas-pkw-markt-im-rueckwaertsgang. jhtml [accessed 14.12.2012].

Schauen, Till (2005). "Englische Autoindustrie (Historie des Untergangs)". Oldtimer Markt, 09/2005.

Uhl, A., Gollenia, L.A. (eds) (2012). *A Handbook of Business Transformation Management Methodology*. Farnham, UK: Gower Publishing.

7

Lean Transformation at Mercedes-Benz

Joachim Follmann (Mercedes-Benz), Sebastian Laack (Mercedes-Benz), Helmut Schütt (Mercedes-Benz), Axel Uhl (SAP)

Abstract

Mercedes-Benz Cars looks back on their lean transformation efforts started more than fifteen years ago. Establishing the Mercedes-Benz Production System (MPS) as a closed system had laid the foundation for lean management principles. Two departments were formed, the MPS Training Center and MPS Support. The educated MPS Experts help analyze business processes, consult with management, and oversee transformation projects. A "model factory" simulates processes and adapts the training content to the existing knowledge of the participants. Collaborative efforts in lean management optimize the processes, saved money, and improve customer satisfaction and employee communication, which solves problems in less time.

*****

"The best or nothing" – Gottlieb Daimler's claim characterizes the Mercedes-Benz brand and is anything but easy to live up to. What originally referred primarily to the ideas and ingenuity of the company's founder has since become more pragmatic. Daimler is now a global organization with over 260,000 staff members and requires a clear vision, experienced and competent managers and employees, stable processes, and a strong corporate culture. The success of the automotive company hinges on the efforts of each individual.

One of the important success factors to this end is a far-reaching production system. Production systems have a long tradition and clear principles. Back in 1831, for example, General Carl von Clausewitz recognized the importance of robust processes, avoiding waste, and ensuring continuous improvement as necessary to achieve goals. The best-known production system currently used is that of Toyota. The production system used by Mercedes-Benz Cars (MBC) also has a long tradition and has become one of the driving factors behind the success of the premium Mercedes-Benz brand – with a pronounced focus on technology, innovation, quality, safety, and sustainability. In 2000, this system was bundled as a closed system for the first time – the Mercedes-Benz Production System (MPS) – by leveraging different developments in the company. This laid the foundation for lean management principles in production and, somewhat later on, in administration.

From a critical perspective, initial success was confronted by the challenges of early lean initiatives. Improvements in the individual business units, for example, could not be made at the expense of other business units (e.g. the historical conflict of assembly processes being compromised in the name of logistics and vice versa, or assuming that active involvement of managers in optimization measures is all that is required to safeguard changes and prevent relapses from occurring).

To meet these challenges and facilitate implementation of the MPS, all resources were bundled at MBC in 2008. The organization was restructured and four new consulting fields were defined: strategic and operative target definition, methods and tools, qualification, and Mercedes-Benz culture. Today, almost four years after the go-ahead, an initial conclusion can be drawn.

"Leadership, qualification, and organization are key factors that determine the success of lean transformation"

Joachim Follmann, Director of Production Strategy
and Mercedes-Benz Production System

The introduction of centralized MPS offices in 2008 provides a standardized basis for the decentralized lean support organization at Mercedes-Benz Cars and anchored it in the "Strategische Planung und Mercedes-Benz Produktionssystem" (Strategic Planning and Mercedes-Benz Production System) center. This center is, among others, responsible for assisting business units in implementing the MPS throughout Mercedes-Benz Cars. Activities started in the production area and have since carried over to administrative areas such as Human Resources and IT.

Two departments were formed to implement the Mercedes-Benz Production System: the MPS Training Center and MPS Support, which leads the MPS offices located in the plants. The training center is used to qualify MPS experts and continuous improvement managers. After receiving training, the MPS experts work on site in the MPS offices to assist plants in applying continuous improvement processes (CIPs) and assume functions directly in the plants after approximately 3–5 years in the MPS office.

In general, the lean support organization comprises two distinct types of expertise: MPS experts who work in the plant offices and are managed centrally via the MPS office, and improvement managers who are assigned to the respective area managers. Qualifying the MPS experts in the MPS training center takes one year and concludes with a certificate from Reutlingen University. The information conveyed is very much rooted in practice; only one-fifth of the content covers theory. The aim of the course is to acquire implementation skills by realizing lean projects and involves coordinating four projects each year coached by an MPS expert trainer. Additional seminars that deal with MPS basics and methods are also provided. The practical projects are carried out in a production or administration environment and lead to the formal qualification of "Lean Manufacturing Consultant" or "Lean Administration Consultant" for the future MPS expert, who is then responsible for analyzing business processes, consulting with management, and overseeing transformation projects.

Improvement managers are qualified in an introductory seminar and a series of workshops, and subsequently assume responsibility for controlling the CIP (creation of measures, CIP workshops, measure tracking) in the respective center (e.g. bodyshell or assembly center in a plant).

Six Sigma green and black belts are additional qualifications. Six Sigma is a methodological add-on in the production system and finds particular application in the MPS when it comes to sustaining and stabilizing processes as well as systematic problem solving processes.

Employees who want to participate in the MPS expert training program must first pass a selection process. This is necessary because not only expert qualification but also consulting and social skills, for example, are also important to successfully embark on an MPS career. After completing the program, the experts work for three to five years in the MPS office, after which they themselves can become MPS expert trainers or assume general or specialist functions. An average of five years should be spent working in the MPS office. "It is important that we come full circle with seminar-based learning, learning by doing, and constructive feedback for personal development", summarizes Guido Gratza, manager of MPS expert training in the MPS Training Center. Describing a particular feature of this, Guido Gratza adds: "All MPS experts worldwide have undergone the same MPS training. The participants know each other, exchange information, and develop a joint understanding of the results we want to achieve with lean transformation." Figure 7.1 provides an overview of the training offered as part of the MPS organization.

"Developing an awareness for lean leadership is one of the key factors in determining the success of lean transformation"

Guido Gratza, Head of MPS Expert Training at the MPS Training Center

Newly appointed managers (team and senior leaders) have been educated in lean management practices since 2011 by participating in a one-week lean qualification program that includes theory, the MPS learning platform (also known as the "model factory", in which participants experience lean principles as they pertain to production, administration and engineering in a practically-oriented, real-world environment), and a lean project conducted in the individual's area of expertise.

The learning factory now simulates not only production processes, but also administration and engineering processes as well as energy efficiency and adapts the training content to the existing knowledge of the participants. Having managers carry out optimization measures themselves brings theoretical and practical knowledge together and increases their motivation to implement them in their respective areas.

One of the key points in understanding leadership as it applies to the lean philosophy is that managers act more as a coach than a problem-solver for employees. The lean leadership principles of motivational ability, goal orientation, improvement skills, openness to change, coaching competency, and customer and process orientation are even being incorporated into the general leadership philosophy at Mercedes-Benz Cars and supplement the existing leadership model.

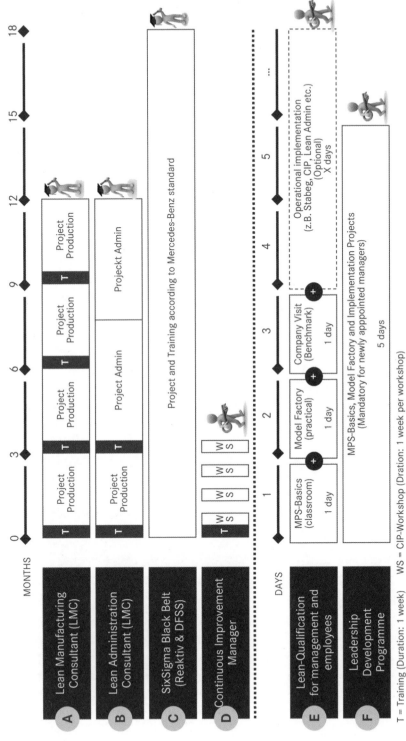

Figure 7.1   Training Overview
Source: Daimler AG PP/SPS.

T = Training (Duration: 1 week)   WS = CIP-Workshop (Dration: 1 week per workshop)

MONTHS

A Lean Manufacturing Consultant (LMC)

B Lean Administration Consultant (LMC)

C SixSigma Black Belt (Reaktiv & DFSS)

D Continuous Improvement Manager

DAYS

E Lean-Qualification for management and employees

F Leadership Development Programme

Project Production

Project Admin

Project and Training according to Mercedes-Benz standard

MPS-Basics (classroom) 1 day

Model Factory (practical) 1 day

Company Visit (Benchmark) 1 day

Operational implementation (z.B. Stabeg, CIP, Lean Admin etc.) (Optional) X days

MPS-Basics, Model Factory and Implementation Projects (Mandatory for newly apppointed managers) 5 days

"We will have reached our goal when lean principles are actively practiced on all levels and in all business units"

Bettina Sandig, Head of Change Management and Communication at the MPS Training Center

Sustained improvements are only possible when employees are convinced of the value of their contribution and commitment. "Lean transformation cannot be forced. Rather, the added value created in thinking and acting from a lean perspective must be experienced and confirmed within one's sphere of influence", explains Bettina Sandig, who heads the change management and communication program at the MPS Training Center.

Lean transformation therefore requires a high degree of self-motivation that translates into employees being genuinely interested in improving quality sustainably. Such a mindset is only possible, however, when problems are viewed as opportunities to improve the system and not as threats. "One could even say that we always knowingly test the limits of our systems and processes until problems become apparent and we can eliminate what causes them. We facilitate this approach methodically by coaching and sharing knowledge gained from experience", adds Sandig.

"Many everyday problems can only be resolved by adopting a team perspective and critically reflecting on collaborative efforts, interaction, common goals, and values. This allows changes in attitude and behavior among employees to be monitored and the willingness to cooperate improves. To ensure that motivation does not dwindle, all suggestions for improvement must be checked and prioritized. Promoting the open exchange of information and discussion with leadership circles is also beneficial. Decisions are communicated in a transparent manner so that everyone has the same level of knowledge", explains Sandig.

"Stable processes and reliable quality must be safeguarded to realize lower costs in the long term"

Joachim Follmann, Director of Production Strategy and Mercedes-Benz Production System

The success of the MPS and the excellent acceptance of the lean initiative have also been substantiated by positive feedback from plant managers who are interested in making increased use of the know-how of MPS experts for their locations. "We focus on realizing genuine, lasting added value instead of pursuing short-term success", comments Joachim Follmann. What has materialized is a solid basis on which sustainable lean culture can be practiced in the enterprise. This experience, combined with the trust that has been placed in the MPS, also makes it possible to resolutely manage crises as well as secure additional competitive advantages. "Only when the waters are rough does it become apparent who has the right strategy and is well prepared", adds Follmann.

Setting qualitative goals does not by any means come to the exclusion of achieving quantitative improvements. On the contrary. "We realize an average sustainable savings potential that is well into the six-figure range (in Euros) for each project", explains Guido Gratza. "This is why we are convinced more than ever that lean transformation is the way to go."

"We thought we were already lean. Thanks to the trained eyes of MPS experts, however, processes could be optimized further and unforeseen potential tapped!"
Customer feedback from a Production Manager for Mercedes-Benz Cars

Lean principles encompass standardization, the just-in-time production strategy, continuous improvement processes (CIPs), shop floor management, and the pull principle. Managers are also assisted in creating the lean vision, translating strategies into key figures, developing an integrated milestone plan, and implementing this plan together with the internal support organization. The various MPS offices currently use a comprehensive box of methods and tools for optimizing processes, and lean awareness training courses, coaching, team development, and qualification are offered for managers as part of cultural intervention.

Mercedes-Benz Cars thus practices a holistic transformation concept with strategic and operative targets, lean methods and tools, qualification and training concepts, and a Mercedes-Benz lean culture. While Mercedes-Benz Cars knows that the transformation is far from complete the direction has been set.

"Applying lean management methods plays an important role in IT as well and helps us streamline our processes"

Helmut Schütt, Vice President and CIO Mercedes-Benz Cars and Vans

IT personnel at Mercedes-Benz Cars and Vans are aware of the strategic role they play in the lean transformation of the company. "Transformation projects that have nothing to do with information systems are basically non-existent, which is why our skills are almost always required and are typically a strategic success factor", says Helmut Schütt, ITM CIO for Mercedes-Benz Cars and Vans. In the past, IT processes were very much a function of managing bits and bytes. Today, the emphasis is on designing and optimizing processes through the use of information technology.

To meet diverse requirements, a program was developed for optimizing and standardizing IT processes and is currently being rolled out. Lean management is geared towards optimizing existing processes. It is in this context that a trade-off was reached between process re-engineering and the classic lean approach, which were carefully weighed and meaningfully combined. "Re-engineering these processes with lean principles in mind makes perfect sense. For example, we realized that specifying only the relevant details for standardized processes can streamline process documentation considerably", explains Schütt.

One critical point is the provision of resources for lean projects, since employees are typically immersed in their operative tasks and ongoing projects. "We therefore have to keep a close eye on the lean initiative and correlating changes from a management perspective, which accounts for approximately 20% of managerial capacity. Implementing changes without express approval from management would be inconceivable", affirms Schütt. IT personnel will continue to pursue the lean process established and carry out workshops with participants after the processes have been rolled out to identify additional optimization measures. A further step could involve integrating the lean methods in all IT projects in the interest of promoting their application throughout the company.

"Lean administration is an investment in the future. It improves customer satisfaction and shareholder value and, not least, it helps to secure jobs"

Sebastian Laack, Senior Manager of Lean Administration in HR

Lean transformation also applies to human resources (HR), whereby the focus is on lean administration. To this end, the head of human resources strives to:

1. Further the leadership culture by promoting the continuous improvement process (CIP).
2. Improve product and process quality in HR.

Not only do companies and HR management profit from structured optimization procedures, streamlined processes, and greater added value, HR employees too enjoy tangible benefits such as clear orientation, the possibility of addressing and resolving problems quickly, and significantly improved collaboration with interface partners.

"Our goal is to have each individual internalize the concept of lean processes in its DNA. CIP culture means that everybody asks themselves each morning what they can do better than yesterday", clarifies Sebastian Laack.

Lean administration in HR is a strategic initiative that is implemented in four stages:

1. Anchor the lean administration mindset and make HR employees aware of the added value it provides.
2. Test and experience lean administration at all levels.
3. Stabilize improved processes and extend their reach via lean administration.
4. Practice lean administration during daily business as part of a culture of continuous improvement.

Leadership and communication are key levers for the established CIP. Shop Floor Management (SFM), that is, being on site – is therefore an important instrument that is consistently practiced in HR. The objective is to quickly communicate important day-to-day issues and challenges to the entire team and determine how best to handle them. This occurs by continually aligning tasks with higher-level and longer-term targets. The meeting takes place every day or once a week and lasts 15 to 30 minutes.

"Our employees have now embraced SFM. Communication has improved considerably and problems are resolved in less time. This makes our employees the best multipliers of the lean concept and colleagues from adjacent departments frequently stop by and ask for more information", explains Laack.

The second central method is that of "small projects". The objective here is to analyze the as-is status of a process, then derive a desired status and apply targeted measures to optimize the process within a week. This does not always occur smoothly, which is all the more reason to educate multiplicators in dealing with conflicts and complex social dynamics in addition to providing information about lean methods.

"We are not merely a consulting organization, but more of a program office that is responsible for coordinating the introductory process in HR from a content and methods perspective. To safeguard implementation in the individual HR departments which, together, employ several thousand people around the world, an implementation organization with tandems and multiplicators was established and educated in one week training seminars", says Laack.

All Senior HR Managers also took a three-day seminar so that they could become aware of lean practices and qualified to practice them. The focus of these seminars was to become familiar with these practices in a simulated environment and to learn how to apply this knowledge to everyday tasks.

In summary, lean transformation in human resources is advanced through the combination of awareness and qualification, simulation, fast implementation (small projects), improved communication, and leadership (SFM).

"The objective also indicates the starting point for lean transformation"

Bettina Sandig, Head of Change Management and Communication in the MPS Training Center

Lean transformation was also successfully implemented at the smart plant in Hambach. "Our first order of business in the 18-month project was to convince everyone involved of the importance of the initiative. This case for action is necessary, since not presenting a plausible reason makes it difficult for the team to justify a change", explains Bettina Sandig. A common goal that indicates the outcome and associated benefits must then be developed in the leadership team. Different communication channels are leveraged to clearly communicate the common goal to everyone involved and include kick-off meetings with management and proper use of interactive events or media such as the employee newsletter and the intranet.

Value stream mapping and a lean check were carried out for optimization purposes. This was followed by systematic planning of all projects. Additional key interventions at the smart plant were the development and initiation of a skills-based qualification program. Today, the plant can be proud of more robust, end-to-end, and order-based processes characterized by their optimal frequency and value stream. The most noteworthy outcome, however, was a much improved attitude toward mistakes coupled with the commitment to implement reliable correction measures. Managers now also spend much more time in the production area and work together with employees to find solutions. "This was the most satisfying feedback of all", summarizes Sandig.

Key Learnings and Lean Transformation Compared to Business Transformation

The following conclusions can be drawn with respect to successful lean transformation based on the experience gained by Mercedes-Benz Cars:

- Lean transformation requires a holistic approach that integrates strategy/objectives, processes, leadership, and culture in equal measure.
- Lean transformation does not focus primarily on reducing costs, but on bettering processes and products and improving quality delivery and processing times, for example. This, in turn, automatically leads to cost savings.
- Proficiency in lean processes is almost impossible to gain without a respective organizational unit that supports line functions in their CIP initiatives. New approaches must therefore be piloted and adapted to the specific requirements of the organization.
- Lean transformation requires time to develop the values and codes of conduct to be practiced by everyone involved.
- Lean transformation can be introduced at any time; crises can accelerate this transformation.
- The importance of managers embracing lean transformation as role models cannot be over-estimated.

- Upper management trusting in the effectiveness of lean transformation and in the ability of the respective organizational units is more important than achieving short-term success.

Acknowledgments

The authors would like to thank the following people for sharing their thoughts and experiences:

- Guido Gratza (SPS/MPST) Head of Expert Training at the MPS Training Center.
- Bettina Sandig (SPS/MPST) Head of Change Management and Communication at the MPS Training Center.

It's All About Culture!

A COMMENT ON THE MERCEDES-BENZ CASE
BY ANDREAS SCHÖNHERR (ZURICH INSURANCE COMPANY LTD)

If you read through the Mercedes-Benz case study on lean transformation, you might think to yourself: "So what? That's nothing new. If your company mission is 'The best or nothing', your daily work should be focused on Lean, Six Sigma, continuous process improvements, and so on."

But in reality, this is so difficult to achieve as you need the commitment and dedication of each and every one of your employees, starting with the product engineer, who not only focuses on the beauty of the car (and with the new Mercedes-Benz SL, they have thought it through meticulously, right down to the smallest detail), but also considers how the production process, logistics, and so on can be optimized. This applies to your entire production chain and does not stop at the Finance or Human Resources departments.

So it is not so much about the methodology itself but how you transform a company with 260,000 employees worldwide into a cross-departmental and cross-functional think tank, making sure that each and every employee improves the way he or she works.

So how did Mercedes-Benz address these challenges in the case study?

1. *Understanding:* Employees will only change their way of working if they see the point of the change and agree with it. This is exemplified by the lean transformation in the Hambach production factory.
2. *Reinforcement:* Measurement procedures and reporting structures need to be consistent with the behavior that people are asked to embrace. The setup with a dedicated central team as well as a sponsor in the top management of Mercedes-Benz has sent out the right "message" that this is important for them.
3. *Skills:* The MPS-Training Center, the "model factoring site", and the dedicated MPS-Certification equip the company with the right skills and methodologies, and the practical application in smaller projects gives them time to learn and absorb the information and integrate it into their existing knowledge.

4. *Role models:* Integrating the lean principles into the management philosophy at Mercedes-Benz and the very practical Shop Floor Management enable role models at every level who "walk the talk".

So the foundation of lean transformation as part of the culture at Mercedes-Benz has been built, and the future will show how much benefit Mercedes-Benz will be able to reap from this endeavor. Unfortunately, these benefits are often impossible to quantify at the beginning of such a transformation and very difficult to prove afterwards, which is one reason why companies are often afraid to even start them. Maybe they should read this case study first?

Simply the Best

A COMMENT ON THE MERCEDES-BENZ CASE BY AXEL UHL (SAP)

Lean transformation at Mercedes-Benz is a best practice for successful transformations. To illustrate this, I will use the BTM² – the Business Transformation Management Methodology.

Lean transformation at Mercedes-Benz is driven by the top management. The person responsible for the transformation reports directly to the Management Board of the Mercedes-Benz brand and has its full support. All management levels are systematically incorporated into the lean transformation process and the lean values are integrated into the Mercedes value system.

At a strategic level, the company management is aware of the transformation need and of the transformation readiness and allows sufficient time for the implementation. The management team stands unanimously behind the initiative and the ambitious pre-defined targets which do not focus primarily on saving costs but on ensuring quality.

The project team consists of outstanding employees, and has been complemented by an experienced academic partner. The implementation involves every discipline of the BTM²: processes and project organization, technical infrastructure, qualification program, the key performance indicators, and responsibilities for achieving value, change management, and program management.

Worthy of particular mention are the certification options for participants of the lean initiative and the consistent focus on implementing all the measures in practice. The project team has found just the right balance between essential specialist knowledge and real-world scenarios. Finally, the interviews and discussions revealed perhaps the most important aspect of successful transformations: the highly infectious passion and enthusiasm with which the team went about its work.

8

Smart Mobility: An Up-and-Down Ride on the Transformation Roller Coaster

John Ward (Cranfield University), Paul Stratil (SAS Automotive Systems), Axel Uhl (SAP), Alexander Schmid (SAP)

Do you remember when you first saw one of the tiny Smart cars on the streets? You may be surprised to hear that it has been around for 15 years now. Learn how the initially unique mobility concept has gone through many phases before it arrived in today's reality of highly competitive, web-enabled, and sustainable mobility.

Abstract

Today, the small Smart automobile is a micro car like many others. However, it has its origins in a revolutionary mobility concept of the New Economy times. Since the first model was launched in 1998 by the joint venture of Daimler and Swatch, the Smart car project has gone through various phases and transformations. This case study highlights important changes, like the involvement of changing partners, the level of integration into the Daimler corporation, the scope of the Smart product range, and the specification of the marketing concept.

The case study illustrates vividly how, even with the most creative and visionary idea, the simultaneous innovation of many parameters increases the complexity of initiatives to such an extent that success is put at risk.

*****

The first Smart Car was produced by Micro Compact Car AG (MCC) in 1998. It was based on the idea of a futuristic mobility concept by the Swiss entrepreneur and founder of Swatch, Nicolas G. Hayek (1928–2010). MCC at that time was a joint venture of Daimler and Swatch. (The Daimler company itself underwent organizational changes during the time described in this case study, being Daimler-Benz AG, DaimlerChrysler AG, and finally Daimler AG. To avoid confusion, the corporation is named "Daimler" throughout the entire article.) The MCC company was managed as an independent entity outside of its corporate parents Daimler and Swatch, which reflected an approach to innovation that was adopted by many organizations within the so-called "New Economy".

The Beginnings of the Concept

The original individual mobility concept had been developed by Hayek and his associates as a solution to congestion and environmental pollution in urban areas. It included cooperation at several levels: with train companies to ensure easy rail loading as well as with city authorities and car parking operators who provided extra small and cheaper parking spaces. Founded on those ideas, in 1991 Hayek signed a deal with Volkswagen (VW) to bring the concept to market. Three years later the relationship was called off by VW. Market research had not been able to find the necessary customer demand for the planned automobile, and other projects of ecological mobility at VW were favored by the new CEO of VW (Lewin 2004, pp. 51–59).

Hayek had to look for new partners. In March 1994, Daimler agreed to establish the joint venture MCC with Swatch (Lüscher and Pellinghausen 2005) – after concessions by Hayek in the areas of branding, design, and technology of the automobile. Daimler, whose average Mercedes customer was more than 50 years old, saw in the concept an opportunity to find a new and younger target group, the 20–30 year olds.

Launching the product in 1998 was a significant achievement: A completely new brand had been developed, whose marketing concept had raised high levels of customer awareness and interest in European markets. A production site had been constructed from scratch. Finally, a dealer and marketing organization had been developed and was ready for the product launch.

In order to share the risks, costs, and also the profits of the innovative product concept, cooperation was a primary feature of MCC's business model. The business model and its highly integrated supply-chain concept went beyond existing automotive industry practices in a number of ways:

- Customers could configure the Smart car online to their preferences, yet order-to-delivery lead-times were counted in weeks.
- The distribution followed a 2-tier model, that is, an order passed through two parties (the factory and the dealer) before the Smart car was connected to the final customer.
- Dealers had to invest in "Smart Car Towers" to stock and display 24 cars (see picture on page 44).
- Suppliers co-invested in the production location and took over more responsibility in the final assembly process.

Consistent with the set-up of the supply chain, the IT strategy also included cooperation. From conception through implementation to the maintenance, all the work was outsourced to an IT provider. The contract included payment after the start of production and a profit sharing of every car sold. At the beginning, this full-service outsourcing model seemed to be advantageous for both sides, as MCC did not need to build up IT knowledge (Computerwoche 2003; Kunz et al. 1997).

Looking back, a lot has happened since then. Today, the first Smart (successor) version of Daimler and Renault-Nissan's cooperation is soon to be launched (Seiwert 2012). This case study will describe the transformations that the Smart project has undergone in-between.

The timespan is divided into four phases of evolution, and associated with those, there were four major strategic transformations:

- Phase 1 (1998–2002)
- Phase 2 (2002–2005)
- Phase 3 (2005–2010)
- Phase 4 (2010–today)

Phase 1 (1998–2002): A Venture in the New Economy

Soon after the launch of Smart in 1998, Hayek left the MCC company due to a disagreement concerning the ecological orientation of the concept, and the shares were taken over by Daimler. MCC became an independent 100% subsidiary, staffed by predominantly young, well-qualified, and innovative staff who reflected the characteristics of the Smart target market segment. In order to encourage new ideas and ways of thinking, every aspect of the Smart business was kept separate from the rather conservative, risk-averse culture of Daimler. The aim was to deliver a strategy of "differentiation through innovation". As it was to turn out later, the arguments in favor of this approach were, according to the words of Pfeffer and Sutton (2006, p. 87), "not based on the best evidence, but on what was in vogue at that time". In the New Economy, companies often established separate organizations with license and funds to create new products and services which were often delivered through new, but unproven business models and processes. The obvious lack of car producing experience of the staff was known and accepted by the management of Daimler. It was considered as a necessary risk if MCC was to create and deliver the new concept and products to satisfy the expected new market. However, no one knew how big that market was and whether the new mobility concept would be a valuable selling proposition for the target customers or whether the business model could satisfy all the parties involved.

The distribution concept was focusing on Europe and on big cities only, which limited the size of the market. In all cases the "forecasts" in this first phase proved to be more than optimistic. Sales were lower than expected. Manufacturing proved to be more complex and costly than anticipated. Profits were lower than planned. As a result, the partnerships – on which the success of the venture strongly depended – were put at risk.

The innovative business model required highly customized and integrated process architecture and IT systems. As mentioned above, the IT strategy foresaw close cooperation and outsourcing of all non-core activities. Since the exclusive partnership with the IT provider involved sharing the sales profits between the two companies, considering Smart's poor economic performance, the IT partner began to compensate its loss of money by charging for change requests. Due to a lack of internal IT know-how, Smart had no choice but to accept it (Computerwoche 2002; Müller and Preissner 2004).

Phase 2 (2002–2005): Turnaround, Integration, and Partnership

The economic constraints, cost pressures, and high shareholder expectations forced Daimler to abandon the original mobility concept. The business had to be "harmonized" with the main car business, adapted and reorganized, in particular with regard to financial controls and systems. In 2004, a new CEO and new management teams were appointed for Smart, mainly from the international parts of the Daimler business, with the intent to introduce a different, far more traditional car manufacturing strategy. The team decided to focus purely on the production of cars. Hence, the complex mobility concept – including cooperation with train companies, car sharers, etc. – was abandoned. At the same time the management decided to go global and to expand the product portfolio, thus expecting higher sales volumes while keeping the previous cost structure. To implement this strategy, it was decided to integrate MCC into Daimler. By then Smart had also become a "strategic asset" as it produced a reduction in the (average) CO_2 emissions of the Daimler vehicle fleet, meeting the statutory provisions (which also had a significant financial value).

The new strategy also included a partnership with Mitsubishi. The goal was to reduce the costs of product development, to allow the fast introduction of new models, and to enter new markets in the USA and Asia. An overall sales target of 200,000 cars per annum was set (Milne 2005), but unfortunately sales still fell short of this, reaching 150,000 in 2004, the best year. Success depended on making a difficult "mixed model" strategy work: on the one hand, the sales organization still worked according to the original Smart business approach with the young target group; on the other hand it had to comply with the traditional Mercedes Car Group's way of doing things. And it also depended on the effectiveness of the partnership work with Mitsubishi, who actually had a competing product.

To achieve increased volumes, the strategy adaptation included a change from a previously "pull" to a "push" production model. With a push model, the production plan is based on forecast sales figures, not the actual consumer demand. This change did not fit well with the customization options that made the car attractive. At the same time, a 3-tier distribution model was built up by introducing a wholesale level between the factory and the dealer. Consequently, the distribution complexity rose, margins were reduced, and dealer inventories increased significantly, holding cars that did not quite match any customer specification.

In 2003, to reduce costs and inventories throughout the network, the sales and marketing channels were changed. The cars were now sold through the Daimler retail and sales organization. However, considering the profit margin of other models, the incentive to sell the Smart cars was pretty low.

The development plan for the Smart cars required complete integration of the Smart company into the Mercedes Car Group (the business division of DaimlerChrysler), which led to a more complex organization. Employees were integrated into the Mercedes Car Group via a matrix organization, which removed the separation of the "Smart world" from the rest of the organization. This resulted in multiple reporting lines and a higher degree of complexity, therefore more communication and coordination was required. However, from Mercedes' point of view this integration resulted in an earlier payback time from innovations. Nonetheless, there were problems due to the clash of different company cultures, project understanding, and approaches to decision making. As a result of the integration, many of the younger, innovative employees left the organization. As the car market became tougher during 2003, the further consolidation and cost cutting made most of the Smart sales and marketing staff leave as well.

By 2004 it was becoming clear that the strategy of Smart would not be able to deliver the profitability planned for 2005. Also the new models, like the "roadster" or the "forfour", were no success. Lewin (2004, p. 10) seemed to be right when he stated: "No one asked the buyers if they wanted a car like this." This perspective, combined with the repeated cost cutting in the Smart project, led to further staff demoralization.

At that time the smoldering conflict between Smart and the IT provider concerning the high IT outsourcing costs escalated. This led to in-sourcing the IT function (Zillich 2004). Immediate cost savings were a quick win, but it was necessary for Daimler and Smart to rebuild the IT and systems "know-how" by hiring some IT people from the IT provider.

In 2005 the new CEO and executive team at Daimler realized that the current operating model and existing range of Smart models would never produce the expected sales figures on which the development plan was based. Hence the corporation's strategy was fundamentally changed once more, involving giving up the vision of a global company being positioned in every market all over the world. And it led to a separation from the partner Mitsubishi.

Box 8.1   The Initiatives of Daimler Mobility Services GmbH
Source: Daimler 2013a.

DAIMLER MOBILITY SERVICES GMBH

Daimler Mobility Services GmbH is driving, for example, the following initiatives:

- car2go: This is an alternative car rental system initiated by Daimler and Europcar. As of March 2013, more than 7,000 Smart cars (around 15% of them with electric drive) are ready to be rented by over 300,000 registered subscribers in 18 cities all over the world (Daimler 2013b). In contrast to traditional car rental, the tenant takes the car at one of the special parking spaces which are spread all over the cities, and has the flexibility to drop the car on any such special parking space after usage.
- car2share: This is a platform where car owners can register to offer their car for rent in the time slots when they do not use it themselves.
- moovel: This is a smartphone app that allows customers to compare travel time, cost, etc., and then choose between car2go, a taxi, getting a ride, or taking public transportation.
- GottaPark: This platform helps car drivers search for, book, and reserve parking spaces in big cities in North America, like San Francisco, Boston, or Miami.
- Daimler Mobility Services GmbH also participates in various cooperations and makes investments concerning alternative mobility services, like the smartphone app "myTaxi", the platform "carpooling.com", and tiramizoo, a platform to find courier services.

Phase 3 (2005–2010): Back to Basics and Traditional Car Manufacturing

Overall cost-cutting in the Mercedes Car Group division and shareholder and analyst pressure due to unreached Smart sales targets were the primary reasons for reducing the Smart product range to the "Smart fortwo" as the one and only core Smart product. The "Smart" brand name was to become completely integrated in the Mercedes Car Group and continued to exist only as one of many brands. The individuality and the unique selling proposition was no longer part of the strategy. Forecast sales targets had been too optimistic since the beginning. It had become apparent that the target group's enthusiasm for the concept was less than had been expected. It was no longer a product which customers bought to distinguish themselves but it had essentially become a "me-too" small car product (Capon and Hulbert 2009,

p. 193). More realistic targets were to be set for the single Smart model. From now on, the main goal was to generate net profit for the manufacturer.

Smart was now delivering benefits for Daimler due to several reasons. A youngermarketwasaddressedwiththemicrocar.Highersalesvolumescombined with lower overall fixed costs finally began to pay back the investment cost. And "European emission standards" – introduced by the European Union to force the car manufacturers to reduce the average CO_2 emission of their vehicle fleet – could be met more easily. Meanwhile, there was increasing congestion in the cities worldwide. With the continuing shift of consumer preferences towards smaller, more fuel-efficient cars and ever tougher emissions targets being introduced, it was perhaps time to revisit the original Smart mobility concept? In 2007/2008, Daimler chairman Dr Zetsche established an innovation team to identify new business opportunities for Daimler, and as an outcome of this initiative, 100 vehicles of the first generation of zero-emission "Smart fortwo electric drive (ED)" were launched as a test fleet in the city of London (Reed 2007; Daimler 2008). In 2009, the second generation was produced in series and leased to customers instead of sold (Daimler 2009). At the same time, Daimler pioneered a car sharing service (Car2go) in Ulm, Germany (see Box 8.1).

Phase 4 (2010–Today): Has the Time for the Idea Finally Arrived?

In a strategic effort to build the next-generation Smart, in 2010 Daimler signed a deal with the alliance Renault-Nissan (The Economist 2010). Small or micro cars powered by traditional combustion engines or by electricity now have a significant role in meeting the increasing demand for fuel-efficiency and also the emissions targets imposed in the EU and other major markets.

Renault and Nissan, who have been working together for some time, both already have products that compete directly with Smart. Daimler is the new party in this threefold relationship. But Daimler can claim to have invented the micro car concept, which should give it a major influence on the development of the new model(s). Furthermore, the experience Daimler has gained from the development and evolution of the product and from experiments with organizational and business models – including complex inter-company working relationships and dependencies – should help the collaboration succeed. However, Daimler also had to accept compromises, including sharing high-end technology with Nissan's luxury line "Infinity" (Cheong 2012).

In April 2010, only three months after the announcement, Daimler transferred the Smart project back from the Mercedes Car Group division into a separate product line within the Daimler group (Stuttgarter Zeitung 2010). Joachim Schmidt, Director of marketing and sales at Mercedes, highlighted in an interview the strategic importance of the Smart product for Daimler, especially in the field of electric mobility and climate balance of their fleet (Rother and Seiwert 2011).

With the incorporation of Daimler Mobility Services GmbH in January 2013 (see Box 8.1), Daimler made a significant step towards alternative mobility concepts – which was an important part of the original idea of the Smart automobile. Hence, in the last of these four phases, Smart seems to have finally returned to its origins in the conception of innovative mobility. In the fifteen years of the Smart car's existence, the business has been through three transformations – and the fourth is starting now. Figure 8.1 on the next page presents an overview of the phases. In the following paragraphs we will look at the transformations more closely.

First Transformation: Starting Several Adventures at Once

At the beginning, the innovative but rather complex mobility concept was introduced by Nicolas Hayek, who was an outsider to the automotive industry. His idea was at that time hard to understand for traditional car manufacturers and difficult to address through market research. Nonetheless, Daimler decided to undertake this adventurous new initiative, which was not only a new product but also – to a certain extent – a social experiment.

From a strategic point of view, for Daimler it was essentially a "diversification" strategy – a new product for a new market. As studies show, this is far from easy to achieve successfully (e.g., Ansoff and McDonnell 1990). In addition to that, a groundbreaking business model was introduced, which increased the risks. But Daimler could afford to take these risks, and this transformation can be considered as Daimler's venture in the New Economy, which at the time was said to have different "rules" and would even lead to the demise of old "dinosaur" corporations.

Given all the interrelated innovations involved, the number of only partially controllable variables, and the inexperience of the management, perhaps it could not be expected to be completely successful. It was successful

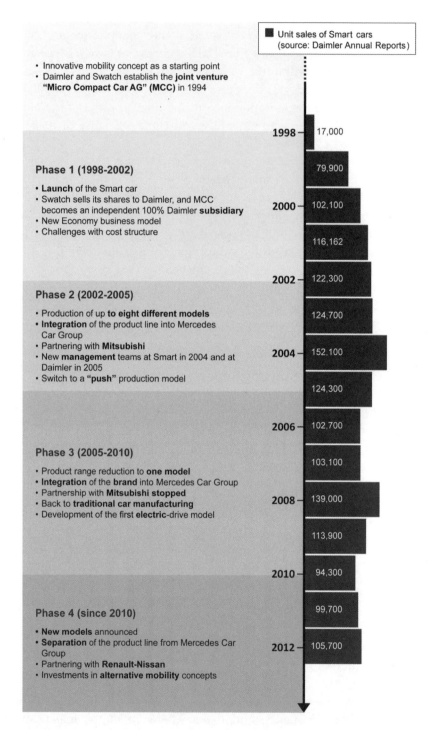

Figure 8.1   Timeline of the Smart Car History
Source: BTA.

in creating a new product that sold moderately well into a new market for the company, but it was not profitable, and the complex business model with its many partners was fragile and only sustainable if there were significant profits to share.

Perhaps there was nothing wrong with the idea, it was just at the wrong time? However, that was not evident at the time – a time when there was a plethora of new business and product ideas, usually developed by enthusiastic, optimistic young people. Many of those endeavors were sustained for too long due to a lack of experience and sound business judgment. Others received such a "positive feedback" that everyone involved hoped to profit from the venture. As other research shows, this combination can lead to "delusional optimism" (Lovallo and Kahneman 2003, p. 58).

The downturn of the New Economy changed it all. New business models were suddenly seen as overvalued and overly risky. Many New Economy business models had run out of money by this time. For Smart, it meant the end of the original business model and a move towards more traditional models of the automotive industry.

Second Transformation: Saving the Product from a Failure of Concept

The transformation from phase 1 to 2 happened very quickly, both in terms of the change in strategy and reorganization to integrate the separate company into the corporate orbit of Daimler. Traditional values of producing quality products in a profitable way were brought in by the new management team, although the innovative thinking remained in expanding the range of Smart models.

The significant change in values and strategy, which involved abandoning the mobility concept, meant that there would be casualties. The culture clash between the original Smart staff and the Daimler organization inevitably resulted in most of the original Smart team leaving quickly, avoiding a protracted "struggle" between the old and new regimes.

It did however involve major contractual and relationship changes with many of the partners involved in the first phase. This required dismantling many of the unique features of the original business model, including the separate dealer network and supplier arrangements. In addition to that, the new collaboration with Mitsubishi was a core aspect of the strategy to expand the product range and to enter new markets outside Europe. These changes were not trivial tasks. Inevitably, significant resources and costs were absorbed to extricate Daimler from its previous arrangements and to develop the new partnership.

However, the fact that the Smart car had become a strategic asset, as described above, increased the motivation of senior management to keep the product in the Daimler organization – despite the circumstance that analysts stated that it would be difficult to achieve significant profits in the short term.

Third Transformation: Regaining Stability and Control

The third transformation was as much driven by the issues which the automotive industry worldwide and the strategy of Daimler as a corporation were faced with, as by the continuing unprofitable performance of the Smart models – something which industry analysts and shareholders thought Daimler could no longer sustain.

The actions taken were really the only ones available: getting back to what Daimler knew it could do well, using its traditional expertise, systems, and business processes in order to achieve higher volumes and at the same time become profitable by sharing the fixed costs. Introducing stability was essential to achieve the required economies of scale. Hence, further product innovation or development was reduced to the minimum. Separating from Mitsubishi and regaining control of all business aspects rather than relying on external partners also helped the execution of the new product strategy. The Smart car became integral to Daimler's corporate strategy. The micro cars enabled Daimler to expand its sales of other models, yet still complying with the increasingly demanding CO_2 emission regulations worldwide.

An important question remains: If Daimler had undertaken this more drastic transformation earlier and brought Smart fully "in-house" earlier, could it have produced profits earlier?

Fourth Transformation: Back to the Future?

Against all odds, the Smart brand was never abandoned or closed down by Daimler. In 2010 they announced the development of a new generation of Smart automobiles through a strategic alliance with Renault-Nissan. The Smart car was separated from Mercedes Car Group again and became a separate business organization with responsibility for product development, engineering, production, and sales. The motives behind this move were not clear at that time. There were speculations that this could be an exit preparation strategy, prior to either shutting down or selling the unit. Or maybe the reason was to form a more dedicated and consequently agile project team in order to develop the next micro car generation?

However, as the last years have shown, Daimler is still willing to invest in the innovation of the Smart project but tries to reduce development and production costs by sharing them with Renault-Nissan. Not only are new models of the two- and four-seat car being launched soon, but there are also considerable efforts made to expand the alternative mobility concepts. The initiator of the Smart concept, Nicolas Hayek, would have been pleased to see his ideas finally becoming reality.

Reflections and Conclusions

After having discussed the phases and transformations, we would like to reflect on the case from two angles: the people side and the market perspective.

Achieving a quick drastic transformation is sometimes only possible with a major change in the management team of the unit concerned. The new team will have a remit to act quickly if their appointment was driven by crisis, as it was in the two transformations at the start of the millennium. But this can only work out if there is sponsorship and support for the new unit team at the top level of the corporation – especially if the financial and IT implications of the transformations are substantial, as it was the case with the Smart endeavor. A feature of the second and the third transformation was that the incoming management teams had been led to believe that the situation was more positive than it actually was. More detailed scrutiny revealed the need for more urgent change than had perhaps been anticipated. But this situation may actually have been an advantage. Major transformations are easier to sustain when the existing situation is clearly untenable and is deteriorating further. It enables the "marketing" of the new strategy to be more straightforward and the arguments for major changes to be more convincing and therefore more acceptable.

On the down side, the almost inevitable result of this type of dramatic and rapid transformation is that many employees involved in the previous regime, including very able people, will be lost. Perhaps this is an imperative necessity to enable the new team to be effective and the new strategy to work, but one should always consider the potentially negative effects on people remaining in the organization.

On the market side, over time the segment for Smart cars changed from mainly the "trendy" young people, for whom it was designed, to the cost-conscious person of any age. The transformations at each stage seemed to follow this trend and to adapt to the implications, leading to less and less support for the brand's uniqueness and more focus on the direct and indirect product costs. In many ways this is the natural and familiar product life cycle. Although Smart has – in terms of market share or profitability – never really been a "star" or a "cash cow" product, external factors, especially the ecological issues and accompanying regulations, have led it to become an important business asset.

In terms of generalizing the lessons learned from this case, a number of observations can be made and questions posed about business transformations, especially those involving the creation of new business ventures:

1. How many variables can be managed successfully at the same time in a business transformation? It is very risky to change too many business parameters simultaneously – in this case: the product concept and target market, business models and relationships, processes, systems, and staff. This is especially true when there is little evidence available that the new product concept or business model will be successful, which is likely to be the case in a major, revolutionary innovation.

2. A strategy requires vision, conviction, and power to implement but also an understanding of the capabilities and resources including financial means needed to deliver it. There has to be a sound business rationale behind it – adjusting to, or perhaps anticipating, external forces and opportunities without an objective evaluation is not sufficient. In this case, the mobility concept was very visionary and well ahead of its time. Perseverance was needed to continue until a strong business rationale materialized – in this case: compliance with CO_2 emission standards combined with renewed interest in the mobility concept, which jointly created an attractive opportunity.

3. To what extent can core activities involved in the transformation be outsourced or entrusted to third parties? It may be necessary to "buy in" new skills and capabilities to create the new product, the business model, and the processes, or to achieve rapid change. But, as discussed above, the longer-term implications of reliance on others, who may not share the same vision or level of commitment to the future business model, need to be considered and the consequences of that potential mismatch need to be anticipated.

Key Learnings

- The transformation complexity and challenge increases with the number of innovative elements involved: it is likely that at least some of the innovations will not work.
- Visionary ideas that anticipate developments need great staying power and patience, that is, a combination of faith in the concept plus the funds to sustain investment until they become profitable.
- A successful transformation needs both a sound business rationale and an understanding of the resources and the capabilities needed to achieve it.
- Most importantly, before investing significant money in a new business model, the value proposition needs to be 100% clear: Who is selling what to whom with which core competence? Who are the main competitors, and what is the main differentiating factor? This provides the basis for a reliable business plan and a realistic roadmap.

Bibliography

Ansoff, H.I., McDonnell, E.J. (1990). *Implanting Strategic Management*. 2nd edn. New York: Prentice Hall.

Capon, N., Hulbert, J.M. (2009). *Managing Marketing in the 21st Century: Developing and implementing the market strategy*. Wessex Inc., Bronxville NY.

Cheong, H. (2012). "Renault-Nissan Deepens Ties With Daimler, Infitini A-Class Likely". Available from: www.cbt.com.my/2012/10/01/renault-nissan-deepens-ties-with-daimler-infitini-a-class-likely/ [accessed 02.04.2013].

Computerwoche (2002). "Fallstricke auf der grünen Wiese". Available from: http://www.computerwoche.de/a/fallstricke-auf-der-gruenen-wiese,1061738 [accessed 03.04.2013].

Computerwoche (2003). "Rückholprojekte bei Porsche, Smart und Zimbo. Dreimal Outsourcing rückwärts". Available from: http://www.computerwoche.de/a/dreimal-outsourcing-rueckwaerts,1056656 [accessed 03.04.2013].

Smart's Backward Loop Into the Future

A COMMENT ON THE SMART CASE BY AXEL UHL (SAP)

The Smart case study impressively demonstrates the impact that strategic decisions have on the success of a company or product.

Hypothesis 1: In retrospect, I am convinced that Smart was and still is a fantastic product, the strategic significance of which can hardly be overestimated.

Smart has provided Daimler with several strategic value potentials at once. These include positive innovative added value for the Mercedes brand and the access to new and younger customer groups. And what is more, the significance of meeting the legal specifications for CO_2 emissions.

The product perfectly dovetails with the requirements of modern societies and the development of megacities, and it complies with climatic and environmental standards.

Although virtually nothing has been invested in the product for a decade, Smart still attracts almost as many buyers as it did at its launch.

Hypothesis 2: The Smart organization had a very high level of expertise in the areas of innovation, transformation, and customer orientation.

The sales and mobility concepts developed by Smart were innovative additions to the core product. Furthermore, it would be very difficult to find another example of a company which has changed its business model so extensively in such a short period of time. Smart had brought on board managers and employees who were extremely innovative and willing to embrace change. Smart developed holistic customer solutions that went far beyond the product itself, such as the special smart parking bays in city centers. In doing so, they created further strategic competitive advantages.

Hypothesis 3: Smart underestimated the costs for an international sales and service concept and had to meet too ambitious economic objectives too early.

Even with innovative products and solutions, international success can only be achieved with considerable effort, significant investment, and plenty of staying power. After all, Smart was not a digital product with low marginal costs, but had to equal the performance of other vehicle manufacturers in terms of production, sales, and service. Although the product was in its growth phase the necessary investments were reduced. Under increasing sales pressure, Smart focused on traditional concepts to achieve success in the automotive industry and invested in new product variants, such as the "Smart forfour" and "Smart roadster". Having been hastily launched onto the market, however, these products were unable to meet the high quality demands or simply had not enough buyers.

Daimler responded to the lack of economic success and the brand's deteriorating image by completely integrating Smart into the Group. If economic success could not be achieved using the previous approach, they would have to implement further cost reductions. This allowed Daimler to limit the negative economic effects, and at least the Group's targets in terms of CO_2 reduction could be achieved, although Smart's innovative strength and Daimler's profile among a younger target group fell behind.

9

Pro3 at Allianz:
A New Dimension of Customer
Centricity

Axel Uhl (SAP) and Oliver Hanslik (Former SAP)

What can a successful market leader do to further strengthen its customer relationship? At Allianz, top management decided to implement Pro3, a transformational program to reach a new level of customer centricity.

Abstract

Allianz SE is the largest insurance group in Germany. To keep its leading position, Allianz Germany has committed to Pro3, a program which will bring customer-oriented consulting to a new level. The reasons for this step are the ever changing circumstances, new media and technologies, as well as increasingly discerning, responsible, and highly involved customers in a saturated market. Those customers want financial service providers who are genuine, unassuming, and down-to-earth, but who also align their services entirely on the ideas, visions, and aspirations of the clients. The transformation of the biggest German sales organization has just recently begun.

*****

Martin Künzel is constantly on the road. He is the rollout manager of an important transformation at the Allianz Beratungs- und Vertriebs-AG, the consulting and sales organization of Allianz Deutschland AG. As a manager with many years of sales experience at Allianz, he is used to travelling, but the sheer number of kilometers he is covering at present is taking on a whole new dimension, even for him. Each week – sometimes on a daily basis – he commutes between Leipzig, Munich, and Hamburg, and never tires of explaining the objectives and motivation behind the Pro3 program in order to expedite its implementation.

A new dimension is also the transformation project itself, as it involves nothing less than changing the largest field sales organization in Germany. More than 9,000 mostly already successful and independent general and main agents, another 3,500 employed salesmen, as well as some 5,000 office staff in the various agencies need to be convinced and enthused about this new sales concept. The program is called Pro3 and it represents a partly shift in Allianz's sales strategy – from "good salesmanship" towards more customer-oriented consulting services.

There has often been talk of consulting in the past as well, but still the focus was rather on the successful salesperson and not as much on the customer-oriented consultant. This time, however, Allianz is serious about it.

"The future of our profession and also that of the Allianz Deutschland sales model, with its general and main agents, will be sustainably changed through this project", says Martin Künzel. To this end, he willingly accepts the burden that this involves; it will take another one or two years until the change will be effectively implemented. That is a long time, especially in sales, where you are measured in terms of your latest figures and where is little room for patience. But this time, Allianz will have the necessary persistence – Künzel is sure of that.

Allianz SE

Allianz SE is the world's second largest insurance group in terms of sales revenue[1] and has its headquarters in Munich, Germany. The company was founded in 1890 by supervisory board members of Munich RE, a large reinsurance company. To this day, Allianz and Munich RE maintain very close contact.

Allianz SE has several business units (see Figure 9.1)[2] and serves some 78 million customers in 70 countries. In 2011, about 142,000 employees generated €103.6 billion of revenue and achieved profits of €7.9 billion (see Figure 9.2).[3] In Germany, Allianz is the market leader in the insurance sector, with numerous holdings in well-known major corporations such as BMW, E.ON, and Siemens. In the public eye, the Group's activities tend to be rather unobtrusive and reserved, and Allianz has so far been spared any scandals such as the one recently suffered by its competitor ERGO Insurance Group.[4]

Allianz Deutschland AG, as wholly-owned subsidiary of Allianz SE, provides insurance services in the areas of life insurance, health insurance, and property insurance. Additionally, banking products are sold through the Allianz Bank. Allianz Deutschland AG relies on independent agents (in accordance with section 84 of the German Commercial Code, HGB) to sell its insurance products and services. The strongest sales branch belongs to the Allianz Beratungs- und Vertriebs AG. As a result of this independence, Allianz has only limited authority over its more than 9,000 agencies.

Customer Orientation – for Good Reason

There are important reasons for the evolution of the Allianz Deutschland sales organization. Insurance sales agents in general have always been a thorn in the side of consumerists. In the public opinion, insurance agents are usually said to put their own interests first when it comes to concluding insurance services.

An insurance policy is a complex product that is supposed to both protect the customer against risks and also to accumulate his assets. However, it is difficult for consumers to deal with the multitude of tariffs, the increasingly long-term commitment, and the diversity of products. These circumstances, according to consumerists, are repeatedly used by insurance agents to intentionally provide consumers with advice that fails to meet their needs. Insurance and investment products are trust-based products – but who can you still trust these days?[5]

Banks, especially those in the field of retail banking, operate in a similar setting and face the same problems. The apparent integrity of banks, which had long since been their competitive edge compared to the seemingly less reputable insurance companies, has suffered enormously since the financial crisis. The former were therefore recently legally obliged to draw up reports of all consultations and have them signed by their customers. The coercive measures imposed by the state to ensure greater consulting integrity, though, have resulted in an immense amount of administration work.

Figure 9.1   Allianz SE and Shareholdings
Source: Allianz.

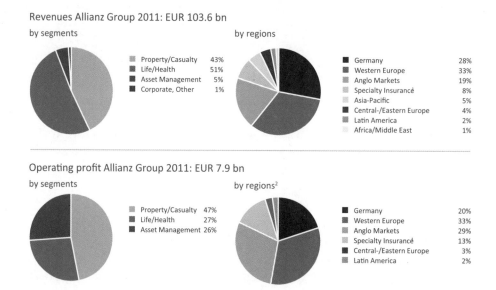

Figure 9.2   Revenues Allianz SE 2011
Source: Allianz.

Figure 9.3   Drivers for Change

Further state regulations regarding the sales of insurance policies are currently viewed with skepticism at Allianz. "We have always invested a great deal of time and money in high-quality training and education", says Jens Grote, board member at Allianz Beratungs- und Vetriebs AG. The education at Allianz is indeed considered exemplary throughout the industry. "We do not allow any agent to have contact with customers without the relevant specialist skills. For further improving our consulting expertise, however, we rely more on a proactive, customer-oriented management than on state regulation."

"After all, it is our customers who are increasingly looking for more support and orientation, which is shown in the feedbacks from the meetings with our clients", says Martin Künzel. "Private pension arrangements are becoming increasingly important, while the financial market has become riskier. This leads to rising customer expectations regarding our consulting expertise. The local salesperson must be fully aware of those needs and act accordingly. In the past, customers were less likely to change their provider. Today, besides high-quality service, close customer contact is a key factor for customer retention." This situation has also been reflected in the industry-wide negative trend in customer satisfaction ratings for years. The most important indicator here is the number of people willing to recommend their insurance provider to others. As insurance products are trust-based products, customers will only recommend their provider e.g. to relatives if there is an appropriate trusting relationship with the insurance provider.

Like the industry as a whole, the market leader Allianz also suffers from low further recommendation rates. This trend is accompanied by a transition in the way younger generations lead their lives. "With smartphones and the establishment of e-business sales channels, we find ourselves right in the middle of a digitalization of the single stages of life. With this comes faster access to the latest information, which leads to a previously unknown level of customer responsibility and hence to an increased consulting demand", explains Jens Grote.

The Internet as the pivotal medium of the 21st century, and with it social media, enables companies to maintain a constant dialog with its customers and thereby actively involve them in the design of products. The Internet is therefore much more than just a quick and inexpensive distribution and communication channel. "These days, it is much easier for everybody to get any required information. But the rapid dissemination of information e.g. via Facebook, Twitter, and comparison portals can have both positive and negative consequences", says Martin Künzel. "The Internet is interactive and principally democratic, and it enables faster product innovations and individually designed services. With the increased presence of direct insurers and comparison portals, a hybrid shopping behavior has established, of which insurance companies are only too aware", sums up Erich Rochlitz, Sales Director at Allianz responsible for Northern Bavaria. "Although an insurance contract is mostly still concluded in an agency, most offers are obtained from the Web. For this reason, contacting customers via new media – in addition to classic means of communication – is becoming increasingly popular. There are approximately 800 Allianz agencies that actively use Facebook to contact customers these days."

Dr Jürgen Schüler, Branch Manager in Leipzig (Germany), sees a further reason behind Pro3 in the amendable innovation activity at Allianz regarding the development of new products. Too little innovation leads to a loss in attractiveness for customers. "This is primarily reflected in the fact that, although customers liked the products, we noticed decreasing enthusiasm", underscores Dr Schüler. "Only delighted customers recommend us to others." With the introduction of new products such as "myCar" or the new home contents insurance product, Allianz is able to enthuse customers again.

Changing economic conditions, new media, and higher customer expectations in the German market are decisive factors that lead to a new way of thinking at Allianz (see Figure 9.3). The customers want financial service providers who are authentic, modest, and down-to-earth, but who also align

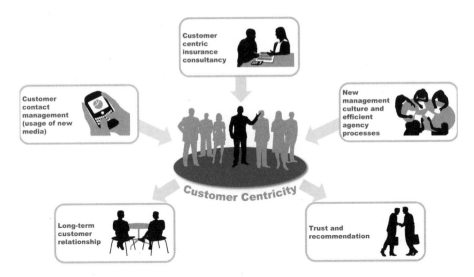

Figure 9.4   Objective of Pro3 – Customer Centricity

their services entirely with the ideas, visions, and aspirations of the customers. In order to deal with the anonymity and abundance of offerings on the Internet and to meet the increased need for trust and information, customer proximity and an intact customer relationship are the most important prerequisites to ensure competitiveness.[6]

Pro3 – Customers, Employees, and the Company

Pro3 introduces a positive change for customers, employees, and Allianz as a company. The integral parts of the Pro3 program are a structured, holistic approach to consulting, significant improvements in customer contact management, the analysis of internal agency processes, and the introduction of a new management culture. Allianz wants to use these measures to achieve a new level of customer centricity, which will lead to long-term customer relationships, increased trust and higher recommendation (see Figure 9.4).

The central component of the program is its focus on holistic insurance consulting. "Above all, it is about actively involving customers in the consulting process and, together with them, analyzing their circumstances, plans, and needs, jointly prioritizing them, and finding the right solutions", emphasizes Rochlitz.

At first, this does not appear to be particularly new – but it is. For many salesmen in the industry, holistic consulting necessitates a new way of thinking and a corresponding change in behavior. Today, insurance salespeople often approach customers with certain products in mind and then attempt to convince them by e.g. pointing out specific risks or benefits. In other cases, they start by analyzing the risk situation, but as soon as the first gap opens up, the product sales process begins.

This "sales mentality" is deeply entrenched in the industry. Insurance policies have successfully been sold this way for over 100 years; many of the agents have been doing this for decades, and it has served them well. Those who close most deals are deemed successful and accepted, and those who complete the most customer appointments in the least time are regarded as efficient. However, customer-oriented consulting primarily means asking questions, listening, and reaching a common understanding about the client's needs. This requires patience and time – two factors that are rarely encountered in sales. But yet, the long-term benefits of customer-oriented consulting are obvious. Salespeople get to know their customers and their priorities, while customers feel better understood and taken seriously, which eventually arranges for a better match of the consultation and the identified solutions. Additionally, the competition will find it more difficult to tempt enthused customers away.

Improving customer contact management is the second Pro3 success factor. It means contacting each customer at least once a year, if possible. This does not always have to be a personal visit; it can also be done by telephone or by sending an e-mail or a letter. Naturally, a personal interaction is more important. For many insurance salespeople, the higher frequency of contacting clients also represents a fundamental change. Most customer visits were previously planned from a purely economic perspective: How likely is it that the contract will be concluded (based on the mostly incomplete information available to the salesperson)? Where does the customer live and what is the travel distance? Does the salesperson already know the customer personally? How did the last appointment go? Such criteria were frequently taken into account when deciding which customers to visit in person. As a result, most business was done repeatedly with the same customers. In the past, approximately less than 50% of all customers were contacted annually, and about 80% of sales revenue could be achieved with 20% of the total number of customers. Therefore, considerable potential remained idle.

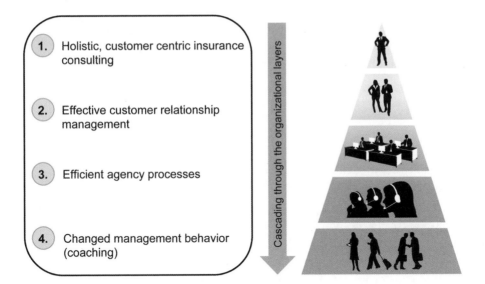

Figure 9.5   Integral Parts of Pro3 and Cascading

From a change management perspective, optimized customer contact thus also means altering the conventional approach towards treating customers equally and impartially and providing all of them with the same consulting services. Customers will now be prioritized according to the criterion when they were last consulted and whether they have ever been consulted at all. From the agents' viewpoint, this – combined with more time-consuming consultations – increases the risk of failing to use their time effectively. This is comparable to changing from being a hunter to a farmer. Instead of short-term notions of concluding contracts, a longer-term approach is adopted. Consequently, there is the probability that the salesperson will not conclude a contract immediately. But the information obtained during the consultation and the improved customer relationship should secure medium and long-term success.

The third Pro3 measure relates to agency procedures, such as answering customer requests, forwarding applications, checking insurance contracts, arranging appointments, processing claims, or preparing quotations. The efficiency of processes varies considerably, with highly efficient, high-quality administration processes in some agencies, and completely the opposite in others. There have been no uniform agency standards in the past, and it was up to the individual agents and their office staff to define their administration processes. A lack of transparency in procedures, long processing times, and an unclear role allocation are just some of the problems that were observed in some agencies. Inefficient agency processes result in agents loosing too much time through administrative tasks – time which could be used more effectively in customer consultations. Furthermore, ineffective agency processes can decrease customer satisfaction, or even create risks, such as a lack of the customer's insurance protection. This re-organization effort of processes must not be underestimated. Some procedures, which have become entrenched over many years, need to be completely reorganized. In addition, process-oriented thinking is a competency which is barely present in many part-time employees working in agency administration.

However, the by far most important success factor is a change in management behavior. In the past, insurance agents have been viewed more as a huge organization of salespeople who, it was felt, operated with military precision and were treated with a rather autocratic style of management. This management culture was increasingly met with opposition by independent and experienced agents, and Allianz has since taken measures to change the situation. Pro3 envisions managers who develop from result focused controllers into trustworthy companions, taking on more of a coaching role. The managers interviewed by us have a management philosophy that is in line with the objectives of Pro3. They base their management style on trust and have weekly coordination meetings with the agents. Those managers have moved away from results orientation towards an activity-based style of improving sales processes.

For the Allianz managers, this initially means an increased burden on their time resources because, as coaches, they must examine the work approach of their sales personnel in much greater detail. Instead of "one-size-fits-all" advice, individual analyses and optimizations need to be carried out, and, together with the sales staff, they discuss how individual success rates can be improved.

To sum it up, many of the desired changes take place at the attitude or behavior level, and are therefore particularly difficult to achieve. In addition to that, the sheer size of the organization further increases the complexity of change processes. So, to bring about this change, all hierarchical levels of the Allianz organization are involved (see Figure 9.5).

From Concept to Implementation

Pro3 is based on the voluntary participation of agents and directly affects a majority of the more than 9,000 independent agency owners, approximately 3,500 sales employees, the agency office staff, and the sales managers.

With this huge number of personnel affected, the implementation phase becomes particularly important. "In previous projects, we usually adopted a 'watering can' type of approach", says Martin Künzel. "This means that we tried to reach the entire organization at once and to implement changes quickly. But that didn't work. We are too big, and you cannot get independent agents to make behavioral changes by simply commanding it."

For this reason, Pro3 is being rolled out in several waves. The first wave started with 2,200 salespeople in April 2012 and has already been completed. The remaining roll-out waves are planned to begin early October 2012, and then April 2013. By mid-2013, more than 50% of sales personnel should be familiar with and work according to the new approach. "We want to convince our self-employed agency owners of the advantages and thus further develop the majority of agencies with Pro3 in the long-run", underlines Martin Künzel.

A comprehensive training concept was developed in order to optimize the consulting process, which will be put into practice by the Allianz field sales academy. More than 100 trainers will carry out the training program over the next few months. Participants have to follow a five-month training plan. This plan begins with four days of in-house training, during which agency managers and salespeople are familiarized with Pro3. The agencies are subsequently provided with continuous support, which is called "sales coaching" and which is executed by the managers. Allianz will be backed by additional coaches to assist the managers on site and provide them with feedback on their management style.

The holistic consulting approach is supported by a discussion guideline for client consultation in traditional paper form and as an IT-supported solution. The IT solution enables the agents to create consultation documents quickly. With its structured approach to carrying out customer meetings, Allianz ensures to provide a consistently high standard of consulting quality across all participating agencies. "We have supplied our agents and junior sales staff with an electronic and physical aid that enables them to enter into a genuine dialog with their customers. The consultant can use it to better assess the needs and wishes of customers and, ultimately, gather customized solutions", explains Martin Künzel.

IT plays a further important role for the success of Pro3. Additional and intensive customer consultations result in considerably more data being collected; this is important on the one hand for following up on consultations, and on the other hand it is of considerable relevance for the development of new products. Also, the new IT-supported consulting process should speed up the identification of the best possible solution for the customer. For this reason, a new HTML 5-based consulting tool was created, which can incorporate existing customer data from available systems and restore it there again. Optimizing agency processes follows best-practices. "In larger organizations, the various outlets do not devise their own processes individually, but use standardized and efficient processes. After all, the tasks in our agencies are usually the same everywhere", says Martin Künzel. A process template that describes model working procedures, tasks, and responsibilities as well as provides checklists is used as the basis for standardizing processes. Sales manager Mike Westhoff illustrates it with the following practical example: "Each morning, the agency owner conducts a check-in conversation with his office manager and discusses the tasks for the day. This is something that rarely happened in the past. In the beginning this conversation is also coached. It is furthermore examined who takes over which tasks in the agency. If the telephone rings, while an office employee, the office manager, and an agent are in the agency, and all three of them pick it up, something is not right. The tasks should be clearly allocated."

However, the most important driver of the change program is the involvement of executives – the so called "leader-led principle". The Pro3 objectives can only be achieved if the managers make their contribution, and for this reason, the approximately 350 managers are given particularly intensive training. The importance of management support in the transformation process is explained by Jens Grote: "In the past, we did not always get close to the sales processes and, consequently, the way in which the agents were managed. We rather concentrated on the results. This time, it is different. The main distinction compared to earlier initiatives is probably not the appealing consulting process itself, but the secret lies in the new sustainable management process, with the managers being the key to success. You can have the best processes available, but without management support, the full benefits cannot be exploited. And that is the reason for my optimism. We accompany Pro3 throughout the organization, from board level to the sales department manager. It is less about 'how much', and more about 'how it was achieved'. Of course, numbers will continue to play a major part, but they will no longer be the sole criterion. We are coaching the salespeople to get them on the right track. We are not leaving those involved in the sales process to their own devices."

Driving the Change – Initial Results and Lessons Learned

When Pro3 was initiated, Allianz Deutschland was not in a perceptible crisis – quite the contrary: 2011 was the best fiscal year since the Allianz Beratungs- und Vertriebs-AG had been established. Naturally, the management was aware that, without changes, a crisis was simply a matter of time, as competitors would catch up. Implementing a program such as Pro3 early on during good times has several benefits: The necessary investments are economically feasible, you have sufficient time for systematic planning and implementation, and the management enjoys the confidence of important stakeholders and employees.

It is important to have a clear understanding of the expected benefits and to know how those can be measured. Allianz wants the investment to pay off both in financial and qualitative terms. An increase in productivity should be achieved by improved processes and tailored consulting. Other qualitative improvements include more frequent and more intensive customer consultations, increased customer retention, greater security regarding existing business, a more contact-oriented management style with a great deal of reflection, and collectively defined next steps.

The principle of free choice plays a fundamental role in implementing Pro3. A sustainable behavioral change can only be achieved if the change is accepted and supported by each person individually. "Without a basic readiness to change of the people involved, it would be a lengthy and presumably unsuccessful process, which is why we started with the agencies that had indicated a strong willingness to change. The success of Pro3 originates from the base and can only be multiplied there", explains Mike Westhoff.

The Pro3 communication concept is also having a positive effect. As early as September 2011, the whole organization was informed about what to expect. All questions that arose were discussed openly, and the importance and necessity of implementing Pro3 were explained. There was also sufficient time available for preparation before the first wave of Pro3 got underway, which has ultimately led to considerable dynamism and speed when currently implementing Pro3. The change was acted out throughout the entire management pyramid (see Figure 9.5). The executive board explained the aims, contents, and necessity of the change to the next lower level, the sales directors explained it to the branch managers, and the latter explained it to the sales managers. This way, all management levels were involved in the implementation, ensuring the necessary understanding and increasing the acceptance of the program.

The project enjoys the support of the top management. In the management board meetings half of the time is dedicated to addressing issues relating to the Pro3 transformation. Top management engages in discussing best practice processes or change management challenges, and actively helps to find solutions. In other words: The top management has changed from control mode to solution mode. Jens Grote: "I consider myself as an element of this process and as a role model for Pro3. This means that I must be familiar with the processes and not just demand them from my employees. Part of my role as a sales director is to be visibly present in the sales department. I will regularly spend a day in an agency and participate in the office activities and sales processes there. In addition to that, I conduct management discussions with directors and hold regular meetings with the sales personnel. Sometimes you get to hear about problems that you thought would not even exist."

An important step in the transformation process was the setup of model agencies in different regions for reference purposes. Those agency managers were asked to make themselves available for an exchange of ideas, best practices, and opinions to find possibilities for optimization for other agencies in a realistic setting.

Next to the communication of the agency managers and their personnel, a regular communication between the agency owner and his Allianz manager is particularly important. They meet once a week to assess the progress of the implementation and to discuss the next steps. They usually identify key focus areas to work on, such as optimizing agency processes and customer contact management, and cultivating the new approach to consulting.

The coaching at all levels of management has proved favorable so far. For example, coaches accompany branch managers during their monthly meetings with sales managers and as well the agent area managers, when conducting their weekly discussions at the agencies. In the next step, the sales managers will coach the agency owners.

Outlook

Although the measurable success in financial terms will only become apparent over time, Allianz's experiences of the first few months of the Pro3 program have been very good. The fact is that first positive tendencies with regards to customer reactions can already be observed and Allianz works hard to further improve this. It is also evident that the feeling of trust between the managers and the agents has deepened. The reasons for this are the weekly conversations and the assurance that common aims are being pursued. It was also possible to ascertain a reduction in the rate of cancellations at the participating agencies, and there is almost zero fluctuation in the sales personnel.

"At any rate, the customers are impressed by the new quality of consultations provided by Allianz", says Martin Künzel – before getting into his car to drive to the next meeting at the other end of the country.

Key Learnings

- The most important driver of the change program is the involvement of executives, the so called "leader-led principle".
- Since insurance products are trust-based products, customers will only recommend their provider to their peers if there is an appropriate trusting relationship.
- To ensure an intact customer relationship, it is key to involve the customers in the consulting process and to jointly prioritize the individual circumstances and plans.
- Holistic consulting necessitates patience and time in order to learn more about the customers, to make them feel understood and find best matched solutions.
- Effective customer contact management helps to create considerable potential for accompanying the customer during his life changes.
- A new management philosophy supports the altered focus at Allianz: Managers are moving away from results orientation towards being activity-centric, trustworthy coaches.
- Efficient business processes will help agents to provide more effective consultations and will lead to increased customer satisfaction.
- Sustainable change can only be achieved if the change is supported by each person individually.

Acknowledgments

The authors would like to thank the following people for sharing their thoughts and experiences:

Martin Künzel, Leiter Rollout Pro3
Jens Grote, Vorstand der Allianz Beratungs- und Vertriebs-AG
Erich Rochlitz, Vertriebsdirektor
Dr Jürgen Schüler, Geschäftsstellenleiter
Mike Westhoff, Vertriebsbereichsleiter

Bibliography

1. Fortune 500 (2012). Global Fortune 500. Available from: http://money.cnn. com/magazines/fortune/global500/2011/full_list/ [accessed 20.08.2012].
2. Allianz (2012a). Unternehmensportrait Allianz Deutschland AG. Available from: https://www.allianzdeutschland.de/unternehmen/ unternehmensportrait/ [accessed 09.09.2012].
3. Allianz (2012b). Fact Sheet. Available from: https://www.allianz.com/static-resources/de/ueber_uns/profil/v_1338888265000/1206_factsheet_eng_final. pdf [accessed 20.08.2012].
4. Rexer, A. (2011). Ergo-Orgien lenken von miesen Riester-Praktiken ab. Welt Online. Available from: http://www.welt.de/wirtschaft/article13524658/ Ergo-Orgien-lenken-von-miesen-Riester-Praktiken-ab.html   [accessed 20.08.2012].
5. Uhl, A. (2000). Motivation durch Ziele, Anreize und Führung. Eine empirische Untersuchung am Beispiel eines Versicherungskonzerns. Dissertation. Berlin: Duncker & Humblot.
6. Fromme, H. (2011). Allianz will Negativtrend mit IT stoppen. Financial Times Deutschland. Available from: http://www.ftd.de/unternehmen/ versicherungen/:neue-software-allianz-will-negativtrend-mit-it-stoppen/60131864.html [accessed 20.08.2012].

A Promise is a Promise

A COMMENT ON THE ALLIANZ CASE BY AXEL UHL (SAP)

Allianz's need for change: Without improved customer focus through better consulting, more up-to-date customer information, and an enhanced image, it will become increasingly difficult – in the face of increased competition – to place the more complex investment and insurance products on the market. The way the information gathering and purchasing behavior have changed – due to the Internet, social networks, and so on – has to be considered as well.

Allianz's answer to that is called PRO3. It is a holistic and integrated solution concept with a sharper customer focus, improved consulting, and optimized qualification and agency processes.

The particular strength of PRO3 lies in its consistent top-down approach. The Management Board has formed a strong coalition which jointly controls and supports the transformation. This is complemented by an experienced program manager who has the necessary methodological skills and is an expert in the field of insurance sales. The Management Board backs him up also in the public and emphasizes the importance of this transformation. This transformation is also seen as an orchestrated, holistic management process. The scheduling is realistic, and experienced partners have been brought on board. This was only possible by providing sufficient financial means, which, in turn, was possible because the organization was enjoying a period of particular success at the initiation of the transformation. Since the risks associated with transformations are well known, the planning was especially meticulous. The behavioral changes are addressed first, which involves developing dedicated training programs. The entire change process is based on voluntary participation and conviction, and it involves all hierarchical levels. Therefore, in contrast to the past, the direct superiors of the representatives are assigned a key role as coaches of the change process.

10

Who's the Leader? Financial IT Integration at a Global Insurance Company

Gabriel Giordano (Ohio University), Annabelle (Lamy) Giordano (Ohio University), Tomasz Janasz (SAP)

What is the best way to approach a SAP financial integration project in an industry with very diverse national regulations? This case covers the ups and downs that the "Lukas Financial Services" insurance company (the real name of the company has been changed for reasons of anonymity) faced in two financial enterprise IT projects, one led by IT, the other by Finance. The case answers the following questions: What are the people- and system-related concerns? Who should lead transformational IT projects, and how should such projects be governed?

Abstract

In 1999, Lukas Financial Services, one of the world's largest insurance companies, implemented SAP systems for most of their European business units as part of a major Finance IT upgrade. However, country business units were still responsible for their own data management, which led to inconsistent reporting and a low level of standardization.

In 2004, there was a push to improve the efficiency and effectiveness of European Finance, and the IT unit launched the EVA project. The goal of the project was to converge all European SAP systems into one system. As the project progressed, many unexpected challenges emerged for the IT leaders.

There was little buy-in from the business unit leaders, resources were limited, and the project fell behind schedule. The pilot sites were dropped, and eventually, the entire project was stopped.

The company continued with decentralized systems until 2009, when a new company focus on globalization and efficiency led to the OCTOPUS Plan, which was a business reorganization plan that called for all of European General Insurance to be based in one country. The European Finance business leaders were in charge of OCTOPUS, and they made the decision to start another SAP convergence project, MASON, to support these changes.

The case ends with the questions that the IT and Finance leaders face as they create their project strategy for the new SAP integration (MASON) and the business reorganization (OCTOPUS). The Finance-led project strategy addresses many of the problems revealed in the first project, although they still face project prioritization, pilot testing, and other challenges that they must account for in their plans.

*****

In January 2010, Francois Rousseau, CFO of European Operations at Lukas Financial Services, had an important meeting with Aart Stryker, the Head of Global Finance IT Strategy. Francois was the project director of a new European SAP convergence project named MASON, and he could not help but think about the challenges and failures of Lukas' previous European SAP convergence project, EVA. Francois knew that there was pressure to transform Lukas Financial Services into a truly global company, and that this project would be a key part of that process. He thought to himself, "How will we overcome the roadblocks that occurred during EVA, as well as handle potential new threats in order to meet our business goals?" When Aart Stryker arrived at the meeting, he could sense that Francois was excited about the future, but that he was also concerned about the past. Aart told Francois the one thing he was certain of: "If we do this again, we have to start with people and governance, not systems and processes." Both of them knew that they needed to look closely at the history of previous projects and to act wisely and carefully to handle the number of risks and pressures that were part of a large project IT project such as MASON.

Lukas Financial Services and its European Business Units

Lukas Financial Services, one of the largest global insurance companies, has more than 50,000 employees based in approximately 150 countries. Two main types of insurance that Lukas Financial Services provides are General Insurance and Global Life. The General Insurance segment provides property and casualty insurance, and the Global Life segment offers life insurance, investments, savings, and pensions. Lukas Financial Services' main European operations are in Germany, Italy, Spain, Switzerland, and the United Kingdom; however, they also have significant representation in countries such as Austria, Ireland, Russia, and Turkey.

Information Systems in the Insurance Industry

Historically, companies in the insurance industry have been organized with decentralized local business units, due to the nature of the industry. Each country has varying regulatory requirements for insurance that require specific expertise, knowledge, and support processes; therefore, insurance companies have traditionally allowed localized business units to act independently and build information systems based on their specific needs. However, since the late 1990s, many insurance companies have realized that inefficiencies stem from allowing business units to act autonomously. Some common issues reported are that information is not readily available for global analysis, data accuracy is not consistent across business units, and reporting processes are time-consuming and expensive. Furthermore, a number of mergers and acquisitions since the 1990s have increased competitiveness in the industry, and customer service, data management, and regulatory compliance are now key success factors.

In response to these issues, many insurance companies have taken on large information systems upgrade projects in order to maintain their competitiveness. One of the most common enterprise systems now used in the insurance industry is SAP, which over 700 insurance companies have implemented.[1] SAP identifies five main areas in the insurance industry that they focus on: customer demands, global competition, innovation, profitable growth, and compliance and governance.

History of SAP at Lukas Financial Services

In 1999, Lukas Financial Services implemented finance and accounting SAP systems for most of their European business units as part of a major IT upgrade. This implementation included 17 country business units, but due to the significant differences between country business units, each business unit had an autonomous SAP system installed, and most information in the systems was not shared between units. The decision to implement independent systems supported the existing business unit design, where power and decision-making were focused at the local business unit level. These differences led to only 10% of the processes in the new SAP systems being common across the units. Until 2004, the company operated under this IT structure.

The EVA Project...

At the start of 2004, Lukas Financial Services was feeling the pressures of the changing landscape of the financial services industry. After severe losses of over USD 3 billion in 2002, in 2003, Lukas Financial Services reported a net income of over USD 1.5 billion. Lukas knew that they needed to make considerable headway in 2004 to continue to be competitive in the industry.

Due to these pressures, the company was operating in a change mode and they appointed a new CEO. This new CEO focused on streamlining processes and approached the company as a truly global organization. The Finance IT unit was asked to review the budget spent on the business unit IT systems and they were given a clear message to increase efficiency and cut costs. In May 2004, after a number of technical reviews and analyses, the Finance IT unit proposed a solution: converge all EU SAP systems into one system. This solution would become known as the EVA project.

A unified SAP program promised many benefits for the company. It would create a highly automated and scalable process platform and it would enable quick posting of local data in the European-level general ledger. At the time, month-end closing could take anything from three to four months, but the new SAP program could decrease this time by 10%. The system also promised to create significant financial savings, generating company-wide benefits of USD 15.6 million by year three.

Box 10.1   IT Integration Projects at Lukas Financial Services:
               EVA Project

EVA PROJECT (2004–2005)

Role of Information Systems in the Company

IT-led and treated as a support project

Important Issues in the Implementation

PEOPLE:
- No business champions to drive the project
- Business Unit leaders did not see the benefits and did not have resources to allocate to the project
- There was resistance to standardization from the Business Unit leaders (at least partially due to the fact that they would lose governance and decision-making power)
- Project governance was not clearly set up, including responsibility of costs
- IT did not have enough access to people with critical knowledge for mapping processes
- There was no clear communication to the Business Units from IT about system benefits

SYSTEM:
- IT-driven, limited local business process integration
- Feeder (legacy) systems were not fully understood
- No pilot site tests (cancelled after the project was running behind schedule)

The project would involve two key actions: the implementation of a common business platform and the implementation of a common systems platform. The objectives for each action were defined as follows:

COMMON BUSINESS PLATFORM

- To implement common Finance processes
- To establish operational Center(s) of Excellence to support common processes
- To integrate information into one Chart of Accounts
- To create standard reporting
- To achieve cost savings in European Finance

COMMON SAP SYSTEM PLATFORM

- To implement one common platform for accounting, controlling, and reporting
- To achieve systems implementation and maintenance cost savings
- To achieve improvement of data quality and handling

Initially, the project celebrated the success of completing the framework for one European Chart of Accounts, although a couple of major challenges emerged in the early stages of the project. First, there were differing opinions in the project team regarding which business segments to target in the convergence. Many objected to including Life Insurance as it was a highly complex and geography-specific business. Second, the Finance IT group was facing difficulties when gathering required information from the individual business units. Even though the framework for the Chart of Accounts was established, Finance IT needed key information, such as local legal requirements, from each business unit in order to continue with the project.

... and its Problems

By November 2004, it was clear that a breakdown was occurring between the Finance IT department and the CFOs of the business units as Finance IT felt that they were missing key information needed to move forward. The IT team had already built basic parts of the infrastructure but they lacked the knowledge of the business units' processes that was necessary to continue with the system configuration. There were thousands of processes to be outlined and integrated into the system and the business unit leaders only provided limited involvement, with most only agreeing to 20% of the requested participation. Furthermore, Finance IT was unable to attain any commitment to the Center of Excellence from business unit individuals or managers, which was a key to creating common templates and a governance structure for the new standardized units.

In the fall of 2004, the Project Director of EVA left Lukas Financial Services and a new Project Director was appointed. The new Project Director quickly sensed that the project was not where it should be. There was little support from upper management or the business units, which meant that it was becoming increasingly difficult to define the business requirements of the SAP system. Doubts also began to arise regarding the ability to have a pilot for the EVA project. Initially, smaller, less complex country units such as France, Spain, and Portugal were targeted for the first pilot sites; however, after another evaluation of the project timeline, it was decided that there would not be time for any pilots.

Even without a pilot, the system was running critically behind schedule as delays continued to snowball and resistance to the project from the business units continued to grow. Finally, in early 2005, an important meeting with upper management and business unit CFOs was called to discuss the future of the project. At the meeting, it was clear that some of the larger business units felt strongly that the system could not be adapted to the complexity of their units, many country unit CFOs felt that they did not have sufficient human resources to commit to the project, and lastly, the country unit leaders mentioned the fact that local legacy systems were not yet fully understood by the project team.

Although the SAP team attempted to regroup, it was decidedly too late. IT management realized that the costs required to complete the project were too high and there were not enough resources, either in terms of time or personnel, to continue with the project. So the project leaders decided that the EVA project should be stopped, and the decision was made to outsource many of the European finance and accounting processes to meet some of the company's efficiency goals.

The OCTOPUS Project and the Center of Excellence

In 2009, after five years of no major changes to the Finance IT systems, upper management at Lukas made another push towards greater efficiency and they decided to reorganize the European business units so that all General Insurance was based in one country, Ireland. This change had projected cost savings of USD 100–200 million per year, since each country no longer had to maintain a full support system. Furthermore regulatory changes for General Insurance only had be taken into account for one country, allowing the business units to focus on expanding sales, gaining new clients, and supporting distributors. Life Insurance was not included in this process since it required all policy holders of life insurance to agree to a new contract based in Ireland and these policies were not updated frequently.

The OCTOPUS Plan created the foundation to establish a Center of Excellence (an EU Accounting Center) and it allowed for the standardization of processes in the General Insurance part of the organization. The Center of Excellence would include specialists from each business unit and these specialists would manage the financial and accounting processes and data for the business units.

The MASON Project...

Both the OCTOPUS Plan and the foundation of the Center of Excellence created a need for a standardized enterprise information system, and so a new SAP consolidation project led by Finance was launched: the MASON project. Overall, the objectives of MASON continued the EVA philosophy, focusing on making Lukas Financial Services a global company. The project had similar financial benefits to EVA, with project leaders indicating that the MASON project would lead to benefits of USD 17 million by year three.

While many of the objectives of MASON were similar to EVA, there was a key difference between the two projects. As a member of the project change

Box 10.2   IT Integration Projects at Lukas Financial Services:
              MASON Project

MASON PROJECT (2009–ONGOING)

Finance-led and treated as a strategic project

PEOPLE:
- The project was led by Finance, not IT
- There was an effort to engage larger country units from the beginning, using workshops and involving them with the pilot site selection
- There was a strain on resources and time, but the team understood these pressures from the start of the project
- The shift of power could no longer be questioned by Business Unit leaders – there was a clear business reorganization initiative that came from the top of the company (project OCTOPUS Plan) that was leading the overall project

SYSTEM:
- Regulatory changes/requirements were very complex, and they threatened to delay the project at critical points

---

management team explained, "We wanted to make sure this would be a finance initiative, and that this [MASON] project would not just be about IT consolidation; this would be about Finance driving for a common Center of Excellence with common processes. SAP would be the enabler rather than being the only thing we are trying to standardize." Furthermore, she explained that this project had an explicit goal of getting 80% of the finance and accounting processes in business units standardized.

... its Strategy...

Finance and IT management agreed that a key part of the MASON project strategy was related to getting local business unit management committed to the change process and open to discussions about the Center of Excellence. Part of this strategy was formally communicating the drivers and benefits that would stem from these changes:

- Support for talent management in Finance: Offer clear career progression and development opportunities as well as helping to develop standard training packages.
- Reduce "key people dependency": Move towards a process-orientated organization rather than a business unit-orientated one.
- Support the drive for best practice: Reorganize activities around common best practices.
- Allow for efficiency gains: Through the harmonization of processes and the implementation of best practices, the Center of Excellence will improve efficiently.
- Common systems landscape: The Center of Excellence will facilitate the implementation of a single SAP platform and Chart of Accounts.
- Cost-saving technical support: Reduction of SAP support and Chart of Accounts maintenance, and decommissioning of legacy hardware.

Finance and IT also planned a variety of workshops in order to communicate these points and ensure the participation and understanding of the business units. Workshops included a high-level introductory course to the project, as well as an SAP course outlining how the system affected day-to-day operations. The workshops also attempted to engage business unit personnel with mapping processes that were standardized in the SAP system. Finance and IT also used these workshops to help them to recruit representatives to do training for the final transition.

Figure 10.1   Business Unit Details[2]

	Estimated number of FI/CO users	Estimated number of processes	IT Budget (USD)
Ireland	52	170	310,500
Portugal	41	150	288, 600
Spain	101	225	587,700
Nordic	33	120	215,000
Morocco	27	90	192,600
Belgium / Lux	27	110	201,800
Germany	797	800	8,932,500
Italy	215	400	2,529,900
UK	576	700+	8,460,000
Switzerland	214	400	4,511,700

... and its Challenges

A key challenge with MASON related to the consolidation of work resulting from the integrated SAP system and Center of Excellence. These changes required a number of key business unit members to relocate to company headquarters. There was a possibility of hiring outside personnel but this could introduce more risk into the project and limit the initial effectiveness of the Center of Excellence.

Another challenge was deciding if there would be any pilot sites. A key consideration was the complexity of the finance and accounting processes at the selected sites. Some small countries, such as Portugal, were less complex with 41 people and an estimated 170 processes, while the UK had 576 employees and more than 700 processes (see Figure 10.1). Finance and IT had to decide if they would go with a small pilot site such as Portugal, a large site such as the UK, or multiple sites. Some project members felt that using the UK as a pilot and successfully converging SAP was needed to convince other business units of the success and benefits of the project. Project leaders stated, "If the UK can do it, anybody can do it". However, if they selected a large pilot and it faced too many problems, the resistance could increase in the other business units.

There were also project risks associated with building the system itself as it would be susceptible to regulatory changes, particularly Solvency II requirements, which take effect in 2012. Mapping and implementing existing processes was already a complex task, and having to account for additional annual regulation changes in a time-pressured setting further increased complexity and it could prove overwhelming for the implementation team.

As with the EVA project, the system also faced competition for business unit resources from other projects, as several IT projects that local units already deemed as higher priority than MASON were underway. One such project focused on system improvements for tax reporting, and another project related to entrepreneurial activity support, and each of these projects required significant resources.

Future Challenges with The MASON Project

Moving forward, Francois Rousseau knew that they could not deliver a global system without establishing global governance, and this required the support of each local CFO as well as top management. Additionally, while the framework for SAP convergence and the Center of Excellence was more established than with EVA, MASON still faced significant challenges, including gaining access to the local business units' expertise, meeting regulatory requirements, determining one or more pilot sites, and handling competing IT projects. Francois felt that he understood the challenges related to Mason, but he now needed to continue to refine the implementation strategy to minimize the impact of the project risks and allow Lukas to achieve their goals with the OCTOPUS and MASON projects.

Key Learnings

- The project needed be fully supported by the key business area involved (having Finance lead the second project solved this).
- Governance needed to be established in order to enforce the project mission and engage the business units.

- A focus on knowledge management and talent management was necessary to handle the organizational change needed for the Center of Excellence (workshops were a key part of this).
- A required level of standardization for all processes was used to drive business change.

Key Ongoing Questions about the MASON Project

- How should the project leaders engage employees to help the reorganization process?
- How should IT manage the challenge of other projects competing for resources with MASON?
- At which Business Units should they start the pilot implementation?

Notes

1 SAP, 2010. "Industry Overview for Insurance," PowerPoint Version 2010.1.
2 Source: Internal Project Reports.

Sometimes You Don't Have to Be a Prophesier

A COMMENT ON THE LUKAS FINANCIAL SERVICES CASE BY AXEL UHL (SAP)

The Lukas Case is a typical example of a transformation that was only able to achieve success after several cycles. Although the project went awry in the first cycle, important skills were developed for the following cycle, which was then more successful.

It is typical for a first, failed attempt at ERP (Enterprise Resource Planning) harmonization that the project was driven primarily by IT, even though the changes would have impacted the business level. Therefore, it also comes as no surprise that the expertise needed for the future solution is only available on the business side of things. However, the project was not supported by the business management, and there was no business strategy which would require a harmonized ERP solution.

What happened then is characteristic of the way failed IT-driven projects develop. First, there is a lack of project resources on the business side – essentially because business has prioritized its own projects, which are not coordinated with the ERP harmonization. As a result, the ERP project comes under pressure due to time and cost restraints. Finally, the ERP program manager sees escalation as the only means of resolving the issue. The material problem then becomes a personal problem – it must be the fault of the program manager. So he is replaced. But the new program manager cannot improve the situation either and the project gets into even greater difficulties. Finally, the management realizes that the project is never going to be a success and breaks it off. For a while, the company is in a state of complete shock and no longer dares to embark on another project of this kind. Therefore, a few years go by before a company makes a second attempt.

Having learned from the failure of the previous project, the next time a number of important strategic steps are taken to put right what went wrong before. For example, the responsibility for the project is handed over to business. The case for change is the desired improvement in efficiency through shared services, for which ERP harmonization is an essential requirement. The necessary expertise for the project is secured by setting up the Business Excellence function. The final and all-important question, however, remains unanswered: Can the local CFOs agree on a common strategy, and then also jointly implement it?

11

Vodafone Answers Call to Transformation

Michaela Kresak[†] (SAP), Lilian Corvington (Vodafone), Frits Wiegel (Vodafone), Guido Wokurka (SAP), Stephanie Teufel (University of Fribourg), Peter Williamson (University of Cambridge)

Michaela was the driving force behind instigating this study and worked tirelessly to build the relationship between Vodafone, SAP and the academic world. Michaela tragically passed away prior to the initial publication of this study, Vodafone and SAP dedicate this chapter to the memory of Michaela who was truly inspirational.

Vodafone's ongoing business transformation project "Evolution Vodafone" has given the global communications company a future-proof business model that saves money and invests in innovation.

Abstract

The "Evolution Vodafone" (EVO) Business Transformation Programme, started in 2006, transforms value chain back office processes. This, in turn, has enabled Vodafone's local operating companies to focus on value creation. EVO is introducing one 'Future State Operating Model' (FSOM) that works across supply chain, human resources (HR) and finance functions to deliver a globally unified set of standardized business processes. Fundamental aspects of this program were the creation of a new Core Business Model, Vodafone Procurement Center, and Shared Service Organization, underpinned by a global SAP platform. EVO is due for completion by 2012.

*****

Achieving large-scale change within any global company is extraordinarily challenging. This is particularly the case for Vodafone. The journey from a merger-and-acquisition-grown company to a shareholder and value-driven consumer business was one of the main drivers behind the transformation project. Another was to help Vodafone become one global firm under a single brand instead of a multitude of independent companies.

That is why Vodafone, one of the world's largest communications companies, set out on an ambitious program in 2006. It is radically transforming the company's back office and support operations by creating a new Future State Operating model. Dubbed "Evolution Vodafone" (EVO), the Business Transformation Programme is helping Vodafone become a more competitive global player. This mission-critical program supports back office, value chain processes: the setup of a shared service organization, a globally centralized supply chain community, and the Vodafone Procurement Centre VPC. The resulting operational savings are enabling further investment in innovative technologies and new business models. This, in turn, is defending and expanding the company's market position.

Finally, these combined efforts are helping Vodafone achieve a competitive advantage through greater buying power, new business models, and effective acquisition integration. The project is due for completion by 2012.

For an overview of relevant abbreviations, see the information box on page 131.

Vodafone – Uniting Local Talent for Global Strength

Since it launched its first cellular network 25 years ago, Vodafone Group Plc. has grown through strategic acquisitions to become one of the world's leading mobile telecommunications companies. In 2010, it had 85,000 employees with total revenues of £44.5 billion. As of 2010, the combined Vodafone companies had 341 million customers. The company has equity interests in more than 30 countries and partner networks in over 40 countries.

Most of the Vodafone Group's mobile subsidiaries operate under the single flagship brand 'Vodafone'. Yet because of the company's acquisition strategy,

---

FUTURE STATE OPERATING MODEL (FSOM)

The 'Future State Operating Model' (FSOM) is designed to:

- Get a "single version of the truth" – a single, global, centralized database that stores all of Vodafone's business data consistently and non-redundantly.
- Simplify business operations, thus freeing up time and talents to focus on increasing shareholder value.
- Standardize global processes that impact the value chain.
- Leverage economies of scale to gain a competitive advantage.
- Identify the best commercial solutions to utilize buying power.
- Maximize technology to support the new global business model.
- Provide a consistent employee experience in a streamlined organization.
- Develop sustainable capability for change and future global strategies.

Figure 11.1   Future State Operating Model

many of these companies operated as stand-alone businesses with their own business processes. As a result, inconsistencies emerged that made it difficult to operate efficiently as a single company. This lack of economies of scale was one of the major drivers behind the Vodafone EVO Programme.

Radical Evolution for a Changing Market Place

In the past, Vodafone had successfully completed a major global customer growth phase. Now it sought to realize the many benefits of its larger scale by becoming a truly global company. At the same time, senior managers wanted to send a strong signal to the market that Vodafone was far greater than the sum of its individual assets. They also wanted to maximize shareholder revenue and establish a 'new way of working'. To achieve these goals, they defined a set of strategies:

- Drive operational performance.
- Pursue growth opportunities in total communications.
- Execute in emerging markets.
- Strengthen financial discipline.

Transforming Vodafone's back office operations became fundamental to achieving these objectives. This move will improve and streamline business decision-making processes with high-quality information, reduce costs, deliver greater value creation opportunities, and offer enhanced service delivery

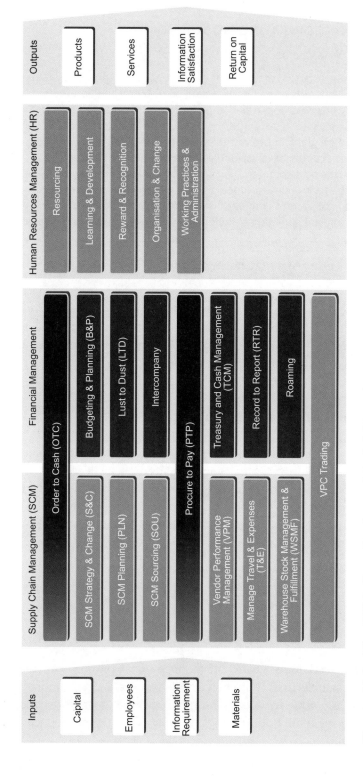

Figure 11.2 The EVO Core Business Model (CBM)
Source: Vodafone.

EVO Abbreviations

3TM	Third-party Logistics Terminals Model
ASD	Accelerated Solution Design
CBM	Core Business Model
EVO	Evolution Vodafone
FSOM	Future State Operating Model
OpCo	Operating Company
VPC	Vodafone Procurement Company

capabilities. An example of this is Vodafone's strategic goal of building in-house expertise. At the start of the EVO Programme, Vodafone did not have the business transformation management experience on the scale of the EVO implementation. Management saw the deployment as an opportunity to acquire know-how for future scope extensions and the implementation of similar programs. These might include customer-facing areas like retail store logistics, back office extensions in real estate management, or mobile platform innovations. Yet the EVO Programme will also allow the Vodafone Group to act as a truly global company. From the outset, the decision was made to exclude customer-facing, front-end processes during the first steps of the rollout. Given the size and complexity of existing billing and Customer Relationship Management (CRM) systems, for example, management teams wanted to limit risks to non-customer-facing, core value chain processes. Another consideration was to build a foundation for future change.

The EVO Business Transformation Programme

The EVO Programme is a large-scale organization. Like a medium-sized, aggressive-growth company, it had the necessary scale and staff size to pursue fast-paced timescales and achieve immediate results. Housed in a completely separate building, team members worked in a company-within-a-company atmosphere. This allowed the program to move forward as quickly as possible with separate, fast-track decision-making.

EVO was supported by SAP in a Value Partnership (VPS) between SAP and Vodafone. Accenture and IBM were selected as implementation partners. Niall O'Sullivan and Lilian Corvington led the EVO central team at Vodafone headquarters in Newbury, UK. Michaela Kresak led a joint roadmap from the SAP side to help Vodafone meet business objectives. After a tragic accident in Switzerland in 2011, Neill Crump assumed her role.

Created as an integral part of EVO, the Core Business Model (CBM, see Figure 11.2) translates Vodafone's Future State Operating Model (FSOM, see Figure 11.1) into a set of standardized global business processes, underpinned by a single-instance SAP system. As the CBM (Figure 11.2) demonstrates, Vodafone will introduce 19 new end-to-end business processes for supply chain management (SCM), human resources (HR), and finance functions. In addition, EVO included the selection of an Enterprise Resource Planning (ERP) platform and an implementation partner.

Vodafone also implemented centralized key business functions to ensure that it gets the right people with the right skills doing the right business activities. To enable SCM benefits, the company created one global community reporting to a single lead. This allowed the Vodafone Procurement Company (VPC) to enable large-scale global procurement from a single location and to eliminate activity duplication.

Finally, the EVO Programme introduced Shared Service Centers, an organization that enables the centralized and standardized processing of high-volume business transactions and other administrative tasks across SCM, HR and finance. It leverages near-shore and off-shore locations to further optimize operation costs.

Vodafone's Approach in Relation to BTM²

Vodafone planned and designed the principles of the EVO Business Transformation Programme in April 2006 at "Accelerated Solution Design" (ASD) events, a series of seven workshops held at Pinewood Studios near London. The workshop participants met in a special, closed-room setting that encouraged open thinking and that was conductive to the "we are one" consensus objective. One outcome – a drawing that shows the transformation drivers and program deliverables of the EVO Programme – is presented in Figure 11.4.

Divided into three phases, the EVO Programme has achieved several critical milestones over the past four years:

2006
2007

Phase 1 (2006 – 2007):
The first step in Vodafone's business transformation begins with the setup of the Transformation project. The design of the Core Business Model, as well as creation of the supporting SAP platform, has its start.

2008
2009

Phase 2 (2007 – 2009):
EVO delivers its first tangible results. The Vodafone Procurement Company and the Vodafone Operations Center are established, followed by the first country rollouts in Hungary, Germany, and India.

2010
2011
2012

Phase 3 (2010 – 2012):
EVO enlarges its footprint to enable Vodafone to become a global player. International rollouts are scaled up, with multiple concurrent releases going live every six months. The Third-party Logistics Terminals Model (3TM) program is created to focus on handset logistics and the EVO Fast Track for emerging countries. The EVO program will be completed in 2012.

Figure 11.3   EVO's Three Phases

The Vodafone business transformation approach that emerged from these ASD meetings bears a remarkably strong correlation to the eight disciplines of BTM². This correlation is one of the reasons Vodafone participated in this case study. For an overview of the BTM² approach, readers will find a detailed description of EVO alongside the eight disciplines of the BTM² below.

STRATEGY MANAGEMENT APPLIED IN EVO

The strategic management discipline is designed to help managers plan transformation projects in a way that benefits the business. Vodafone's primary interest in transformation was to make the move from a merger-and-acquisition-grown technology company to a shareholder-driven, consumer company. It also sought to join its multiple subsidiaries into one global company. The effort has made Vodafone a more competitive, global player. The resulting operational savings can be invested in other innovative technologies. The newfound flexibility also supports new business models that strengthen its market position with greater buying power, lower transaction costs, and economies of scale. These benefits should then help pave the way for new acquisitions in emerging markets.

In the meantime, the EVO Programme has already tapped into several potential value areas. With the end of the rollouts, a new EVO phase will begin. It will focus on hidden value potentials and operating model 'fine-tuning'.

VALUE MANAGEMENT IN EVO

Value management organizes and manages business transformation projects like EVO to realize maximum potential value. This discipline offers tools and techniques to help organizations better identify business value, build the business case, and manage necessary changes.

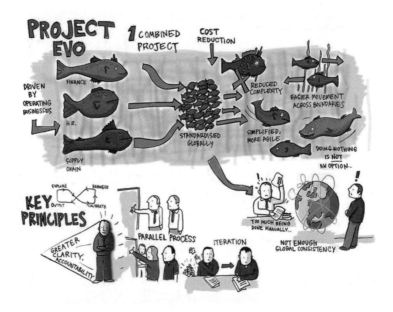

Figure 11.4   A Schematic Illustration of Project EVO
Source: Vodafone.

By consistently applying these concepts, techniques, and frameworks, the EVO Programme is achieving annual cash savings of over €550 million. Vodafone has, for example, realized savings through Shared Service Center standardized transaction processing and lower total cost of ownership from IT. By the end of 2011, over 60,000 employees will be using EVO processes, systems, and new ways of working.

RISK MANAGEMENT IN EVO

The risk management discipline within BTM^2 gives organizations a comprehensive and enterprise-wide view of strategic risks. These risks are defined as external risk drivers that could impact – either negatively or positively – the company's ability to achieve its strategic objectives on a two to five year horizon. Vodafone continues to use this discipline to identify risks at both the local and global level. By avoiding potential pitfalls with a predefined risk clarification framework, EVO is able to document the probability and impact of potential threats. It can then take mitigating actions. Instead of exploring risks during the different project phases, the EVO team initiates risk workshops at the very beginning of every rollout. Based on project scope and lessons learned from previous rollouts, as many risks are identified as possible. Mitigating actions are then assigned to each of them. The most common EVO risks involve legacy IT system integration. Another area deals with competition due to critical parallel projects. Other risks include top resource availability, external partnership dependencies, executive sponsorship, and key stakeholder buy-in over a five-year program. Among the most efficient risk mitigation actions were commercial and legal safeguarding. This included changing the original Accenture contract into a multi-vendor contract. They proved to be especially valuable in times of crisis for the program. Thanks to risk management, Vodafone has been able to realize business case benefits better and to move to an operational business-as-usual model while managing rollouts.

PROCESS MANAGEMENT IN EVO

CBM process standardization and simplification are the key EVO Programme drivers. As a fundamental part of CBM, they make shared services possible. As a result, they lower transaction costs. Prior to EVO, process management at Vodafone was done on a market-by-market basis with different process modeling methods and tools. EVO developed one global process standard in the Architecture of Integrated Information Systems (ARIS) toolset. Based on this standard, new processes are created for supply chain management, human resources, and finance. They provide a consistent employee experience and simplify the way the CBM is operated.

More recently, Vodafone has also made a strategic move toward working with a multi-vendor EVO approach in the future. CBM technical documentation is now stored in the SAP Solution Manager, a centralized support and system management suite. SAP Solution Manager provides an extensive set of features in the IT Support area for enhancing, automating, and improving the management of SAP systems. ARIS and SAP Solution Manager are now fully integrated and published on the Vodafone intranet. In doing so, the team has created a leading-edge portal for the CBM. This investment now provides a consolidated platform for Vodafone. It enables continuous improvement, effectiveness, and an efficient business-as-usual mode across the model's entire lifecycle.

PROGRAM AND PROJECT MANAGEMENT IN EVO

Program and project management is a comprehensive discipline. It makes it possible to manage various program elements centrally to achieve specific business objectives. It also supports project leaders in making informed decisions on a number of related elements to achieve specific outcomes. Vodafone used this valuable discipline to define its rollout strategy, track the business case, achieve good governance, handle scope, manage risks, and plan resources. To ensure this, Vodafone used a standard program management method. As a result, project leaders continue to provide governance and a common set of tools and processes to support EVO implementation teams' IT projects. EVO Programme management has also paid specific attention to a key challenge that any complex program faces: ensuring information flow visibility among the program's various groups. The team is also responsible for making certain that explicit approval mechanisms are in place at each program stage. The program also produced another very tangible result: Vodafone won the SAP EMEA Quality Award as a GOLD Winner.

Every large-scale program faces a tipping point where the business support organization outgrows the program organization. The business owners' agenda is driven by operational objectives that are not equal to roll-out completion. At the time of this writing, the issue has been identified. The resolution, however, is still in progress.

IT TRANSFORMATION MANAGEMENT IN EVO

IT transformation management helps change an organization's technology systems to reduce costs, achieve lower total cost of ownership, and enhance quality and performance. In terms of this discipline, Vodafone hired a group of people in the Vodafone organization with extensive experience in global transformation programs and extensive technical expertise. After a detailed selection process, SAP was chosen as the ERP value partner for its standard, out-of-the-box, best-practice processes. Additional business software products were chosen from Informatica, Opentext, Readsoft, Sabrix, Redwood, HP, and Remedy for their ability to integrate within an SAP-based IT landscape.

One of the key challenges for Vodafone was the consolidation of all local legacy ERP packages. Project managers were confronted with large numbers of interfaces, users, and legal requirements. To add to the task's complexity, the IT organization had to shift from a mostly independent, local IT department working structure into a more collaborative global model. Finally, the EVO Programme had to accommodate sheer scale. For instance, by 2012, more than 80,000 people will be using EVO in multiple locations around the world. Each year, Vodafone processes more than 50 million SAP IDOC (Intermediate Document) "messages", a standard SAP document format used for data in purchase orders, for example, or the supplier profile information in a supplier master record. 1,000 interfaces will connect legacy systems. Two data centers in Germany and India will also host more than 280 dedicated servers.

CHANGE AND TRAINING MANAGEMENT IN EVO

Change management defines and addresses the things that cause change. Large companies like Vodafone use it to make radical, complex, and necessary change for future success. It also defines why change is necessary in the first place. In doing so, it enables people, teams, and organizations to adopt change. It also supports managers in successfully leading change processes. Recognizing that enduring, meaningful change requires organizational buy-in at all levels, Vodafone used the change management discipline to lead by example. Yet change management and training have proven to be quite a challenge for the EVO Business Transformation Programme. This was because Vodafone operating companies (OpCos) began the EVO Programme from very heterogeneous starting points. As a result, it was difficult to design and build a "one-size-fits-all" training library that addressed the adoption needs of all end-users.

In terms of systems, the OpCos began EVO with very different legacy IT landscapes and user experiences. For OpCos who were already using SAP, for example, the new user experience was an extension of the existing one. For OpCos transitioning from Oracle, however, the profound technical and end-user changes represented a complete break with the past.

From a process perspective, EVO forced all employees to work and think differently than they had before. A prime example was the introduction of a new three-way matching system (purchase order, receipt, and invoice) within a purchase-to-pay process to approve invoices automatically for payment.

There are several major challenges in driving a global change program, among them the "not invented here" syndrome, cultural differences, and lack of ramp-up time. To overcome these, Lilian Corvington was convinced that an accelerated, intensive preparation program was necessary before any rollout started in local markets. She introduced the 'Fit for EVO' approach, which proved very successful. The sessions brought together local teams, local senior management, global teams, system integrators, and local IT vendors in a conducive, one-team environment. This not only facilitated knowledge transfer, but it also created positive momentum and convinced "change-agents".

Additionally, 'EVO ambassadors' have been appointed. These are key project members who have already gained deep EVO knowledge in one country. They are then re-appointed to support another country with their business transformation know-how. As a result, lessons learned are employed at every new release.

To cater to all training needs, a "Core Training Library" was set up. It consists of over 1,000 training assets and covers all business processes and functionalities provided by EVO. To accommodate local EVO language requirements, materials are provided in English, German, Spanish, and Italian. Finally, each of these efforts has been managed to be as cost effective as possible.

A Tale of an Implementation Journey

Hungary and Germany were the two countries selected for the pilot. Because of the delays described earlier in this study, the go-live dates for both countries were staggered. Hungary was the first to deploy because of its size. Germany went second.

The experiences provided by the initial setup of the procurement center and the first shared service center in Hungary proved to be extremely valuable. The subsequent rollouts in Hungary and Germany also provided a study in contrasts for the kinds of challenges faced by the EVO Team. Due to their different IT landscapes, corporate cultures, requirements, and expectations, the countries approached pre-, during-, and post-launch experiences in very different ways. This required the EVO Programme to develop adaptive response mechanisms that anticipate future rollout challenges and that avoid one-size-fits-all strategies.

The implementation started with the creation of the Vodafone Procurement Company (VPC) and the Vodafone Operations Centre in Hungary (VOCH) shared service center based in Hungary. Within a matter of weeks, complex structures were created in record time to help OpCos operate globally. Hundreds of top-skilled internal and external Vodafone professionals began working together in new facilities using the CBM processes for the first time.

In spite of the significant investments in both time and money, the first rollout was ultimately delayed. Teams engaged in lengthy strategic design discussions. Yet their plans failed to reach the execution stage. Senior management ultimately decided to force the issue by setting down a hard deadline for deployment. This prompted EVO teams to change the style and substance of their deliberations and planning. Discussions became more focused and solution oriented. The ground rules had clearly changed.

Rollout Hungary

Headquartered in Budapest, Vodafone Hungary is a midsize company that employs 2,000 people. Before EVO, it had a legacy Oracle environment with basic functionality. This made the EVO launch in Hungary less complex than at many of its larger counterparts in Western Europe. It also made it an ideal counterweight to its more mature trial partner, Germany. Due to the above – and the fact that Hungary had a relatively small IT platform and a strong need to strengthen process and controls – it offered little resistance in changing its IT systems and business processes.

During the actual go-live, senior management had high expectations for the EVO team and employees. Not only would the program ultimately force the organization to adapt to new business processes and to a new shared services organization, it would also change the very way colleagues worked together.

Although the Hungary EVO team was well prepared for the actual launch, it did not foresee the amount of hands-on support that end-users would require. During the early days, weeks, and months following deployment, the high volume of support requests greatly exceeded initial estimates. This had a significant impact on resource availability for both Vodafone core teams and Accenture teams. As a result, personnel, assets, and materials that could have been devoted to the next EVO release were held back. This experience and key learning went on to have a profound impact on the large-scale deployment scheduled that launched in Germany just weeks later.

Rollout Germany

In contrast to Vodafone Hungary, Vodafone Germany is a very mature company. From 2009 to 2010, it earned €9.04 billion p.a., which represents more than 20% of Vodafone's total revenue. Headquartered in Dusseldorf, Germany, it has 13,000 employees.

Germany was also an attractive choice for the pilot. It was Europe's largest market, and it had a mature SAP platform. Project managers reasoned that if they could achieve a successful go-live in Germany, they would be able to bring the remaining entities on board. Teams within the German organization were also motivated to participate. As experienced SAP users, they wanted to influence the implementation's final design.

The EVO deployment posed a greater challenge to Vodafone Germany. The organization had over 130 legacy systems and had been an experienced SAP user for over a decade. Over time, it had adapted its systems to local requirements and working styles. This included many customized business processes. The pending deployment meant that much of this dearly-held functionality would be standardized and eliminated. As a result, there was significant skepticism among many internal stakeholders.

The deployment also took on a socio-political dimension – a factor that was absent from the rollouts in Hungary and later in emerging market countries. The work split with the newly established procurement and shared service centers conflicted with employees' strongly held values of social fairness and job security. The deployment was perceived by some employees as a potential "job killer". As a result, the rollout was sometimes met with significant resistance.

To minimize risk and give Vodafone Germany ample time to adjust to change, a phased, incremental approach was chosen over a "big bang". Thanks to the early experiences in Hungary, the EVO team also moved quickly to provide hypercare – one-on-one, on-location support – to all employees affected by the transition.

Support teams dressed in red T-shirts were dispatched throughout the Vodafone Germany campus to answer questions, solve problems, and liaise with project leaders. This direct support effort provided the EVO team with a critical set of quick-wins to overcome resistance and drive adoption. Support was complemented by comprehensive education sessions and training events. Senior corporate executives also personally assisted in adoption efforts. OpCo Board-level managers participated in a large-scale communications drive, making themselves visible to employees throughout the deployment and expressing their explicit support for EVO. Finally, the EVO team offered important compromises. Some solutions were adapted to better meet local requirements, most notably the decision not to implement the order-to-cash process. At the same time, not all workers were moved to the shared services center during the first phase. This helped to minimize the degree of sudden change in such a large organization.

Vodafone and Accenture also faced major challenges and risks to their commercial obligations. Because of the program's enormous size, scope, and complexity, commercial issues emerged with Accenture and an escalation ensued. This forced the global leadership teams from both parties to agree to new terms and conditions to be able to continue the EVO Programme.

Unlocking Unexpected Opportunities

Over the course of the project, EVO teams also had the opportunity to apply the lessons learned in Hungary and Germany. This added value to two unexpected opportunities, leading to a successful extension of scope of the EVO Programme. For a related discussion of the project's working culture, see Figure 11.5.

The first opportunity emerged from the Third-party Logistics Terminals Model (3TM). As a mobile operator, Vodafone provides connectivity to its cellular and data networks. The original scope of the EVO Programme was designed to address this aspect of its business. Yet Vodafone is also a large-scale retailer. It sells handsets, devices, and accessories, and pairs them with services

---

Challenges of Business Transformation

Over the course of the first rollouts, EVO teams learned how to provide immediate, effective solutions to common problems. By creating a culture that acknowledged and learned from mistakes, the program achieved several important objectives:

- Maintain momentum over multiple years
- Cater to changing business models
- Manage people and change actively
- Get to 'business-as-usual' as quickly as possible
- Adopt a global platform
- Manage the initial negative effects of the implementation on the local market

---

Figure 11.5   Challenges of Business Transformation

in its own retail stores and through other sales channels. Recognizing the need to harmonize processes across the Vodafone business, the EVO team created a new common terminals operating model, 3TM. This model was quickly handed to EVO as the delivery vehicle of choice for implementing global large-scale transformation programs. A 3TM pilot program was successfully implemented in July 2010 for Vodafone Netherlands, and it received overwhelmingly positive feedback from internal and external stakeholders.

The second opportunity emerged during an unexpected pan-Indian EVO rollout called "Project Tiger". India's Hutchison Essar was acquired by Vodafone to become Vodafone Essar in May 2007. Because India was not part of the Vodafone family when the EVO Programme was launched in 2007, integration of the new business was an unexpected additional task. Through its "Project Tiger", Vodafone set out to help Vodafone Essar consolidate and standardize processes in order to sustain planned growth. The pan-Indian rollout was completed by July 7, 2010 – with zero disruption to the business during the entire implementation phase.

Empowering Transformation Success

In overcoming all of these challenges, finance, supply chain, and HR have successfully converted their business operations to the 'new Vodafone way of working'.

In SCM, the 'One Supply Chain Management' element of the EVO Programme has succeeded in streamlining operations. Now they are more consistent, and they foster collaboration as a community. The project has also introduced a newly appointed global head of supply chain, a consistent way of getting things done, and a unified organizational structure. Vodafone now qualifies its suppliers. This allows the company to take advantage of volume purchasing through eProcurement tools. Instead of managing 19 separate local markets, Vodafone now deals with one location and with one contract.

In HR, teams are focused on delivering great employee experiences. This is helping the company achieve its strategic objectives through its people. EVO does this in several ways. Line managers, for example, are empowered to strengthen relationships with their employees. They achieve this by promoting operational excellence through self-service learning, events, and personal data management.

Today, finance is also evolving to become a high-performing global team. EVO enables this transformation with a single finance platform and shared service centers that use consistent business principles and processes. In the future, Vodafone also hopes that these services will shift administrative and volume transaction processing responsibilities from the OpCos to let them focus on value creation aligned to strategic objectives.

Key Learnings

- Keep launch commitments, even if it means temporarily overriding internal resistance.
- Involve key individuals and organizations in project design and planning as early as possible.
- Simulate new business processes at an early stage to avoid threats to service quality and stakeholder buy-in.
- Delays and challenges are inevitable. Be ready for them with strong structure and superior skills.
- Turn big challenges as 'scope creep' into new opportunities by creating spin-off projects.
- Be able to quantify, track, and continually communicate your program's financial and strategic benefits.

- Get the best people on your team as soon as possible. At the same time, understand that high performers in existing roles may not be suited to high-stress project management roles.
- Do proactively address performance issues in the program and drive the solution of these issues. The urgent nature of transformation projects leave little time for potential difficulties.
- Put strong commercial and legal arrangements in place quickly.
- Continually evaluate the performance of all suppliers.
- Create an environment where people can be very open about their issues and mistakes. This also applies to communications with senior management.
- Stay on budget! Make sure that financial support is big enough before you start. Avoid appropriating additional resources after the fact.

THE AUTHORS WOULD LIKE TO THANK:

- Andy Halford (Chief Financial Officer for Vodafone)
- Niall O'Sullivan (Program Director for the EVO Programme at Vodafone)
- Giovanni Chiarelli (Program Delivery Director)
- Marcus Cotes (Global Head of Enterprise Resource Planning at Vodafone)

for sharing their experiences and lessons learned in the transformation program.

Think Global, Adapt Local

A COMMENT ON THE VODAFONE CASE
BY WERNER SCHULTHEIS (RANDSTAD DEUTSCHLAND)

The EVO case study provides an overview of how global companies are challenged to drive large-scale transformation programs for new business models and further growth. The EVO vision and strategic roadmap to increase shareholder value follow well-known patterns that we have seen in many other international companies before. This case study nonetheless shows why multinational transformations could not be executed within a simple copy-and-paste approach.

The EVO case also underscores how different languages, cultures, and corporate DNAs, like management, processes and systems, can be significant drivers in any whole-scale transformation process. This is particularly true for Vodafone – a company forged by a series of international mergers and acquisitions. Acting independently, each of these regional companies had established its own powerful financial, human resources, and procurement departments. This fueled resistance to change during country-by-country rollout phases. That is why the EVO project team's decision to conduct small-scale rollouts was the right way to go, particularly in Hungary – home of Vodafone's new HR and financial back office. Hungary provided a critical first lesson in business transformation management. And it would prove to be an important lesson learned for subsequent roll-outs in bigger and more powerful Vodafone countries.

During the rollout in Germany, the EVO team also made several crucial key learnings:

- Manage expectations up front.
- Involve top management early, often, and extensively.
- Give people time to learn and adopt new ways of working within a different process and system environment.

Only when these prerequisites are fulfilled can true change happen.

That is why the EVO case study is an example of the challenges that companies face during global business transformation processes. At the same time, it also demonstrates how other organizations can benefit from experiences like this 3TM project to drive future change.

The EVO project followed a well-known, logical business model pattern. Yet a business transformation blueprint for a smooth international transition – one that fits all industries, countries, and cultures – remains elusive. That is why Vodafone's decision to invest in building up its own institutional knowledge for transformation competence was a wise one. As a result, the global company has succeeded in creating a framework that designs future business models globally – and adapts them locally.

12

Shell Human Resources Transformation

Dominic Houlder (London Business School),
Guido Wokurka (SAP), Robert Günther (SAP)

Great Ambition, Greater Challenge

Headquartered in its administrative seat of Holland, The Hague, Shell is a global energy company with businesses in upstream, downstream, and, as a third stream, projects and technology. In *upstream*, Shell searches for and recovers crude oil and natural gas. The *downstream* businesses refine, supply, trade, and ship crude oil worldwide and also manufacture and market a range of petrochemicals and products for industrial customers. The *projects and technology* stream manages the delivery of Shell's major projects and drives the research and innovation needed to create technology solutions.

With about 3,300 employees and a budget of US$810 million, Shell's Human Resources (HR) function is one of the largest among multinational corporations. Traditionally, HR offices at Shell were largely administrative, handling transactions while also providing services, such as recruitment and training, as well as advice to those leading the businesses. Until the late 1990s, Shell HR was fully decentralized geographically and offered flexible support and problem solving as its offices were designed to cater to the needs of individual countries and business units. HR IT systems were aligned with this decentralized business model with different systems at country level or even within countries for different business units. The high level of flexibility, however, had resulted in inconsistent policies and processes and held back the development of a professional business advisory capability. Because individual countries and business units shared neither a single infrastructure

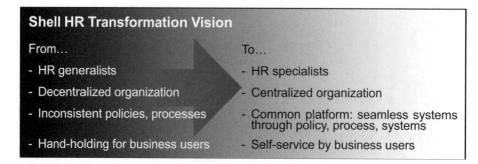

Figure 12.1   Shell HR Transformation Vision

nor a common way of working, the decentralized HR functions constantly replicated solutions when trying to deal with similar problems.

In the late 1990s, Shell's HR functions moved from a country-based to a regional grouping in order to gain some scale and commonality in work processes. Between these mega regions, however, there were still great differences. HR management realized that in order to be more efficient and professional, they had to move towards a centralized global organization and make a major investment in a common IT platform purchased from the software giant SAP. The goal went beyond merely standardizing IT and work processes. Shell's HR leaders wanted to transform the function from a traditional administrative office – in which all roles were combined in an ad hoc manner – into a structure in which administration would be done through online self-service software, creating space for its people to grow from HR generalists into specialists who could give valuable strategic advice to the businesses (see Figure 12.1). The structural transformation would also allow Shell to develop global centers of excellence in high-value services, such as recruitment and training.

Convinced by their vision, HR management launched the transformation process but soon ran into obstacles.

The Beginning: *Shell People* as the Global Platform

In 2000, *Shell People* was launched with the aim of harmonizing processes and harvesting the benefits of commonality through a global IT platform. The plan was to roll out the platform country by country across the world.

The project steering group, led by senior HR managers, organized extensive road shows to communicate the vision to business units after presenting the vision and business case to Shell's top management. Behind the transformational vision was a simple reality. As Group HR Director, Hugh Mitchell, commented: "*Shell People* was a consequence of the condition of the existing infrastructure rather than our identifying a new way of doing things out there … We had to spend a huge amount of capital anyway on fixing and upgrading the existing infrastructure, so it was evident that we should include a new system."

The steering group committed to executing *Shell People* in line with Shell's corporate culture. Notwithstanding the standardization goals of the project, the *Shell People* steering group was ready to listen to individual voices and offer adaptation to local needs. The promise was that *Shell People* would be a win-win situation. It would fulfill HR's transformation vision, offer local business units a much more efficient and reliable system, and would not cost the company extra money.

The new IT platform was offered to local business units as a service. HR provided the development funding while local businesses were asked to pay for the implementation cost. A Shell business manager in Asia believed in the transformation and was prepared to take the risk. "He was our pioneer", said Senior Project Manager, Arthur Williamson. "Once we had the pioneer, then we had some early adopters to follow."

The followers were far fewer than HR had wanted. By mid-2002, only six countries out of 100 had implemented the *Shell People* platform. Local business units argued that since they were paying for the implementation, they wanted it customized. "We lost sight of all our common process and data goals", said Williamson. "There were constant challenges between local teams, which got to a point where we had spent all of the money that was budgeted and still had the rest of the world to go."

Amanda Manzoni, Vice President HR Shared Services, reflected on the problem: "Everybody loves standardization as long as it is standardization according to their own rules." There was a lot of disbelief at the receiving end, she recalled. "People didn't take the time to understand the strategy behind *Shell People*. When change hit them, they didn't want to be there. So they largely ignored it." This typical reaction to change spoke for both business and HR communities at Shell. "They tried to ignore it for as long as possible until that point where they could no longer do things the old way", Manzoni added.

Four years after the initial launch of *Shell People*, the result was devastating. In spite of a major investment, the project was massively over budget and over time, not well received by business units, and the user interface was described as "obnoxious". The failure of *Shell People* started to loom large on the Board agenda.

Crisis as Opportunity

Despite the negative perspectives on *Shell People*, the Board did not give up on the HR transformation because it believed in the ultimate value of the program, even with significant outlay of funds. Determined to make it work, Shell's then Chairman, Phil Watts, intervened personally. He replaced the steering group that used to consist exclusively of HR people with a Program Board that included the CFO, HR Director, and IT Director under his personal direction. He introduced completely new funding and governance models that followed a top-down approach, which was the opposite of the former consensual approach, and brought in five senior managers to run the program.

"The corporate restructuring in 2005 – combining the two companies into one –", said Williamson, "meant that as we moved to the next phase of the program, we had far less movement of minds to do." By 2005, the HR transformation program had stabilized under a hierarchical governance model, championed by the new Shell Group CEO, Jeroen van der Veer, steered by key business heads, and led by the new Group HR Director, Hugh Mitchell, with a clear mandate for action (see Figure 12.2). The funding model also became top-down with the corporate center allocating the budget. "Without that backing, you just get buffeted about", said Mitchell. To support this change, a small team of senior change process managers acted as the mediator between HR and business units.

Alongside this top-down approach, Mitchell cut back on local customization. During *Shell People*, he remarked, they gave too much space for local customization, so now they decided to "take the keys away" from local business units. He said: "You have to show a high level of intolerance to local needs because everybody is different by definition. If I asked the businesses, 'Do you like this?', they would say, 'No, we prefer it our way'".

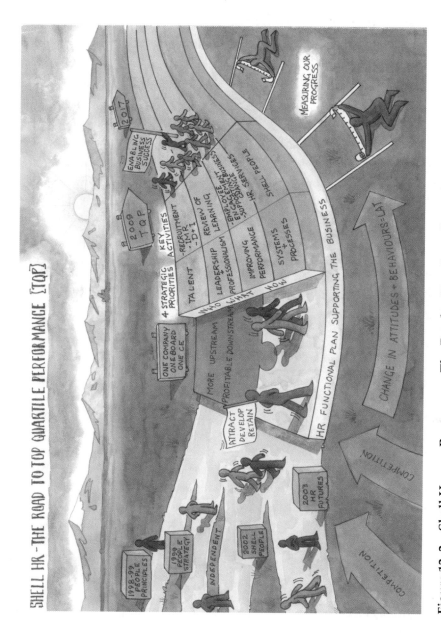

Figure 12. 2   Shell Human Resources – The Road to Top Quartile Performance (TQP)
Source: Shell HR Brochure.

Shell *HR Online*

The next phase of the program was focused on *HR Online*, which took three years to complete from July 2006 to June 2009. Its initial rollout in September 2008 took place in 84 countries and affected 96,000 people, including the user community, business managers, employees, and supervisors. Built on the global platform of *Shell People*, it supports a single global HR policy, uniform transaction process, and self-service functions. Shell Business Service Centre Vice President, Mike Sinclair, said: *"HR Online* is really cool. It has a search facility that is almost 'Google-like' and is continuing to improve. The web forms are outstanding: When it is time to give somebody a bonus or promote somebody, you just click, up comes a web form pre-populated with the data, and with two clicks, the transaction is processed. Previously, there would have been all sorts of dialogue and exchange of e-mails, and it might still take a long time for things to get done timely."

The rollout of *HR Online* coincided with a major wave of organizational change after Shell's current CEO, Peter Voser, took over. In Voser's view, Shell had grown into a "quite complex organization" that needed "urgent restructuring". *HR Online* directly facilitated this restructuring and helped drive efficiency in many areas of the company.

The benefit was immediately apparent in Shell's expatriate management. A first initiative that *Shell People* and *HR Online* made possible was the implementation of a new expatriate policy. Expatriates used to call their local HR office once relocation had been agreed, share the special needs arising from conditions in the country to which they were being asked to move, and discuss options with local HR managers about such things as cars, flight tickets, and children's education. With *HR Online*, the situation altered. Expatriates no longer interacted with HR managers directly. Instead, they would have a phone briefing from HR and receive an e-mail outlining the movement package. A self-service web site offered choices about cars, tickets, and other benefits within a limited number of standard options, which considerably simplified the process for staff.

Williamson offered, "Because Shell's HR systems bring data across the world together and information is no longer at a country level, HR now can easily locate an expert for a certain type of task. In the past, identifying the right person for a specific job in a remote region was always challenging. Also", observed Williamson, *"HR Online* allows employees to see and update their own data, so the accuracy of the information has been greatly improved. It is now standardized and so of much greater value."

Shell People and *HR Online* also helped move key HR staff from focusing solely on administrative tasks to performing a more strategic Business Partner role. Shared data began to drive more strategic thinking among HR people. "Businesses have massive appetites for data", said Mitchell. "If you can show them trend lines and charts and tell them stories through visualization, your analyses are incredibly powerful." Mitchell is deliberately cultivating this mindset to encourage his HR Business Partners to actively use the data.

This new system helped overcome difficulties posed by differences in language and culture, and Shell employees found HR to be more transparent and trustworthy. "We turned HR from being an inefficient system to one that is ready to show you everything about you", said Williamson.

Lessons Learned

From 2005 to 2009, Shell successfully transformed its HR from a decentralized organization to an efficient centralized organization. Shell HR can rise to its full potential in the now clearly differentiated activities of transaction processing, centers of excellence, and business partnering, winning top management recognition as a "best-in-class" function. Because administrative processes are largely simplified, Shell has achieved significant cost savings.

Key Learnings from the HR Transformation at Shell

- **Take advantage of events that help to push forward fast.** Slow progress in the first phase of HR Transformation put pressure on the company to improve project management and decision processes. This was underpinned by the cultural change that accompanied Shell's Corporate restructure. The coincidence of these events accelerated Shell's HR Transformation. In Mitchell's words: "At the end of the day, the arguments for change were compelling, but the Corporate Restructure crystallized the arguments into a strategy which drove things forward in a way that may not have happened otherwise."

- **Create a powerful guiding coalition.** In response to slow progress, Shell introduced a tight top-down governance body to manage HR transformation – championed by the Group CEO, steered by key business heads, and led by the Group HR Director – with a clear mandate for action. With this new governance model, decision-making power was recentralized, enabling Shell to push the transformation forward. As Manzoni said: "Without strong leadership, we would not have progressed as expected."

- **Reflect on events and learn from them.** Shell learned from the first phase of its HR Transformation, following an emergent rather than deliberate path and always looking back to make the most of what worked and adjust what didn't. Like any journey of change, as Manzoni observed, "one needs to go back and reinforce, time and time again, to ensure that the learning is truly embedded, and then one can leverage from there."

- **Make a holistic case for change.** When compared to other investment opportunities, the case for an HR Change project will never be won based on financial indicators. However, management believed in the necessity of such transformation to support a global organization reliant on highly skilled resources and also to remain cost competitive. As Mitchell put it: "Only by looking at the transformation holistically can one drive it on course." Shell followed its sense of reality to make the transformation happen.

- **Enact clear governance.** Shell implemented a tight and clear governance model rather than the consensus model previously used. Mitchell remarked: "The transformation is an activity that has to be done. While change is difficult for some, they ultimately realize that, overall, things work for the better and at less cost."

- **Get alignment.** A transparent cost allocation model aligned to governance structures drove project decisions and outcomes in the right direction. In the phase of *Shell People* when local market units were asked to fund the project, they wanted it customized to their tastes. In the phase of Shell *HR Online*, funding came from headquarters so the market units had to comply with what headquarters demanded, making it possible to get all of Shell moving toward the same goal.

- **Make the most of a big win for some key stakeholders.** The *HR Online* rollout was aligned with the introduction of new Expatriate Policies and processes to support them. *HR Online* underpinned this change, supporting self-service and automation. The new way of working was quickly recognized as a big step forward. From the experiences of this large group of influential managers, a more positive attitude toward the HR transformation emerged in the wider employee community.

- **Leverage well-networked middle managers as cultural bridges for disruptive change.** To manage HR transformation, Shell leveraged the knowledge and skills of middle managers who knew both business and IT. They are the link between senior management and IT professionals, ensuring that direction given by the top will reach the work floor and be well understood. These middle managers also have extensive networks within Shell, knowing whom to call for particular issues, which made the execution of HR transformation much easier.

The Authors wish to thank the following people at Shell for sharing their thoughts:

- Hugh Mitchell (Group HR Director)
- Amanda Manzoni (Vice President HR Shared Services)
- Arthur Williamson (Senior Project Manager)
- Mike Sinclair (Shell Business Service Centre Vice President)

Note

This case study was written with the assistance of the Rotterdam School of Management Case Development Centre.

Right Moment, Right Governance

A COMMENT ON THE SHELL CASE
BY PAOLA BIELLI (BOCCONI UNIVERSITY)

Many suggestions and points for reflection for practitioners can be drawn from the Shell case study. Its main focus (IT-driven change management in global organizations) is a very hot topic in the management community, and the in-depth description of the project (Shell *HR Online*) offers the reader some interesting suggestions.

First of all, there is the issue of *IT alignment* with company strategy. The case illustrates how, at one time, Shell had several IT platforms for HR departments around the world, which no longer supported the company's need for an integrated view of business and organization. This led to the first Enterprise Resource Planning (ERP) project mentioned in the case, which aimed to align technical needs and organizational change. The case study does not provide evidence that businesses should pursue the utopian situation in which IT and information systems (IS) platforms are always aligned with business evolution. On the contrary, it suggests that major IT initiatives are followed by years of continuing utilization and adaptation of existing platforms, until the right moment for change arrives.

The second issue concerns the *"Trojan horse effect"*. In other words, ERP and major IS projects are often a good "opportunity" (or some might say, excuse) to introduce new management rules or to change corporate culture. As Shell *HR Online* shows, a precise (ideally upfront) definition of the desired business processes enables organizations to implement changes within the company that are led by new software procedures. Speed and a shared vision are the advantages of IT-driven projects for change.

Thirdly, the case also challenges calls for the *personalization of software*. Although everybody is different, software customization is often just an attempt to maintain the status quo in businesses where uncertainty and rapid change threaten traditional business practices. In global environments, a local focus often prevents companies from exploiting their international potential (their most promising young managers) as they simply replicate the same services in different geographical locations. On the other hand, a stronger focus on centralization leads to improved efficiency and effectiveness, for the group as a whole and also for individual companies.

The "happy ending" in the Shell *HR Online* case is an important take-home message for academics and practitioners, and shows once again how a sound IS governance system is a prerequisite for many technology projects. By "IS governance system" I mean a clear definition of responsibilities, decision rights, funding mechanisms, and measures. The direct involvement of top management, with clear guidelines and project priorities, is mandatory for any strategic, corporation-wide project. Nothing new? Maybe not, but sometimes it is useful to reinforce traditional wisdom with recent success stories.

13

A Global HR Transformation: How a Leading Company Leveraged the Innovative Power of IT

Theresa Schmiedel (University of Liechtenstein),
Jan vom Brocke (University of Liechtenstein),
Axel Uhl (SAP), Stefanie Zeitz (SAP)

This article reveals the unexpected potential of a global player's HR transformation. It presents the corporation's challenges and benefits of IT-driven business process innovations.

Abstract

Introducing an integrated IT system and harmonizing the business processes of a global player in the consumer goods industry with 50,000 employees is complex and challenging. Focusing on the Human Resources (HR) function of this corporation, we look into the specific challenges and benefits of the global transformation. While, at the beginning, the business value of the new HR system was concealed, the IT system proved to be a major driver not only of HR process improvements and innovations but also of strategic and cultural change. This case is an insightful example for the enormous business benefits that can be gained through IT-driven process transformation. Based on the findings, we derive key learnings that may support similar transformation projects of such scope.

*****

In the year 2000, the consumer goods company Alpha (the name of the company has been changed for reasons of anonymity) took a decision of significant impact. Aiming at globally harmonized processes and standardized data, the corporation launched a global process of business transformation called GIGA (name changed). The sheer size and complexity of a corporation employing around 50,000 people in almost every country in the world was the main challenge for this transformation. In fact, GIGA was Alpha's most ambitious reengineering program. At its core, an integrated SAP system was introduced at Alpha as one standardized business solution. Being one of the largest projects a multinational company has ever attempted, GIGA affected almost all functions of the Alpha corporation, such as finance, supply chain, generating demand, and human resources.

In this article, we focus on the challenges of the IT-driven business transformation at Alpha Human Resources (HR). Taking a closer look at the HR function, we study an interesting phenomenon: "We almost didn't know what to do with the IT system!" Being one of the first statements we heard exploring the roots of GIGA HR at the Alpha headquarters in September 2009, it refers to the starting point of the project when the value of the IT-driven transformation was not fully transparent to the HR function. The perception of the GIGA HR system points out to one of the probably most important issues in business transformation: the "value creation". While the value of IT has been discussed extensively in the literature (Carr 2004; McAfee and Brynjolfsson 2008), the actual value of a specific IT system for the business may be difficult to determine. This article aims to examine the GIGA HR project regarding the leverage of the remarkable investment Alpha put into reorganizing global processes and data. We do not intend to quantify the IT value, but rather focus on the transformational power of the GIGA HR solution.

With a lack of value perception in the first place, GIGA HR faced an obviously difficult situation to start from. In this article, we show how Alpha managed the transformation project to achieve sustained success and to gain significant comparative advantages through GIGA HR. With a new vision in place and extensively utilizing IT, Alpha presents a good example to learn about business transformation in practice. First, we describe the initial situation in more detail. We then report on challenges and measures taken to manage the transformation. Finally, we conclude with lessons learned and also reflect on future evolutions at Alpha inspired by the innovative use of IT in business processes.

The Beginning

The initial purpose of GIGA was to provide a platform that should be used to improve Alpha's business process performance worldwide in order to remain competitive. GIGA HR was started as part of the overall GIGA project and was supposed to deal with the HR transformation in one go along with other functions such as finance and supply chain. Yet, the senior HR business management did not really expect that support functions like HR could highly increase their contribution to Alpha's overall business performance. This was also due to the fact that HR felt more connected to people business than to IT. We can observe a rather typical phenomenon here: Even though the overall GIGA project was about harmonizing processes and standardizing data, GIGA HR was essentially perceived as an IT project by the HR function. One reason for this viewpoint may lie in a missing value perception.

"Wrong birthdates are not as bad as wrong finance data!"

The implementation approach of GIGA HR firstly focused on the backbone of HR (administrative processes like HR master data maintenance, organizational management, payroll including parts of compensation management), even though the strategy blueprint for HR intended to move HR from an administrative to a more consultative role within the company. Thus, GIGA HR's business benefits, especially for the consultative business, could not be immediately realized and were not obvious right away, and so in the beginning the acceptance of GIGA was low. Therefore, it was difficult for the HR management to support the change at that time. Both from a technological and from a cultural point of view, the implementation and development of the IT system in HR were special compared to other functions. "Imagine a supply chain system: if it is down, there are immediate cash problems. You cannot deliver to clients, clients have to wait longer, they buy less, and you have less income (…). If you look at the HR system, it doesn't really matter. You can very well shut off the system for a whole week."

Based on the special situation of GIGA HR at the beginning of the project, Alpha faced a number of challenges regarding the HR transformation. The following examples may give a first impression: With the value proposition of the HR project remaining blurry, the strategic alignment of business and IT turned out to be an important issue. A transformation of such size required special skills, particularly in bridging business and IT. On the one hand, the integration of the overall IT system needed to be ensured. On the other hand, finding a solution to the problem of harmonizing processes and standardizing data required profound business knowledge. Benchmarking was the method Alpha adapted. Alpha started to design generic business processes in order to determine the best practices within the company. This turned out to be tricky – considering the decentralized structure of Alpha – and posed a further difficulty, taking into account the governance of the project. Coming along with the decentralized organization of the corporation, further challenges lay in Alpha's culture, which was very market-focused. People in the different markets were not used to think in global terms.

In order to analyze Alpha's GIGA HR case in more detail, we structure the various challenges focusing on different areas relevant for business transformation. Drawing from studies on Business Process Management (de Bruin and Rosemann 2007; Rosemann and vom Brocke 2010), we analyze the transformation regarding (1) strategic alignment, (2) governance, (3) methods, (4) IT, (5) skills, and (6) culture.

The Transformation

GIGA HR resulted in a fundamental change of the HR function. Traditionally, HR was organized independently in the markets around the world – with GIGA HR, one large global system was implemented enabling harmonized processes and standardized data. Looking at the different challenges of the project, the core of the organizational change and most visible part of the transformation, IT, remained a central but only one out of many areas in which Alpha had to face difficulties. The huge impact the global IT system had on the corporation's transformation becomes obvious when taking a closer look at how Alpha dealt with the different challenges.

1. STRATEGIC ALIGNMENT

Aligning strategic HR business goals with the new IT system was a first fundamental challenge for the GIGA HR project. Initially, the strategic direction of HR was rather implicit in the function's action, and only a blurry idea of the benefits from the new IT system existed. For these reasons, it was difficult for the IT function to demonstrate how GIGA would support strategic HR goals. Particular goals for GIGA HR, such as the implementation of a payroll system, were initially defined by the responsible IT people. For the IT function it became more and more important to identify the business needs and priorities in order to deliver a proposal on how to support the HR business. "If the way we address human capital management and the way we want to support this with an HR IT system are not completely mirrored, the HR organization will not be interested in the technology." To ease the alignment of business and IT throughout the GIGA project, Alpha established the so called Center of Excellence (CoE) (name changed). CoE can be seen as a competence center giving direction for HR IT subjects. At the beginning, it was organizationally allocated to GIGA. Only later, CoE was reassigned to the business function. This organizational change generated more ownership for the HR function regarding the developed best practices and also assured the continuous improvement of these best practices directly out of the function. With the development of an HR roadmap, the HR function proactively defined its priorities that had, until then, only been immanent in the actions of senior management.

> *"We conducted workshops with HR directors as soon as we had developed the template in order to validate it."*

GIGA HR strongly facilitated HR's new vision and structure. Supporting the transformation from an administrational business towards a consultative business, this new vision and structure included the introduction of employee self services and Shared Service Centers (SSC). These allow HR to focus on its value-adding roles as business partner and expertise center. The SSC project started with the setup of a new Global Alpha Shared Business Services organization (GASBS). It covered mainly payroll and HR master data maintenance. Despite the fact that GASBS would have never been possible without GIGA HR, a significant amount of administrative tasks remained local due to the complexity of cross country collaboration. Similar projects were realized in regional SSCs around the globe, such as in Latin America and Asia/Pacific.

2. GOVERNANCE

A transformation of the size and complexity of Alpha's GIGA HR project requires special attention to governance. Alpha's decentralized structure was challenging for the project due to the local organization of the markets and their differing maturity level. Since the local organization of different markets and different companies in different countries had to be managed, it was impossible to control the transformation with only one global hub in the headquarters. Alpha, thus, established three GIGA Centers worldwide for bunding several markets during the project. For these organizational units people were recruited from companies of different countries including SAP-experienced people, who were in charge of the implementation of the system. The CoE staff in the GIGA Centers were responsible for the definition of the processes.

"Follow the best internal process within Alpha!"

Apart from the centers, a GIGA Steering Committee coordinated the project execution. The organizational structure Alpha created in order to manage GIGA was very supportive to the huge global project. However, the different levels of maturity of the single Alpha markets were a special challenge. "For the UK, our solution was a step backwards. An SAP HR system already existed in the market and had received much in-house development. (…) Canada, on the other hand, was not developed as much in the area of HR IT and, thus, improved a lot regarding the information that can now be provided." That means that some markets, as the UK, were very advanced in their process-oriented thinking and had long implemented IT tools serving different purposes of the HR function as opposed to other markets. It turned out to be difficult for Alpha to keep all markets happy to the same extent, aiming at an equal implementation of GIGA worldwide. For example, advanced markets are ready for "getting amazing data" from Business Warehouse reports. Their business requirements have increased and need to be prioritized because of budget constraints. They are eager to see the enormous impact GIGA can actually have on their business. Since it was difficult to create processes that fit the level of maturity of all markets, Alpha developed a template solution, i.e. a set of predefined functionalities that could flexibly be enhanced with country specific additions. "What we decided to do is to have a set of non-negotiables and say, 'As long as you are meeting those requirements you have sufficient flexibility to take it even further, but these are the minimum requirements we will expect you to apply.' Pakistan will say, 'Fine, we can do that!' and the US will say, 'Well, we did this 10 years ago! We are now here!' and that is fine." By establishing this common basis for the overall corporation, Alpha is able to build on a solid foundation in the future.

3. METHODS

Regarding the management of the transformation, Alpha's approach towards harmonizing HR processes and standardizing data was based on a global benchmarking initiative that was launched to find the best HR solutions within the corporation. International project teams were in charge of determining best practices. At the beginning of the GIGA project, best practices were defined in workshops of business representatives. This was an ambitious task because it meant brining together "60 countries (…) and you have to walk out of a three days meeting (…) with one common way of how to hire a person." The definition of best practice processes required many agreements. "If you're looking at hiring: Who is going to do the first steps of recruitment? Is it going to be the manager or is it going to be HR? (…) Who is going to interview the person? (…) What kind of data do you need for hiring? (…) Who does the data entry?" Finally, what was the one ideal solution how to hire a person at Alpha? By posing questions like these, uniform processes were designed for all companies. Based on the international comparison of Alpha HR practices, Alpha developed an increasingly deep understanding of the meaning that benchmarking internal HR processes had for the overall corporation. Yet, finding global solutions was not always as simple as it may sound. There were many local specifications that needed to be considered. "There are also areas, however, that cannot be standardized that much in a global environment, because you have different legal requirements (…) and you have specific ways of doing things in different countries. In Latin America, if you publish a recruitment request, sometimes they get 10,000 replies (… whereas here) you may have 10. You need a different tool, you need a different approach, and you may actually need different publishing tools." Against this background, it was challenging to find best practices while keeping in mind all the differences. In order to address this, Alpha developed generic processes allowing for both, safeguarding a global standard and facilitating local adaptations at the same time.

4. IT

IT served as the enabler of the huge transformation project. From the very beginning, the new IT system was intended to support the HR business in general and the needs of the corporate users in particular. In the early stages, Alpha focused more on providing the right functionality and less on usability. But as the users struggled with the initial user interfaces, Alpha had to change its implementation strategy: having a system that is easy to use is as important as the overall functionality. Another top priority was the concept of data standardization. The system was required to include an efficient data structure, which means that the right type of data is available to the user. Alpha, thus, considered essential principles of the well-known Technology Acceptance Model, i.e. (a) ease of use and (b) perceived usefulness (Davis 1989). Furthermore, the one-vendor approach for IT was not followed anymore. For certain areas, Alpha decided to integrate a few global solutions into their global SAP HR system, sacrificing "integration for simplicity". This resulted in a global hybrid HR system which integrates several solutions. However, Alpha mostly uses SAP solutions and also builds on SAP as data warehouse. The decision for a multi-vendor approach was encouraged when customizing an IT solution for succession planning turned out to be more complex than expected. Additionally, the perceptions of the HR and the IT functions differed fundamentally regarding ease of use and the usefulness of the system. Finally, Alpha decided to define value from the perspective of the client (HR) and less from the perspective of the IT function. This seemed to be the right approach: today's hybrid solution affords less customizing in certain areas and the integration of the GIGA system was easier than expected.

5. SKILLS

GIGA HR required special skills in many ways. First of all, interdisciplinary skills were necessary for the transformation. Since CoE was established as a function to ensure the alignment of business and IT in the project, people had to be recruited for this specific task.

> "You look for HR people who can 'talk technology' to drive HR technology projects."

It was difficult though to find people for CoE. Among the HR personnel a rather general phenomenon occurred: IT was perceived as an unpopular domain and the HR people were therefore not eager to work for 'an IT project'. Today, the HR function is very well aware that CoE is a key position for change in the organization. According to the nature of the CoE, it neither clearly belongs to business nor to IT. "We realized that two types of people were required: HR people who were not afraid of technology and were able to deliver within a technology project. And IT people that understood enough of HR processes so that they could consult their HR counterparts in how to utilize the technology." Thus, Alpha created specific job profiles for CoE for which people were trained in both areas. Fostering double skills of the CoE employees, Alpha eased the communication flow between the two areas. Another important skill that was required through GIGA HR is process orientation. The traditional HR scope was very administrative. Therefore, people responsible for administrative tasks "usually have problems in thinking in terms of processes. They think in terms of isolated activities." Changing employee's thinking from focusing on one task to focusing on a whole process was a process itself and took much time and effort. Alpha's approach lay in forming international project teams.

Working together in one place, the team members developed a common understanding of the Alpha HR processes. HR employees who have been working on global projects, for example to define a best practice solution for a specific process, acted as change agents once they were back working locally. Through these agents from all over the world, Alpha's global thinking was passed on to the local environments. Including process thinking skills into the local functions was an effective measure to slowly but steadily turn away from administrative business and rather approach consultative business. Finally, another dramatic change CoE has introduced was the delivery of specialized project management methodologies and skills to Alpha HR. Today CoE is the recognized project management provider delivering services to both system and non-system related matters.

> *"The hardest part is from brain to heart. That is sometimes the longest journey!"*

6. CULTURE

Culture turned out to be one of the major pillars of transformation. At first glance, the idea of GIGA to have one central way of doing HR business contradicts Alpha's decentralized culture with its very local and market-specific business. "In a Prague office, for example: Who takes care of hiring? A person in Prague." HR is a very local business. The global project, thus, evoked resistance, especially among the HR management in the markets and challenged Alpha's undertaking. The strong support of Alpha's CEO throughout the project and the clear announcement of the transformation goals diminished resistance to change, "Nobody could opt out." Intensive communication helped to decrease the impact of conflicts and improved identification with the GIGA project and the GIGA Centers as new functions in the organizational structure. Thus, the CEO commitment was a key success factor to overcome middle management resistance. The lack of IT affinity by the HR management was resolved only very slowly. Alpha's stamina paid off though. Despite the missing business value proposition at the beginning of GIGA HR, the tremendous potential of the transformation slowly emerged during the course of the project. The HR team is now on its way to change from delivering administrative to consultative services. Thus, GIGA contributed not only to implementing process change but also to implementing a strategic change. These fundamental changes further required a mindset and culture change (vom Brocke and Sinnl 2011). Taking a closer look at Alpha's culture, specific elements of it were very supportive of the GIGA project: the consensus orientation of the corporation helped to overcome the isolated, market-oriented thinking. Being aware that reaching consensus is not always possible, Alpha took a very pragmatic approach discussing issues where necessary and pushing decisions where it was obvious that agreements could not be found. The approach Alpha took was to "select battles". Battling for consensus was avoided in cases where a standardization agreement was obviously not possible due to very specific local requirements. In these cases, Alpha pushed decisions top-down. Acceptance for this procedure may have been high because of another cultural facet: Alpha's long-term orientation. Taking a conservative-steady approach once again turned out to be the right thing to do. In combination with a "keep on going" attitude, it further drove on the transformation.

The Benefit

By 2009, GIGA HR created a strong foundation for the HR business. Around 50% of all HR tasks, such as organizational management as well as payroll and people administration, were already supported by the GIGA IT solution. The system comprises around 10,000 HR users, 20,000 manager self-service users, and 50,000 employee self-service users. Looking at the rollout of GIGA, the start-up phase has been successfully finished with getting all Alpha markets online. "Now we need to be in a different phase (…) of making GIGA deliver the business benefits (…) by improving the processes, applications and the effectiveness of what has been deployed." More and more opportunities for the HR function become obvious through the further development of the IT foundation. Some of the key projects that build on this foundation are talent management, succession planning, learning management, and e-forms. GIGA HR is putting Alpha far ahead in terms of synergies, and today Alpha has started to exploit GIGA HR's huge potential.

GIGA HR has not only enabled the internal transformation of the HR business but also increased external competitiveness. Using the same terminology in the HR processes worldwide, GIGA HR increased the comparability of the data and their analysis. "There is one Alpha! (…) When I want to know how many marketing people across all of the divisions are under 30, what their performance rating is, (…) whether they are male or female… if I asked for that across Alpha, this would be hard work, a big project. (…) Let's just push a button on this!" Alpha is on its way to making IT matter extensively through the harmonization of its processes and the standardization of its data. So far, globally, only Key Performance Indicators (KPIs) like headcount and turnover reports have been possible. GIGA HR now allows for different KPIs, providing answers to more fascinating questions, such as "Have employees in the talent management pool left the organization and for what reason?" There is tremendous potential for Alpha HR to be raised on the basis of the global system. In the following, we analyze the main potentials of GIGA HR according to the six dimensions introduced above.

1. STRATEGIC ALIGNMENT

The strategic alignment of different functions, businesses, and markets will be facilitated through GIGA HR. The system allows for joint initiatives and collaboration ranging from recruitment and talent management to common training. Many synergies can be created on the basis of the GIGA HR system. GIGA HR will simplify the execution of performance reviews and support the management of strategic Alpha goals.

2. GOVERNANCE

Up-to-date global information will be available for decision making. Organizational decisions, such as outsourcing or bargaining with unions, will be supported and as a result be more effective, because a direct comparison of different markets will be possible. Furthermore, the acquisition of new companies will be easier since harmonized processes already exist.

3. METHODS

HR administrational self-services for employees, e.g. through online-forms, will ease the management of HR processes and disburden the administrational HR body. Furthermore, the comparison of global data will allow for a continuous improvement of internal processes.

4. IT

GIGA HR incorporates an IT system that is based on the latest technology. Alpha can now use a business warehouse instead of Excel spreadsheets. Thus, the availability of global data will rise significantly through GIGA HR. Reliable up-to-date data will be available at the touch of a button, thereby having a huge impact on sustaining operational efficiencies, for example global reporting or planning and controlling of HR processes.

5. SKILLS

Regarding the skills and knowledge of people, the potential of the new HR system is manifold. It provides the opportunity to find top employees through a Talent Management System. Succession Planning will further improve the allocation of skills in the corporation. Global Job Posting will allow worldwide mobility of employees. E-learning and global training will increase skills. All in all, Alpha will be able to extensively profit from economies of scale.

6. CULTURE

GIGA HR has a tremendous impact on Alpha's culture. The involvement of HR people in defining global best-practice solutions for HR enhances process-oriented thinking in the function. Combined with the common language that has been created through GIGA HR, the project facilitates one Alpha which in turn will ease leveraging the potential of GIGA HR.

Alpha's GIGA HR project provides some general implications for similar transformation projects of such scope. We differentiate between general, HR-related and IT-related implications and identify in each case six recommendations according to the six areas relevant for business transformation. Please see the Key Learnings opposite.

Conclusion

The example of GIGA HR shows how to successfully build the foundation for a huge transformation process. It shows that the implementation of IT does not necessarily create value directly, but it enables processes which then generate value. GIGA has facilitated Payroll and HR administrative processes, data standardization, and HR Shared Services. It is a unique kernel for managing organizational data, enabling of global reporting and is a solid platform for value added processes, e.g., Talent Management or Compensation Management. Over years, Alpha invested in implementing the core system worldwide. Today, the starting point of "We almost didn't know what to do with the IT system!" is history. "Ironically, the new IT system finally made Alpha acting as one!".

Key Learnings

IN GENERAL:

- Clarify the roles of business and IT.
- Create an organizational structure that supports the transformation.
- Benchmark internal processes (as you do with external processes).
- Match business requirements with IT system capabilities.
- Build up international teams for a global project.
- Achieve strong CEO support and communicate properly.

FOR THE HR FUNCTION:

- Conduct a business benefit analysis on the basis of the functional strategy.
- Identify functional project managers.
- Define business processes including a market perspective.
- Embrace technology at the right moment.
- Find HR people who can "talk technology".
- Support a mindset change through project management.

FOR THE IT FUNCTION:

- Understand the business needs and deliver simple proposals.
- Define minimum requirements for the implementation of a global system.
- Find the right balance between standardization and flexibility.
- Balance ease of use and usefulness of a system.
- Make sure people in the functions understand the language you are using.
- Reach consensus where possible.

Bibliography

Carr, N.G. (Ed.) (2004). *Does IT Matter? Information Technology and the Corrosion of Competitive Advantage*. Boston: Harvard Business School Press.

Davis, F.D. (1989). Perceived usefulness, perceived ease of use, and user acceptance of information technology. *MIS Quarterly*, 13(3), 319–339.

de Bruin, T., Rosemann, M. (2007). Using the Delphi technique to identify BPM capability areas. In Proceedings of the 18th Australasian Conference on Information Systems (ACIS 2007), Toowoomba, Australia.

McAfee, A., Brynjolfsson, E. (2008). Investing in the IT That Makes a Competitive Difference. *Harvard Business Review*, 87 (7/8), 98–107.

Rosemann, M., vom Brocke, J. (2010). The six core elements of business process management. In: Rosemann, M., vom Brocke, J. (Eds.), *Handbook on Business Process Management. Introduction, methods and information systems* (Vol. 1, pp. 109–124). Berlin: Springer.

vom Brocke, J., Sinnl, T. (2011). Culture in business process management: A literature review. *Business Process Management Journal*, 17(2), 357–377.

HR Is Just a Different Animal

A COMMENT ON THE GLOBAL HR TRANSFORMATION CASE BY AXEL UHL (SAP)

IT projects which are conducted in the Human Resources (HR) function are special transformation projects because the HR clientele usually has only a small technological affinity – although, in fact, technology plays an important role in efficient HR processes, particularly in the more administrative processes of personnel administration, payroll or time management. Only gradually does the realization prevail that this also applies to the so-called "value-added processes", such as learning and training, succession planning, compensation, or performance management. So far, the importance of analyzing the employee data for decision making, e.g. in personnel planning, has been completely underestimated.

In general, the interest in technology decreases with the hierarchical level of the HR employee. An HR manager who supports the top management often deals with the recruitment of executive officers as well as with their discharge. After a one-and-a-half-hour meeting with the board member responsible for personnel of an international group, I was told that he had learned more about his HR processes than in the past 25 years. Is this an exception? Rather not. Therefore, it is no surprise that introducing a global HR system was not the idea of the HR function. It was the financial and logistics sectors of the company which came up with this idea, as they were not able to use work flows due to a lack of a global organizational structure – which is part of the HR solution.

That is the reason why HR was "forced" to introduce a global HR system as well. One can vividly imagine how big the enthusiasm and the buy-in of the HR organization for this project were. Ultimately, they were "motivated" by the CEO to promote the subject. Although you can force people to do something, you cannot force them to like it. The project was first driven by IT, then by the newly founded HR Business Excellence Organization, and in the end, somehow, the system was up and running. Although the system is running stable, is efficient and modern – HR does not love it. And, whenever there are discussions about the future development of IT systems, all other alternatives are explored before the most obvious solution is approached – to further develop the existing system. HR does not hold grudges – but HR can never forget anything.

14

Titoni Ltd.:
An Independent Swiss Watch
Brand in China

Matthias Messmer (Titoni)

Chinese people's interest in Western products is best reflected by today's shopping frenzy of Chinese consumers in shopping malls, and especially their delight in buying international watch brands. How did this enthusiasm for Western watches and the success of a small watch company like Titoni Ltd. in China all come about?

Abstract

This article tells the story of how the Swiss watch brand Titoni Ltd. was launched on the Chinese market more than 50 years ago, and how Titoni has evolved to become one of the most famous foreign brands in that country. We start with a brief history of Western watches in China, before going on to take a closer look at the arrival of Titoni watches on that market after the People's Republic of China had been founded. Later on, we will review the challenges, risks, and even threats faced by small and medium-sized enterprises such as Titoni Ltd. after the Chinese opening-up policy and the globalized market environment that soon followed. The factors and decisions that helped Titoni Ltd. stay successful in the 21st century will be revealed and discussed. In the "lessons learned", we will touch on topics dedicated to cross-cultural sensitivity: Without knowledge of the basic principles of How to Behave in Chinese Culture and Society, Titoni Ltd. would not have remained such a thriving enterprise up to this day.

*****

The Italian Jesuit missionary Matteo Ricci arrived in China back in the sixteenth century, bringing with him, among other things, a clock as a present for his hosts. The Chinese expressed great interest in clocks, mechanics, astrology, mathematics, and maps. Along with new missionary stations, Western knowledge spread rapidly, and soon a few Chinese craftsmen and scholars began to take an interest in mechanical timepieces.

During the Qing Dynasty (1644–1911), an imperial clock-making enterprise was set up, drawing most of its know-how from Western experts. Western watches imported from England or France were sought-after between the sixteenth and eighteenth century. Then, Swiss watches slowly began to gain popularity and, from the nineteenth century onwards, dominated the Chinese market because of refined watch-making skills and aesthetics.

Titoni Ltd. Enters Via Singapore and Hong Kong

When the communists came into power in 1949 and founded the People's Republic of China, Switzerland's diplomatic recognition a year later furthered the friendship and exchanges between the two countries. Due to the Cold War and the isolation of China on the international scene, however, it was not easy for Swiss companies to establish or maintain business relationships with China at that time. The few Swiss watch companies that had previously done business with China quit the market.

In fact, it had been only thanks to good luck, great intuition, and the enterprising spirit of the CEO's son, Bruno Schluep, that Felca Ltd., the manufacturer of both Felca and Titoni watches, made its first contact with the Chinese world. The Swiss family enterprise had been founded in 1919 in the watchmaking town of Grenchen, at the foot of the Swiss Jura Mountains. Twenty years later, it was already selling its high-quality "Felca" brand watches to other continents, including some parts of Southeast Asia, like Singapore and Hong Kong. Because many Chinese sailors stopped in Singapore and bought watches to take home to China at that time, the Titoni brand was already known in Beijing (Peking).

In 1944, shortly before the end of the Sino-Japanese War (1937–1945), Schluep received a letter from Koh Mui Yew, a Chinese businessman. Koh, a refugee based in Singapore, had written to several Swiss watch companies, hoping to take over the Southeast Asian regional agency for one or more Swiss watch brands. However, only Bruno Schluep, relying on his keen business acumen, replied with interest, and the two businessmen reached an agreement for cooperation. This partnership was to prove very helpful for Titoni at a later time.

In the late 1950s, the Chinese State Import Authority, responsible for monitoring and supervising articles imported from the West, was looking for a supplier of fine Swiss watches at the most favorable prices. In 1959, the management of Felca Ltd. decided to invite a delegation of the China National Light Industrial Products Import and Export Corporation to visit Switzerland. Knowing "Chinese customs" – thanks to the partnership with Mr. Koh Mui Yew – the Swiss family business succeeded in establishing good relationships with the officials from mainland China and convinced them that Felca Ltd. was the right company with which to do business. Only one year later, a contract with the Chinese State Import Authority was concluded for the delivery of Titoni brand timepieces.

One important factor for a brand's international success – or failure – is, of course, the translation of a company or product name into a local language. The Titoni brand name was cleverly translated into Chinese as "Meihua", literally meaning "plum blossom." This name, symbolizing vigor and permanence, and the stylized plum flower-shaped logo soon won the attention and interest of many Chinese customers (see Figure 14.1 for an advertisement with the logo).

As the sales of watches bearing the Titoni brand name were beginning to account for an increasing share of the total sales of Felca Ltd., the company name was extended to "Felca & Titoni Watches Ltd." in the 1960s. While the same standards of highest quality and greatest precision applied to the manufacturing of both the Felca and Titoni brands, a geographic bifurcation of their distribution channels gradually evolved. Whereas Felca-branded watches were mainly offered in Europe, the Near and Middle East, and in Australia, Titoni-branded watches were sold in China, India and many other Asian countries. In China, a Titoni timepiece was considered a precious symbol and a family treasure to be handed down from generation to generation. During the era of Mao Zedong (1949–76) and long afterwards, many Chinese people saved for months or even years to purchase a Titoni product.

**Figure 14.1   Titoni Advertising, Showing the Meihua (Plum Blossom)
Flower in Singapore and Malaysia in the 1950s and 1960s**
Source: Courtesy of Titoni Ltd.

Growing Competition in the 1980s and 1990s

In the early 1980s, China's economy developed from a planned economy towards an increasingly open market environment under the guidance of Deng Xiaoping. This marked the beginning of a transitional period that started attracting Western companies and changed the distribution channels in China. The former sole import through government agencies was fragmented and substituted by imports through other channels, and the previously solely state-run department stores were complemented by private shops and shopping malls.

Daniel Schluep, Titoni's current CEO, recalls: "We had strengthened our presence and grown under the communist regime, despite major governmental constraints, like a limited number of models, taxes of up to 180%, and a prescribed maximum manufacturer's price of CHF 80. When the economic opening of China happened, it shook the watch sector in this gigantic market, but our long-standing presence gave us decisive advantages."

Titoni Ltd. experienced enormous growth in the following decade, as more Chinese consumers could now afford high-quality Swiss watches. The then already well-known Titoni brand was for many the first choice when buying a foreign watch, and demand soon surpassed supply.

One interesting point to note is the harmony of interests between local department stores and foreign watch brands. On the one hand, the rather shabby-looking state-owned shops were eager to find Western brands to give them a proper "face-lift" at this time of growing competition. On the other hand, a watch brand like Titoni was happy to provide them with attractive store decorations, such as an elegant counter or – later on – fancy shop-in-shop furnishings. In a nutshell, this was a win-win situation for both partners. This concept also launched a whole new design of department stores that was to quickly spread to other countries.

As the state monopoly on imported goods and government control of distribution channels slowly slackened and the import of Western goods became increasingly important, the grey market also grew. Luxury goods in particular were smuggled into China through Hong Kong, and the problem of counterfeit goods emerged and posed a serious threat to Western companies, especially foreign watch brands.

Fortunately, the situation for Titoni Ltd. was slightly different. By that time, Titoni Ltd. had been cooperating with Chinese government officials for almost three decades, and the fact that some of these officials were engaged in the privatization of the import-export sector helped Titoni to safely avoid some pitfalls of this transitional period. Thus, the import of Titoni watches remained more or less unaffected.

China's booming economy in the 1990s was attracting increasing numbers of international watch companies to the Chinese market. As the competition grows, a small independent company like Titoni can only succeed with a long-standing reputation, reliability, and a good sales network nationwide, as well as the knack of reliable partners, especially in a country where personal relationships are highly valued. The long-lasting cooperation between Titoni Ltd. and the Koh Mui Yew family has continued to this very day, and it has helped Titoni Ltd. to overcome a number of challenging times.

"In contrast to the big corporations, we are not replaceable managers", says Daniel Schluep. "For us as an independent family-run business, everything depends on long-term personal relationships and the mutual trust we share with our clients, most of whom are independent dealers, too. Of course, the power of the large competitors concerns us, but our networks are solid. We inspire trust, or rather our products inspire trust."

In the meantime, the problem of counterfeits did not leave Titoni unaffected. Fake Titoni watches appeared on the Chinese market, especially in Internet shops – which is no surprise since, in a transitional period, people try to make money at every opportunity. This is the reason why Titoni has so far avoided setting up its own online shop, despite the potential of this distribution channel. It took Titoni some considerable effort to track down illegal dealers. Even today, Titoni is working together with its Chinese partners to closely monitor the Internet to ensure that no suspicious shops sell fake Titoni watches.

More Risks or Opportunities in the 21st Century?

The new millennium started with a few new short-term threats for the watch industry in China. In 2003, the SARS pandemic alert throughout China made it impossible to move freely within the country, thus presenting challenges for the logistics and distribution processes of Titoni watches for several months. Furthermore, the unstable exchange rate between the Swiss franc and the Chinese Yuan, along with the increase in the price of Swiss-made watch movements due to growing demand, forced Titoni to adjust the retail price. Compared to other more luxurious Swiss watch brands, however, the rise in Titoni's prices was not dramatic, and Titoni watches are still considered to be excellent value for money.

Besides these challenges, Titoni Ltd. was also confronted with heightened competition from major international groups, such as LVMH, Richemont, and Swatch, who were armed with glittering advertisements and a huge marketing budget. For example, these competitors hire international and Chinese celebrities as brand ambassadors. Along with the competition, the race for prime shop locations in cities has driven up the rent prices.

Given the country's communist history and the gross annual national income per capita of only USD 4,260, one might wonder whether the Chinese luxury watch market potential is indeed big enough. However, the considerable size and projected growth of the Chinese upper class population does make China an interesting market for luxury goods (Bain and Company 2011). According to such surveys, "showing off assets and status" is the reason why rich businessmen often purchase a luxury watch worth several tens of thousands of Swiss francs. On the other hand, as Chinese media and Internet users have discovered, one must also be aware that luxury watches are sometimes "effective" presents with which to win government support for business projects.

Rejuvenating the Marketing Strategy

Due to its long presence on the Chinese market, Titoni was a very familiar brand at the turn of the millennium. Some Chinese consumers were even misled into thinking of Titoni as a Chinese brand, because the Chinese brand name Meihua, which had heightened its degree of popularity in the 1970s and 1980s, sounded so traditional to them. The doubts about the origin of Titoni were further nourished due to the fact that quite a few once proud traditional Swiss brands had been taken over by foreign companies after a major crisis had severely hit the Swiss watch industry in the late 1970s and early 1980s. This crisis had two components. First, the Swiss watch industry had not taken the technological leap towards electronic quartz watches seriously enough, and was surprised by Japanese mass production of these new cheaper and more accurate quartz watches. Second, the floating of the USD – Swiss Franc exchange rate (due to the decoupling of USD and the gold price and after the cancellation of the Bretton Woods agreement) weakened the Swiss position on the very important US watch market.

Although the quartz crisis had also affected Titoni Ltd., its management had opted for a reasonable balance between producing mechanical and quartz watches. This decision helped Titoni stay entirely independent despite these challenges; but, given the rumors mentioned above, the Chinese market had to be informed about this independence. Thus, at the turn of the millennium, it became apparent for Titoni that it could not continue to rely solely on "word of mouth" and its "traditional reputation" to convey its brand values. A "rejuvenation" of the marketing strategy was urgently needed. After long and meticulous internal discussions, while sticking to their priorities of high quality and reasonable prices, the management decided to start planning mass marketing campaigns to reach the Chinese consumers (see Figure 14.2). As a result, branding, communication, and public relation experts have been involved in Titoni's marketing work ever since. Image campaigns that reflect Titoni's contemporary values around the pursuit of a modern spirit and outfit whilst still retaining its classic heart are now launched every few years.

Figure 14.2   Titoni Advertising in Shanghai in 2011
Source: Courtesy of Titoni Ltd.

Nonetheless, the idea of inviting ambassadors to promote the brand is still considered unnecessary. "We don't want a celebrity to be the face of our brand. We want our product quality and design and our technology to speak for themselves and for our brand. Besides, I think that consumers are smart and will soon understand that they are paying the advertising bill", explains Daniel Schluep.

In 2006, Titoni Ltd. took a further step and for the first time appointed a Swiss manager to be based in China. The presence of a Swiss representative in China, his knowledge of the Chinese culture, as well as his in-depth and up-to-date insight into China's complex market and dynamic consumers' needs are important in winning the confidence of clients and fostering good relationships with the media.

Titoni's new marketing strategy proved to be effective on the market. Sales of Titoni watches have continued to grow at a steady rate despite the aforementioned tough competition from many companies with high-budget marketing campaigns.

Figure 14.3   The President of the Swiss Confederation, Doris Leuthard, and Mr Sun Liansheng Pose in Front of the Swiss Cities Pavilion, Sponsored by Titoni, at the 2010 Shanghai Expo
Source: Courtesy of Titoni Ltd.

Besides mass-oriented advertising, Titoni also began sponsoring various events related to China. Examples include joining the Swiss City Pavilion at the Shanghai EXPO 2010 (see Figure 14.3), the adoption of panda bears in Chengdu, sponsoring a Beijing Opera exhibition at the Cultural Museum of Basel, and supporting three young Chinese artists to study at Zurich University of the Arts. Each event brought Titoni's brand spirit closer to the Chinese audience and improved the brand awareness level.

The company is also constantly on the lookout for inspirations in watch technology and designs. Limited editions, like the "Artist Watch", which was designed by the famous German-Chinese artist Zhang Qikai, and the Shanghai-inspired "Cathay Edition" watches (see Figure 14.4) have brought fresh blood to this traditional and classic watch brand. At first glance, these designs may step out of line in the eyes of existing Titoni customers. However, these models managed to become topics of conversation, and the wide media coverage of the two aforementioned special editions supports the brand's rejuvenation activities.

Figure 14.4   The Limited "Cathay Edition", inspired by Shanghai
Source: Courtesy of Titoni Ltd.

Another important marketing activity is the annual visit of Chinese journalists to Titoni's headquarters in Grenchen. This provides the Chinese market with first-hand information about Titoni's watch-making process and helps the Chinese consumers understand the "soul" of the Titoni brand.

Swissness and Intercultural Sensitivity are Important

Nowadays, the brand is going strong with around 700 sales outlets in Greater China (see Figure 14.5 for an example), as well as roughly 50 service centers. Nonetheless, challenges never stop.

Figure 14.5   Titoni Gallery in Shanghai, Opened in March 2011
Source: Courtesy of Titoni Ltd.

The "Made in Switzerland" label, which was developed over centuries by Swiss watch campaigns and supported by the Swiss government, currently runs the risk of losing value since many famous Swiss brands are now outsourcing parts of their supply chain and/or production process abroad, due to Switzerland's high labor costs. Many international watch groups even transfer their design or marketing activities to other countries. For a small Swiss family-owned company like Titoni Ltd., however, this new situation is an opportunity to stand out from the crowd; it meets the challenge by re-thinking and improving its value proposition, design, and marketing.

Another threat is also lurking. Over and above the competition from international brands, the launch of high-quality Chinese watches made the competition in China even more exciting and complicated. Chinese brands have the advantage of better knowing the local markets and tastes, but this does not mean that the Chinese consumer automatically prefers domestic brands over Swiss ones. In order to win over potential new customers, these Chinese producers will have to make a concerted effort with not only up-to-date technology, but also with convincing design, production, and marketing skills.

China has been the leading market for Titoni over the last few decades. Apart from the "lucky timing" of the market entry mentioned above, this is also due to the intercultural awareness and reliable intuition of Titoni's management in predicting the Asian Shift several years before it became apparent to others. Respect, open-mindedness, trust, and excellent communication skills are at the heart of Titoni's international business success. For more than fifty years, Titoni Ltd. has had to deal with various challenges in China caused by cultural differences, ranging from cooperating with the government to communicating with the local Chinese partner staff. As expectations and priorities of different stakeholders usually vary to a great extent, the way things are communicated often has a huge influence on the results. Thanks to their vast international experience, Titoni managers know when to listen to their local partners and when to take the lead. Naturally, however, this does not mean that Titoni Ltd. always found it easy to understand the thoughts and opinions of its partners.

Another lesson is that it is essential to understand and monitor consumers' needs and wishes, especially in today's rapidly changing world. Since the Chinese economy opened up, local consumers' tastes in watch design have changed considerably. Furthermore, Chinese consumers also differ throughout the country, as those in large cities want a chic watch design and the latest technology, looking for a comfortable shopping experience in pampering surroundings, whereas those in smaller cities attach greater importance to high quality and reputation. Titoni has thus developed strategies to deal with these heterogeneous markets and needs. Feedback and opinions from local clients and staff, as well as the annual visits of Titoni's current CEO to China help shape these strategies. However, despite the regional differences, Titoni strives to maintain a constantly professional and friendly service standard by establishing training programs for shop assistants in collaboration with its Chinese importer.

To sum up, overcoming cultural differences and reacting to a fast-paced market environment are two pivotal lessons when doing business in China. Only constant learning by doing with an open mind will lead to success; and the two-generation partnership between Titoni and its Chinese importer, as well as the company's widespread network within China resulting from this, have proved priceless, too.

For the coming decade, investments in the latest technologies and communication with consumers through image campaigns, events, positive shopping experiences at Titoni showrooms, and after-sale services will be the key strategies for Titoni Ltd. Although faced with tough competition from many major international watch groups in a market with about 300 watch brands, Titoni is determined to uphold its fine watch-making tradition on a small family scale.

Key Learnings

- Take a lot of time when doing business with Chinese – and never show any sign of impatience (even though you might occasionally feel impatient).
- Check twice before you decide to trust a potential business partner – he or she may try to impress you more with a Potemkin-like façade than showing you the reality.
- Do not act as a wisenheimer – even if you know something better than your business partner, you should try your best to give them some face.
- Never lose your temper – the wisest attribute when in the company of Chinese people is to be good humored. Even if you are not in the mood or are yourself the center of a joke (which foreigners often are), always try to laugh at their jokes even though it might be embarrassing or not funny at all.

Bibliography

Bain and Company (2011). 2011 China Luxury Market Study. Bain Point of View. December 2011. Available from: http://www.bain.com/publications/articles/2011-china-luxury-market-study.aspx [accessed 24.04.2012].

Everything Remains Different

A COMMENT ON THE TITONI CASE BY AXEL UHL (SAP)

When a Swiss company has long been successfully doing business in one of the world's toughest markets, it must be doing something right. In these 50 years in which Titoni has been active in the East, China's market has changed more than any other market in the world. Even now, with all the glitz and glamor of megacities like Shanghai and Beijing, we must not forget that it is still a communist country and consider just how quickly it has evolved into the China of today. Its inhabitants are uncertain about the state's ubiquitous authority. This uncertainty expresses itself in the business world in the form of a great need for trust. It is virtually impossible to do business without relationships that are built on trust. Having maintained good business relationships for decades, Titoni has established this sense of trust which gives them a competitive advantage that helps it to overcome crises better and seize opportunities more quickly than the competitors.

The sustainable success of Titoni is also typified by the fact that it has never viewed China as a source of cheap labor to produce goods for the global marketplace, but rather it has always been interested in Chinese customers and therefore has concentrated its efforts on their specific requirements. One can well imagine that both the country and Titoni's business partners perceive this as a form of sincere appreciation, which is still the basic principle of all good relationships.

15

The Evolution of SAP Services

Oliver Müller (University of Liechtenstein),
Jan vom Brocke (University of Liechtenstein),
Thomas von Alm (SAP), Axel Uhl (SAP)

SAP Services is constantly transforming its business model to meet the ever changing customer demands in the IT services industry. This case study charts the evolution of SAP Services and highlights how the company manages to actively drive change on a global scale.

Abstract

The software industry has changed significantly over the last two decades. Especially in the enterprise software market, the role of software-related services is becoming more and more important. In this case study we investigate how SAP Services, the services arm of SAP, senses and reacts to changing customer needs and reinvents the market for software-related services. A radical overhaul of SAP's service portfolio and new service delivery models are at the heart of the current transformation initiative. From a change management perspective, the proactive involvement of key customers and employees from the field proved to be important enablers for change. Yet, the company also faced some challenges, such as changing its consulting culture and convincing key business partners to follow the new strategy.

*****

The software industry has changed significantly in the last two decades. In relative terms, traditional product revenue has declined, while services revenue is on the rise. In 1990, software firms generated about 70% of their revenue from products and the remaining 30% from software-related services. Since then, the

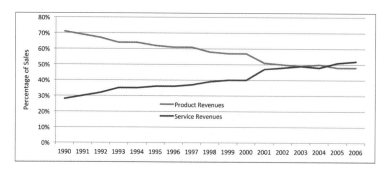

Figure 15.1   Crisscross of Product and Service Revenue in the Software Industry
Source: Cusumano 2008.

revenue share of products has decreased steadily (see Figure 15.1), and in 2003, services sales crossed over to exceed product sales. The growing importance of services is especially apparent in the enterprise software market.

Against this background, the Business Transformation Academy (BTA) and the University of Liechtenstein initiated a joint research project to investigate how the service portfolio at SAP has evolved and is still evolving. Over a six-month period in mid-2011, we conducted interviews with executives of SAP Services, the services arm of SAP, as well as IT managers of two of SAP's major customers. This article presents selected findings of this study.

SAP Services' Business Model

Our first aim was to gain a better understanding of SAP's motivation for offering software-related services. In the software business, the margin of services (typically 20% or less) is much lower than the margin of software products (up to 99%), given that the marginal costs are nearly zero to copy a piece of software. Hence, in theory, it is advisable to put a strong focus on the software side of the business. However, the reality is that SAP's solutions fulfill complex customer needs and require substantial effort and specialized knowledge to set up, customize, and integrate. As it is not economically reasonable for most customers to build up the required skills and resources, there exists an enormous demand for software-related services. On the other hand, "that does not necessarily mean that SAP has to perform this job", as one SAP executive explained. "Today, there are many companies in the market that

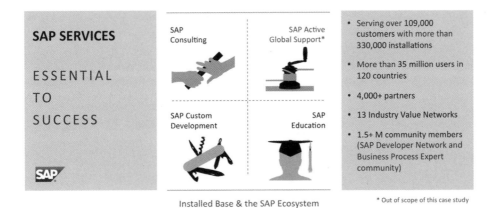

Installed Base & the SAP Ecosystem   * Out of scope of this case study

Figure 15.2   SAP Services Fact Sheet

can offer SAP implementation services. So we can basically decide how much software-related services we want to offer and how much we want to offer in cooperation with our ecosystem partners."

In this context, it is worth noting that the business model of SAP Services differs fundamentally from that of the pure-play service providers (see Figure 15.2). The goal, for example, of a typical standalone consultancy is to generate revenues from service projects through tailoring and adapting solutions to customer requirements. The software products are nothing more than a side note. In contrast, SAP Services – as a subsidiary of a product company – seeks to act as a catalyst for the adoption of SAP's products, for example, by promoting innovations in the market or facilitating the implementation and use of existing software solutions.

Charting the Evolution

To better understand the evolution and ongoing transformation of SAP Services, we took a look back at its recent history and identified a three-phased evolution (see Figure 15.3).

SAP Services started out with an experts-on-demand business model. Its value proposition was based on providing consultants with specialized technical skills and extensive SAP know-how for projects managed either by third-party service providers or by clients themselves. Two market trends induced SAP Services to depart from this model as its primary source of revenue. First, due to

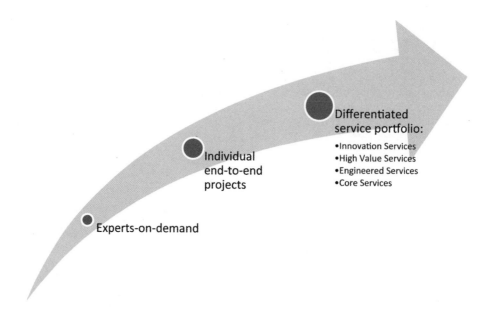

Figure 15.3   Evolution of SAP Services

global competition and technological innovation, SAP Services' capabilities and offerings were subject to an increasing commoditization. According to a global services manager, "many of the traditional services we provided in the past are recognized as commodities today". Second, as IT became more and more essential to the business of most companies, clients increasingly demanded that SAP, as the original software manufacturer, takes full accountability for the successful implementation of its solutions.

The changing customer requirements marked a turning point. Soon after, SAP Services began to grow its involvement in end-to-end projects. Compared to the experts-on-demand business, this model resulted in longer-term engagements with clients, giving SAP Services stronger levers to ensure high-value and low-risk implementations for them. Internally, it allowed SAP Services to leverage economies of scale through the set-up of dedicated organizational structures, the build-up of specialized capabilities, the facilitation of learning and knowledge transfer, and the application of resources across geographies and markets. Yet, with the transition to the project business, SAP Services suddenly found itself in direct competition with the many IT consultancies that have specialized in enterprise software implementation projects. Following their rationale, SAP Services tried to win projects by demonstrating how its software solutions can be customized and adapted to best fit the individual needs of a client.

Sensing new developments in customer expectations, the company decided to further transform its business model to be able to climb to the next rung on the evolutionary ladder. This step included a refinement of the value proposition of SAP Services towards a differentiated service portfolio. Extensive tailoring of solutions and projects is not necessarily in line with the interests of both customers and SAP itself. Today, the majority of the costs of an enterprise software project are not determined by the price of software licenses, but by the total cost of implementing a solution. As one SAP executive pointed out, "for every dollar you spend on software licensing, you have to spend another five dollars for implementation services". While this situation is actually beneficial for pure consultancies, it represents a drag on the core business of any company making and selling software. One of the interviewees made it clear that "the best way to strengthen SAP's position in the competition is to drive down the total cost of implementation". This is especially true in times of increased competition from less service-intensive, on-demand solutions, such as the competitor, Salesforce.com.

Listening to the Voice of the Customer

After gaining a comprehensive picture of SAP's transformation journey, we continued to collect opinions of two of the company's major customers, Hilti and Zurich Financial Services. We were first interested in learning how – from their perspective as customers – the overall enterprise software market changed during the last decade. Both interviewees named the increasing modularization of traditional enterprise applications, for example, Enterprise Resource Planning (ERP) and Customer Relationship Management (CRM), and the emergence of software-as-a-service solutions as the most significant changes over the last few years.

These developments in the software market have interesting effects on IT project management. Both companies are trying to turn to smaller, more focused projects, and it seems that these projects are increasingly managed in-house and not by external consultancies. One IT executive of Zurich described the staffing of future IT projects as follows: "I shop a few experts on the risk modeling platform, I shop a few experts on the data management, I shop a few experts on the integration, and I integrate them into an overall project governed by in-house program management". Likewise, there is a clear trend towards more standardization in back-office functions. One of the interviewees even brought up the metaphor of an "app store" for downloading and deploying standard business processes such as payroll processing or e-procurement: "I know that such standard processes are never 100% perfect for me because they are not individually programmed for me, but it would be great if I could choose between two or three different flavors and I just go for the one that I think best fits my requirements."

We proceeded to discuss how the customers perceive SAP Services. What would they consider the core competencies and unique value propositions of SAP Services? How has the company changed over the last few years? Again, both customers were generally unanimous in their opinions. One of the interviewed managers described SAP's journey as follows: "SAP developed into a company that is able to provide professional services. That was not the case 10 years ago. Back then, they had only very few people and were more like software engineers than consultants." In regards to core competencies, the customers perceive SAP Services as highly specialized experts for SAP-related technology. "When a problem gets really difficult, when we need something really innovative and challenging, then we turn to SAP Services", one interviewee concluded.

On the other hand, according to the interviewees, SAP Services still has potential to increase its reputation for expertise in more business-related issues. In their opinion, the key for SAP Services to provide real business value is in extracting and leveraging knowledge from SAP's huge customer base. Both interviewees expressed great interest in learning from the best practices of their peers and also from developments in other, more innovative industries. "SAP provides cutting-edge solutions to hundreds of customers from virtually all industries. This makes them unique compared to other consultancies. I think it would be a low-hanging fruit for SAP to better exploit this knowledge", one interviewee summarized.

Reaching the Next Level

After having understood the history of SAP Services and collecting feedback from key customers, we continued with a detailed analysis of SAP Services' current transformation efforts. How does the company react to the changing customer requirements? What is SAP's answer to today's highly focused projects and the demand for faster time-to-value and reduced total cost of ownership? How can SAP Services position itself as a partner with sophisticated business know-how? And how is SAP managing the transformation process?

Although SAP's transformation did not have a clear-cut beginning, the process received a substantial push through the appointment of new leaders both at a corporate SAP level and at SAP Services. Following an update and sharpening of the overall SAP corporate strategy, the new President of Services, José Duarte, articulated a vision for the ongoing, evolutionary transformation efforts of SAP Services: "Move from being relevant to being essential." The goal of SAP Services, perceived as being a big but not necessarily unique player in the market, is to become an indispensable partner for two constituencies: SAP's customers and the overall SAP group. In specific terms, "being essential means to differentiate from other service providers in delivering solutions that you will not get somewhere else", as one interviewee explained.

As a logical consequence of the changing customer requirements, a complete overhaul of the service portfolio was at the heart of the transformation. In a series of workshops and off-site leadership meetings, four distinct service categories were defined (see also Table 15.1):

- Innovation services are related to SAP's latest technological developments and solutions, for example, In-Memory, Mobility, and Analytics. As the ecosystem partners have not yet built up capacities for these brand-new innovations, customers perceive SAP Services as being the only one who is able to deliver these solutions. From the perspective of the product business, SAP Services acts as a market maker in these areas.
- The area of high-value services comprises value propositions that are unique in the market in the medium to long term because they involve rare SAP-specific resources. These highly people-centric services are provided by individuals with specialized knowledge and expertise, such as planning SAP-centric IT strategies and system landscapes, industry-specific business process consulting, and custom development.
- Engineered services deliver results that are also offered by other providers but involve less time, cost, and risk. This is intended to be achieved through applying the principles of industrialization, that is, engineered services are standardized in scope, involve predefined technical content, leverage remote delivery capabilities, and are highly repeatable. They act as facilitators for the implementation of SAP's software products. Due to their industrialized form, however, these services are only unique in the short to medium term, and competitors will surely start reusing this model.

- The category of core services comprises the more traditional software implementation projects, for example, ERP implementation. In this area, SAP does not necessarily offer uniqueness in comparison to the value propositions of other players, and customers perceive SAP Services as one of many service providers. Here, SAP is especially in competition with large pure-play IT consultancies. Nonetheless, the traditional implementation services are still in high demand in specific market segments, for example, among customers in fast-growing regions like Brazil or India.

According to the predicted future customer demands, SAP's investments will focus on the first three of these service categories, whereas efforts in the area of core services will be relatively scaled down. It is envisioned that in 5 years' time, roughly a quarter of revenue will be generated by engineered services, and major parts of the remaining share by innovation and high-value services. A significant share of the core services will be provided in cooperation with partners. The following, deliberately exaggerated statement from a regional manager depicts this strategy: "If SAP's ecosystem takes on 100% of the traditional implementation projects, it would actually be a brilliant outcome of the transformation. Yet there will always be customers who want us, as the software vendor, to take responsibility for a project."

Table 15.1   New service categories

Service Category	Description	Examples
Innovation Services	Delivered in a market-maker capacity, they ensure SAP remains in the first-mover role with SAP innovations by adopting new technologies.	– Mobility – HANA/In Memory – Cloud
High-Value Services	These help differentiate SAP Services with unique, people-centric services that deliver tangible mid-term and long-term value for customers.	– Platinum Consultants – Business Transformation Services – Performance Insights & Optimization – Custom Development
Engineered Services	These assemble-to-order services focus on higher efficiency providing quality through reuse, specialization, and built-in scalability, and are designed to reduce the services-to-software ratio for customers.	– Focused Business Solutions – SAP Rapid Deployment Solutions – IT Transformation Services – SAP MaxAttention & Safeguarding

Important Change Agents

A key lever for achieving the defined objectives was to introduce a new delivery model that consisted of three tiers: local, near-shore, and off-shore. Within each of these levels, there are consultants who can work on site, potentially involving extensive travelling activities, or remotely, using advanced communication and collaboration technologies, like the telephone, Web, and video conferencing. One of the interviewees described SAP's ambitious goals in transforming its delivery capabilities as follows: "Currently, almost 90% of our services are provided at the customer's site, while only a small portion is delivered from remote sites. We want to come to a more balanced distribution in the future." One of the next steps will be to identify appropriate prescriptive delivery models for each service offering. The idea is that customers do not have to worry about modes of delivery and instead can focus completely on the outcomes of a service. However, the interviews also revealed that there is still a lot of work to do in this area, for instance, building up the right resources for these new delivery models and increasing acceptance among sales executives and customers. One regional manager concluded: "That will be part of the transformation in the coming years."

Another important enabler for professionalizing delivery capabilities is to enhance the deployability of software, a good example of which is SAP's new rapid deployment solutions. These packages combine software with essential functionality, predefined configurations, and best practice business content with fixed-scope implementation services at a predictable price and delivery date. One of the regional heads said: "With this mass customization approach, SAP promises to deliver a running 80% solution in a couple of weeks, instead of a 99% solution in several months or even years. Most customers like this idea because they can still decide to improve the solution to more than 80% requirements coverage once it is up and running."

These are just a few examples of the transformation areas and goals. As one can imagine, organizing change activities in a global, established, and very successful organization of 18,000 professionals is not an easy task. The decision was made to install transformation managers in all dimensions of SAP Services' organization, that is, business areas, for example, Consulting, Custom Development, Education, geographies, that is, Asia Pacific and Japan, EMEA, Latin America, and North America, and functions, for example, Portfolio Management, Sales, Delivery, HR, Finance. These change agents, enjoying the support of a global transformation management function, are located right in the field, within the local teams. This choice was considered indispensable in avoiding resistance to a transformation program designed outside of the business. As one manager from the global transformation team summed it up: "We strongly believe that the transformation has to be led by the business units in the field. Global functions, like transformation management, are important facilitators, but they cannot execute a transformation alone. Ultimately, the transformation needs to happen in the field, in our customer engagements. Otherwise, it's just talk."

In line with this thinking, SAP is also in a conscious dialogue with its customer base to ensure that the transformation efforts are in line with their needs and expectations. In particular, SAP set up a customer advisory board comprising about 25 clients who, together, represent roughly 10% of SAP Services' revenues. The direction and current state of the transformation process is presented to this panel in intervals of six months. As the interviews with both SAP managers and customers revealed, the feedback and recommendations of the customer advisory board have been absolutely essential in steering the transformation. The head of SAP Services EMEA even went so far as to state that "we actually worked out the repositioning together with the customers".

Challenges Along the Way

Unsurprisingly, the transformation team also faced a number of challenges. A recurring central theme in several interviews was the concern about changing SAP's consulting culture, that is, the mind-sets, practices, and routines of service professionals. In the experts-on-demand and tailor-made-projects businesses, architects and consultants were used to solve customer problems by developing and implementing individual, and sometimes even unique solutions. One of the interviewees compared this job to "creating your own piece of art – which our employees love". While creative problem-solving skills are still essential for innovation and high-value services, consultants in the engineered services model are expected to deliver the same or similar results over and over again. Intellectually, this is not very challenging. On the other hand, the standardization and repeatability frees up resources to do things other than merely installing technical solutions, and, most importantly, to deal with the business problems of the client. Convincing the workforce to take an active part in this shift in focus will certainly be one of the major challenges of the current transformation activities.

Another equally demanding task is to convince SAP's ecosystem to follow the new strategic direction. As previously outlined, the ecosystem partners do not currently see the benefit of reducing the software-to-service cost ratio of SAP's business solutions. As SAP Services is handling only 10–15% of the worldwide SAP implementations, however, it is crucial to get the ecosystem on board. Otherwise, "SAP's efforts will just be a drop in the ocean", as one regional manager depicted. Hence, SAP's plans in the area of engineered services are to train and certify ecosystem partners, license out intellectual property, and co-develop service offerings with special expertise partners. SAP is confident that, in the future, this will be a source of revenue of its own. The company is facing a similar situation in the area of innovation services. External service providers are reluctant to develop service offerings for disruptive innovations like In-Memory or Virtualization. They would rather wait and see until a critical mass of customers is adopting a new technology before investing. One regional executive characterized the situations as follows: "Parts of the ecosystem have become risk-averse. They make billions of dollars on the back of SAP without taking risks, without driving innovation."

First Success Stories

SAP Services is still in the middle of the transformation, so it is still too early to draw reliable conclusions from our study. Nevertheless, first success stories can be told. Early customers of engineered services implementations report dramatically shortened implementation times, for example, about 12 weeks for a clearly scoped CRM solution. In North America and other regions, the customer demand for some innovation and high-value services is exceeding available capacity. Here, SAP urgently needs to invest in human resources to keep up with the growing market.

Analyzing the interviews, we were able to identify some critical success factors that were crucial in reaching the current state. Three aspects were repeatedly mentioned. First, make the transformation transparent; allow employees to connect the dots by explaining what remains stable and highlighting what will significantly change over the course of the transformation journey. Second, involve customers and business partners; transforming against the direction of market trends is impossible. Third, try to reach your revenue and profit goals while transforming; "When you're not paying your bills, transformation is almost impossible. The better our financial performance, the more bandwidth we will have for transformation", one of the regional heads subsumed.

This article presented an overview and some preliminary findings of our case study on the transformation of SAP Services. It tells only a fraction of the whole story, however, and as the transformation journey of SAP Services is not over yet, our case study will also go on. It will be interesting to see how the enterprise software market in general, and SAP Services in particular, will evolve over the coming years.

Key Learnings

- Make the transformation transparent: Highlight to employees what will remain stable and what will change over the course of the transformation journey.
- Involve employees and key customers: Transforming an organization against the interests of these stakeholders is impossible.
- Make sure to reach your financial targets while transforming: The better the business performance, the more bandwidth for transformation.

Acknowledgments

The authors would like to thank the following people for sharing their thoughts and experiences:

- Ross Wainwright (Executive Vice President of Services for North America, SAP)
- Mark From-Poulsen (Executive Vice President of Services for EMEA, SAP)
- Holger Lemanczyk (Head of Services Business Transformation, SAP)
- Nicolas Schobinger (Head of Services Strategy and Business Development, SAP)
- Dr Martin Petry (Chief Information Officer, Hilti Corporation)
- Andreas Schönherr (Head of Global Finance Solutions, Zurich Financial Services)

Bibliography

Cusumano, M.A., 2008. The Changing Software Business: Moving from Products to Services. *IEEE Computer*, Vol. 41, No. 1, January 2008, pp. 20–27.

"Walking the Talk": Difficult but Essential

A COMMENT ON THE SAP SERVICES CASE
BY ROBERT WINTER (UNIVERSITY OF ST. GALLEN)

"The Evolution of SAP Services" case study shows how SAP Services plans to address the software industry's transformation challenge of shifting from (software) goods-dominant logic to service-dominant logic. For the services unit of a world leader in its domain of enterprise software, this transformation challenge is significant and might provide many insights even far beyond the software industry.

Comparing the presented sketch of new or extended service offering types (innovation services, high-value services, and engineered services) or reduced service offering types (core services), their desired revenue contributions, and their respective ecosystems to SAP Services' past and present gives an idea of the extent of the ongoing evolution. Transformations of this extent need to be planned, implemented, and controlled with regard to all direction and enablement dimensions that Business Transformation Management Method (BTM²) comprises. While the case study summarizes some outcomes of strategy management tasks, including need analysis, business vision design, and business model design, many links to other transformation functions and dimensions become apparent. As a consequence, SAP Services needs to "walk the talk", that is, to apply its own BTM² approach to maintain transparency and ensure a systematic process.

In addition to a systematic, transparent "change engineering" approach, the case study points to "maintain profitability while transforming" and customer involvement as transformation success factors. While the former can be associated with the value management dimension of BTM², customer involvement is "hidden" in many, if not most, BTM² transformation activities. Even if not explicitly mentioned, an "outside-in" perspective is key to successful transformation, and it should include not only the "usual suspects", that is, existing large customers, but also stakeholder groups such as financial analysts or union representatives.

It is clear that transformations of this extent also need to incorporate a large-scale evolution of not only skills but also leadership and often mindset (in this case service-dominant logic instead of goods-dominant logic), to mention just a few "soft" factors. BTM² has a competence and training perspective that addresses skills, while culture, mindset, and leadership are part of "meta-management". With growing certainty about how to capture the transformation-specific aspects of such "soft" factors, I expect additional perspectives to be added to BTM^2 in the future.

Furthermore, greater emphasis could and should be given to patterns. Are all geographical and product markets similar with regard to the intended shift toward service-dominant logic? And if not, which configurations exist? Are all service offerings similar with regard to the required competencies, and which product or service components can be reused?

Many of these questions might already have been answered and could provide valuable insights for the BTM^2 community. I would love to learn more and see how "the talk is walked" so that not only SAP but also BTM^2 customers will benefit.

16

How Hilti Masters Transformation

Jan vom Brocke (University of Liechtenstein),
Martin Petry (Hilti), Theresa Schmiedel (University
of Liechtenstein)

Abstract

In 2000, Hilti launched a major business transformation project bringing all eight production plants, more than 50 sales organizations, and over 20,000 employees into one single global ERP system. The project was one of the biggest transformation projects of its kind for the company and it substantially changed the way Hilti is doing business today. In this study, we report on the transformation project referred to as "the Hilti Case". We begin by presenting relevant background information and specifically defining the need for action along with the goals, vision and strategy. We then report on the project's realization, its major results, and also the lessons learned as reflected by the managers involved in the project. We base our study on interviews and intensive document analysis conducted between 2009 and 2010. The results are presented in the form of a case narrative to allow for different perspectives of analysis in future studies. We very much encourage fellow researchers and practitioners to engage in the discussion in order to contribute to the body of knowledge on global business transformation management.

*****

Hilti is a global corporation in the construction industry. It provides tools, systems and services to customers worldwide. With an annual revenue of 3.9 billion Swiss francs in 2010, Hilti employs almost 20,000 people around the globe, of which roughly 1,700 work at the headquarters in Schaan, Liechtenstein. Two-thirds of all employees worldwide work directly for the customer in sales organizations and in engineering, which means a total of more than 200,000 customer contacts every day. Hilti has its own production plants as well as research and development centers in Europe and Asia.

Hilti launched its transformation project called "Global Processes and Data" (GPD) in 2000. The objective was to overcome local data and process silos by introducing global standard business processes and standardized data structures supported by a global system solution and one globally managed IT function. The project was coordinated centrally from the headquarters in Liechtenstein. By the end of 2010, over 95% of Hilti's revenue, more than 50 sales organizations, and all eight production plants were operated in one global system. This means more than 18,000 users working with SAP Enterprise Resource Planning (ERP) software and 6,000 users also working with SAP Mobile solutions and applications.

Call for Action

The idea of a globally integrated work system first surfaced as early as 1963 according to Michael Hilti quoting his father. Although it was not feasible at the time, the idea has been in the Hilti genes for quite a while, resulting in several efforts to achieve a more globally integrated corporation. In the 1980s and in the 1990s, Hilti tried to move in this direction but the solution was only being sought in the IT function, resulting in too little effort on the business side. In order to pursue a global path, the initiative needed to be broader, including a global business application landscape, global processes and global process owners.

In 2000, the Hilti Corporation's business strategy included overall targets such as customer satisfaction and productivity being achieved through operational excellence and a consistent, global implementation of strategic initiatives. Based on this strategy, Hilti IT derived a new strategy considering the local and global business initiatives at that time. It became obvious that many of the global initiatives were hindered by non-harmonized process and data structure landscapes. Furthermore, different IT systems in use were adding to difficulties in global initiatives. However, the main reasons for the transformation project were process landscapes that resulted in slow, inconsistent, and not necessarily global ways of implementing operational excellence initiatives. So Hilti IT decided to implement globally harmonized processes, data structures, and system landscapes. and with this approach, the GPD project was launched.

Goals, Vision and Strategy

The vision of the GPD transformation project was to achieve global and integrated processes, data structures, and system landscapes to realize business opportunities beyond the level reached at that time. In the first phase of the transformation, the project team focused on the 25 top sales organizations, all plants, and the headquarters, this phase being concluded in May 2006. Building on the success of the program, other sales organizations were included in the project in the second phase in order to create "one Hilti". As Hilti continues to grow as a global corporation, it has now reached phase three of the transformation, which aims to also include, for example, new sales organizations at the corporation.

The IT strategy has been discussed and communicated on a large scale in the management team and even beyond as senior managers at Hilti IT went to the sales organizations themselves to communicate and discuss the vision of a globalized IT. In a very early phase of the transformation, before and after the strategy approval, communicating the vision was very important to ensure that everybody understood the strategy of Hilti IT. The longer the project continued in this direction, the more important it became to deliver tangible outcomes rather than "new slide sets", otherwise people would have become nervous. So intense communication at the beginning needed to be followed by clear visible progress in terms of the content. The more in line with the communication the deliverables were, the greater the credibility the project acquired.

Apart from the overall goals of standardized processes and data and an integrated IT system, Hilti aimed at a very smooth implementation, namely compromise instead of confrontation. Specific goals of the transformation project related to optimizing the logistics performance, for example. This included targets such as a 95% customer perfect order (cpo) or three days repair cycle times. It is important to notice that all targets were defined including a target value. Furthermore, new initiatives such as fleet management, consistent pricing, or consistent definition of customers were launched as elements of GPD. The latter was necessary to be able to implement global customer initiatives. Generally, it is interesting that most KPIs arising from the project are business-related rather than IT-related.

To actually create additional business value and also have a reliable infrastructure, Hilti decided to spend a huge amount of money on implementing the IT strategy. Since GPD was the opposite of an IT cost-cutting strategy, business value and a reliable infrastructure needed to compensate for the money spent on the GPD project.

Realization

GAINING SUPPORT FOR A TRANSFORMATIONAL PROJECT

The GPD project was communicated in an open and honest way with clear targets. Despite the huge impact of the transformation, the management team tried to downplay the scale of the project somewhat in the beginning so as not to scare people but to calm everyone down to a degree that is helpful and necessary in the early stages of a project. Knowing about the revolutionary character of GPD, the management team decided to handle the transformation not by fueling consternation but by supporting the perception of a major change in the right direction. The awareness of the change needed was a very important factor in the success of GPD, especially since the transformation was not forced by the company's economic situation.

Looking at general management and plant managers, there was an overall high level of supportiveness, understanding and willingness to be part of the project. One or two were naturally somewhat more hesitant in the beginning but typically regretted later that they had not become more involved in the early stages. On the whole, GPD received enormous support thanks in particular to the backing the top three people in the company.

The main sponsors of the GPD project were the Hilti CEO and two more members of the Executive Board (EB) who had all been with the company for over 25 years. Support for the project from the corporation's senior management was a first fundamental factor in its success. Still, it needed an idea on how to launch a project leading in this direction. In fact, it was the former and present Chief Information Officer (CIO) presenting the idea of GPD that was basically derived out of the IT strategy development.

BUILDING A PROJECT MANAGEMENT TEAM

For the first three to four years, the GPD project management team consisted of the chief process officers, their counterparts on the IT side, representatives of the IT infrastructure, as well as the former and present CIO. The weekly meeting was relatively large because it served as a multiplication point where, especially in the first couple of months, fundamental issues were clarified. Everyone involved brought ideas from their teams to the meeting and took the results of the discussions back to their teams. About 15 people usually attended the meeting, although there was a certain amount of rotation over the years. Altogether, there were around 30 to 40 people in this meeting during the project.

The weekly coordination team meetings were perceived as the engine of the project and involved discussion of the general proceedings, including the design of common terminology. This has been extremely important in being able to address an audience that is not used to projects involving major technical changes. Furthermore, the technical course of action needed to be defined and explained to the affected persons, including questions such as "What is an integration test?", "Why do we need a unit test before the integration test?", "How long might it take and why does it take that long?", and "Can we do that earlier?" The project management team went through a lot of discussions in their regular meetings in order to get everybody on board.

In the first few years, the GPD project was more about education than execution because it was necessary to introduce the IT team to the SAP system, to integrate the entire business environment coming from various different areas, directions and functions, and to integrate new people into the IT team. At the same time, it was necessary for the project management team to amalgamate as a people speaking the same language, which is very important due to the confusion that can arise from ambiguous terminology and procedures. So it was crucial to get this type of alignment.

The project management team was basically led by the former and present CIO, who promoted their idea about how to run the project smoothly by providing detailed explanations and thinking ahead which enabled them to always stay one step ahead of the team. This way, they managed to persuade people by presenting valid ideas. So the project was clearly led by these two, although not in an authoritarian, dictatorial way but in a way that encouraged people to support the suggestions based on sound arguments.

In fact, the idea of a culture where the strongest argument wins was agreed upon in the very first coordination team meeting: "We had a major discussion and we couldn't find a common denominator. One person said 'We do it the Swiss way and just vote'. Someone else said, 'If we start voting, I will leave immediately.'" In the end, they agreed that decisions should be based on the strongest argument. The idea of the strongest argument also concerned the project management. Still, it was obvious that certain arguments needed to be pushed to prevent the project from becoming too complex.

The general management style at Hilti is one of a culture of situational leadership, which means that a manager adjusts his style of management to the skills of the specific person to whom he is delegating a certain task. For example, an enthusiastic beginner requires support and attention that is different from that given to an experienced expert. This simple rule provided very effective support to the leadership in the GPD project.

IMPLEMENTING THE GPD PROJECT

In addition to the project team, approximately 120 people were involved in the implementation process in Vaduz, Buchs, Schaan, and in the local organizations. Throughout the project this resulted in around 150 full-time equivalents at any one time after the start of GPD. The number of people involved shows a clear commitment and dedication of resources to the program. Even in tough times such as 2001/2002, when the construction industry was not so strong, Hilti further pushed the project despite of cost pressure.

In terms of implementation, the project team decided to have one release as a dry run at a very early stage to synchronize everything before going live. So one release was used to develop all processes, process documentation, systems, and test procedure. A clear advantage of this strategy was that the actual implementation was very quick.

Developing the process landscape and the system as well as implementing them was almost flawless. A huge roadmap helped to visualize the implementation. It was also decided that GPD should be launched and qualitative improvements added during the global roll out, which included both geographical and functional improvements. The process and system landscapes were augmented from country to country, adding different legal requirements and also functionality since it is not possible to implement everything from fleet to contact center at the beginning. So to avoid deviations from standards and different set-ups in organizations, it is necessary to keep rolling forwards and backwards, which poses a challenge to the project and puts considerable pressure on the project team.

As they implemented GPD around the globe, Hilti developed the concept of cross-fertilization, where people from different sales organizations, for example, synchronize themselves. This peer support proved to be more effective than sending global process experts to try to convince sales organizations how to conduct their business. It was felt that it would be better to push transformation by having people learn from peers who actually use data structures, processes and systems than having someone from Schaan translating theory into practice. In terms of shared service ideas, the cross-fertilization concept even intensified in the last two to three years.

Concerning the systems implementation, intensive collaboration with SAP was essential for the project success. Having SAP as a strong IT specialist, Hilti was able to focus on their unique business needs. Thanks to a strong involvement of SAP also on the EB level, a very productive collaboration was achieved. Today, Hilti has an outstanding relationship with SAP regarding support and respect.

Even though the GPD project was characterized by a very smooth implementation, it is obvious that a project of this significance also faced some resistance. Generally, this resistance was overcome with the support of the Hilti EB which helped the management team to promote certain facets. Today, Hilti is actually conducting its business in accordance with global standards initially defined through the GPD project. In practice, it is not an option to do things differently. However, not all processes have yet been standardized. So the global process owners and the lines of business are still in the process of establishing which local options to omit and which local best practices to implement globally. At present, there are no difficulties regarding a deviation from the standard, but rather questions about how to further standardize. In this respect, everybody understands the extra effort associated with local options that prevent the overall company from pushing on and making more immediate.

Auditing in terms of process reviews is important when it comes to maintaining the standardized processes. So global process owners and the IT function review processes based on insights gained, for example, from Hilti KPI reporting and SAP system statistics, thus enabling weaknesses to be identified. These process reviews are called "business process approval processes" and help to optimize operations.

Results and Achievements

The GPD project resulted in a transformative change in the way Hilti does business. Even though this was clear to the management team at the very beginning, there were still aspects that remained unforeseen. At the start of the project in particular, the management team did not have full clarity on shared service centers, for example, and these have only been discussed in the last three years. Considering the overall development of the project, the more GPD progressed, the more the entire company became involved.

Globalization of the IT function, common data structures, processes and the IT system is today perceived as a springboard for the entire company undergoing transformation. Global business application landscapes provided opportunities to optimize logistic structures in a multi-national way. Similarly, new ways to organize sales and customer services arose, using opportunities to combine sales organizations into hubs or shared service centers to optimize the sharing of knowledge and execution of marketing and sales activities. Today, integration of the business process organization into the overall line of business is permeating through the entire company.

So the most important benefit of the transformation is having laid a major foundation for the future: the availability of global processes, data structures, and systems, as well as a skilful global IT team that is aware of how to further improve and build on this. Furthermore, reliability in business process execution is another significant achievement at a more detailed level. On this basis, great opportunities can be harvested in the future regarding structural optimization and process services.

Further achievements relate to customer satisfaction. During the project, a manager from Austria came up with the idea of faxing all customer data to the customers themselves, asking them to provide feedback on their data. Many customers very much appreciated this because they realized that Hilti cares about them and Hilti also received feedback from the customers expressing their satisfaction about orders and repairs.

Lessons Learned

At the beginning of GPD, its overall impact was thought to be considerable for the IT organization and beyond, but its actual impact turned out to be even greater than expected. The transformation affected day-to-day work in the markets but also management processes and structural changes, and today, changing a service or allocating it to another country is much easier. Many opportunities that GPD entails were not fully appreciated 10 years ago because, despite their awareness of the impact on business, people were more focused on the IT.

In the GPD project, Hilti did not standardize completely because one of the goals set at the start was to have a smooth implementation. Pushing the implementation of further standards would have meant facing more confrontation and risking people no longer supporting the GPD idea. So Hilti managed to find a balance between full standardization and smooth implementation, and this balance will have to be kept in mind in the future too.

For the overall success of the project, it was very important to get the full support of senior management and other management levels. It is also essential to have a dedicated and capable set of people in the transformation team. And finally, it is necessary to deliver results step by step, continuously implementing the vision of the project.

Since GPD was a major transformational step, many detailed aspects needed to be considered, especially in terms of combining the IT system and business processes. This means it was important to address a number of minor issues in order to achieve the overall vision. It is interesting to learn that small details can fundamentally challenge an initiative like GPD. In 2003, a critical incident occurred as the newly built Data Centre North suffered a power outage. At that time, the GPD rollout was about to start in BeNeLux and had already been completed in Austria. Following the incident, it was unclear whether the entire system needed to be recovered or whether data was corrupt. This could have led to several days of down time, severely ruining the project's credibility in terms of reliable delivery.

Even though such an incident would not mean the end of the project, it can still do considerable harm to its reputation since it was built on trust that needed to be honored, otherwise difficulties were more likely to occur despite the support of senior management. So it is important to have different types of people in the project management team: those who can deliver and fix details and those who give directions and see the bigger picture.

Even though there was substantial communication at the start of the project more tangible training at all levels would have been helpful since a number of people underestimated the impact of the project. GPD required competence at all levels, yet some managers believed GPD was "a back-office type of thing" that would not influence business. In fact, GPD completely changed the way business is carried out in order to be compliant with the GPD foundation.

Having learned from this experience, Hilti organizes peer visits for the current GPD projects. This means that entire management teams visit another market organization that has already implemented GPD and in one week they learn how that market organization is actually conducting business in their environment.

Hilti's transformation can be perceived as a two tier change, with GPD as tier one, laying the foundation for a global Hilti, and tier two building on top of this, including smaller projects such as contact centers. These smaller projects still represent a major transformation for the departments involved because of the way their work and their interaction with customers is changing although the changes are not as fundamental as GPD. Establishing contact centers completely modifies the way specific user groups or job functions work, although it does not involve people in the warehouse, for example. So tier two is between the fundamental change of GPD and an incremental change of continuous improvement.

Key Learnings

- Have a clear vision of the value contribution for business.
- Aim high and be persistent.
- Involve dedicated and capable people in the project team.
- Build a management team with a common language and skill set.
- Gain senior management support.
- Push the project with forward thinking.
- Establish a culture of "the strongest argument wins".
- Communicate in an open and honest way with clear targets.
- Build on a strong corporate culture.
- Strike a balance between a strong vision and smooth implementation.
- Visualize the implementation through a comprehensive roadmap.
- Have a dry run very early on.
- Establish cross-fertilization through peer support.
- Earn credibility by delivering tangible results step by step.

Bibliography

vom Brocke, J. and Sinnl, T. (2010). Applying the BPM-Culture-Model: The Hilti case. ACIS 2010 Proceedings. 21st Australasian Conference on Information Systems, 1–3 Dec 2010, Brisbane, Australia.

vom Brocke, J., Petry, M., Sinnl, T., Kristensen, B. and Sonnenberg, C. (2010). Global processes and data. The culture journey at Hilti corporation. In *Handbook on Business Process Management. Strategic alignment, governance, people and culture*, J. vom Brocke and M. Rosemann (eds), Vol. 2, Berlin: Springer, pp 539–558.

Holler, Stefan (2008). Unternehmensporträt: Hilti-CIO Martin Petry in den CIO-Videonews. CIO, http://www.cio.de/knowledgecenter/erp/856177/.

IT Innovation is a Social Process

A COMMENT ON THE HILTI CASE
BY BEATE BRÜGGEMANN AND RAINER RIEHLE
(INSTITUTE FOR INTERNATIONAL SOCIAL RESEARCH (INFIS))

The Hilti case is an example of a successful innovation that emanates not from IT but primarily from the set objectives and the protagonists who should reach these goals with the help of IT.

In the 1980s and 1990s, Hilti tried to coordinate and standardize the data and process flows in all areas of the company with the help of new IT concepts. It became apparent that the basic issues relating to transformation projects and IT projects are not primarily at a technical and organizational level; IT innovations are social processes with all and for all those involved. Thus, in 2000, a project called "Global Process and Data" (GPD) was launched. The current phase aims to realize and optimize global cooperation and transformation for further market development.

The most important strategy in all three phases has always been to continuously communicate the aim and the vision, so that all people affected or involved understand, follow, and support the transformation process. Consequently, the new IT strategies were discussed not just by the senior management but in all suborganizations. The longer the project continued, the more important the communication about visible success and progress became. Without questioning the vision or the objective, the company focused on cooperation instead of confrontation, on smooth transitions, and on small steps, especially in the business area. (For example, not all data has been fully standardized yet.)

The awareness of and readiness for much-needed change (not primarily for economic reasons) were important factors for the project's success, and the support provided by the senior management for a more decentralized communication structure was of fundamental importance. Especially in the first few years of the project, the GPD team members, who came from different levels of management, met on a weekly basis. These 30–40 people were important communicators and multipliers in their teams, providing real "drive". They devised a common terminology that was comprehensible to everyone, because the process character of this project – beyond the technical innovation – requires a language that integrates, explains, convinces, and above all, embraces. A language that must be appropriate for "new" situations, for a "culture of situational leadership". In other words, the management style must be sensitive and flexible to cater for the employees' responsibilities and abilities. "This simple rule provided very effective support to the leadership in the GPD project." The ongoing exchange of information between the individual subdivisions and the project team, as well as between peers (and not just through the senior management) promotes and intensifies the transformation process. An accompanying evaluation at the various sites allows to identify weaknesses as well as improvement opportunities and to exchange this know-how.

Lessons Learned

In retrospect, the past 10 years have brought about a successful transformation in terms of structure, organization, and habits. This transformation was and still is successful because first and foremost the aims and visions were clearly conveyed, resulting in transformation strategies and operations. It was successful because considerations related primarily not to IT concepts but for the most part to those who were involved. Constant, intensive communication and the exchange of ideas and experiences about progress and setbacks, not only at management levels, enable to strike a balance between smooth transformation, technical standardization, and economic optimization.

As a general rule, transformations, i.e. technical and organizational innovations, are processes that are always associated with more or less pronounced changes to old structures, habitual procedures, and established routines and practices, and they exist at all participant levels. They alter the patterns of day-to-day social relationships and affect the formal and informal hierarchical patterns, roles, responsibilities, and mutual expectations. Thus, established communication relationships, patterns of behavior, and habits are devalued, questioned, and this can be perceived by individuals or groups as a threat and lead to latent or open defensive posturing. This leads to the conclusion, that business innovations and transformations are only successful when change management takes this into consideration in its processes, concepts, and strategies. Thus, a basic condition of successful IT innovations and transformations lies in understanding the implementation as a social process that depends on motivation and interaction, as well as actively integrating all protagonists in the process with largely equal rights. This process requires time, since it must avoid excessive demand. But in the medium term, such a process is more effective and efficient –last but not least also in terms of operating profit.

Slowing Down Speeds Up Growing Success

A COMMENT ON THE HILTI CASE
BY PAUL STRATIL (SAS AUTOMOTIVE SYSTEMS)

Vision is needed to plant the seed and reap the fruit but vision in itself is not enough to get there, the seed needs to be watered and an organizational vision needs to be fostered. Organizational readiness is essential as the soil to nourish and fuel a sustainable transformation over many years.

The Hilti case changed the business of the company in 2008. The idea of "One Hilti" was born by the founder already and was woven into the DNA of the company, but various attempts at creating the "Globally Integrated System" had fallen prey to failure. The implementation of a global IT system was considered the right way of creating a globally integrated corporation, not taking into account that the business owners had to become actors in this transformation process rather than being just the audience while IT accomplished some "back office type of a thing".

Success came when the approach to implementing "One Hilti" was changed in 2000 by the CEO and focus was put on the business processes becoming truly global, with global process owners in charge and with overall targets on productivity, customer satisfaction and operational excellence. This acted as the catalyst, which together with the commitment from the board were the starting point of this transformation.

All 20,000 employees expected changes yet nobody could imagine the many tangible benefits later achieved. Everybody who participated in the project was proud of being part of the team and of the results implemented on SAP ERP and on SAP's mobile solutions. Each process owner taking ownership of the changes was another key success factor as was the fact that the results could be measured: shared and consistent knowledge base, increased performance, ability to relocate business easily from country to country and structural optimization.

Going for the cooperative rather than a confrontational model eased the way to convince even reluctant process owners of the benefits of process standardization and harmonization, finally getting their buy-in. "Standardization to the max" was not imposed on anybody. Hilti as an organization agreed on a set of rules about how to do the job rather than what the final outcome would be in detail.

It was the "Swiss way" of taking firm decisions by voting for the best idea and refusing a different, more aggressive approach.

Generally, this approach might not be right if a company is stuck in stormy waters, when quick and tough decisions are necessary. But with the secure financial situation of Hilti, it created trust and confidence to accept changes. Taking into account how this company struggled to set up its transformation initiative, how long it took, with several unrewarding attempts, and how they finally succeeded, this case provides real insights in understanding why some transformations succeed and others do not.

The CEO of Hilti set global measurable business goals which could no longer be achieved with the traditional way of doing business. Thus he challenged the entire organization to get going in a pre-defined direction. The expectation of such an initiative is to grow business, increase profitability and to achieve additional benefits such as business flexibility, agility, stable business processes, robust IT infrastructure. In the case of Hilti these expectations were exceeded.

Such an approach proves very successful to get a company prepared for the future while it is doing well, instead of being in a reactive mode during an adverse economic situation, under cost and time pressures. Hilti did not change course despite economic challenges and despite some technical problems during the set up phase of the solution.

Another intelligent move was the way the transformation was managed in order to achieve consistent and sustainable changes. It might have been due to the Swiss mentality to care for democratic decisions in the team, for open communication and peer to peer learning among all participants to promote the re-use of solutions across business units and plants. At the first glance this seems to reduce the speed and efficiency of a project implementation, but in fact it established a stable foundation to execute decisions across the entire corporation in high quality and with the desired precision expected.

The GPD core team formed the operational headquarters to prepare project decisions and to set the speed and direction. They developed a phased approach considering organizational and technical complexity, skills available and resources as well as the risks and benefits of each step of the project. This paid off as the team was always one step ahead and driving the discussion.

They could demonstrate good project results which increased the trust in their work and acceptance across the various business units.

Hilti did not do everything right from the very beginning. Nevertheless the company was able to keep the vision on the horizon and implement a straightforward strategy of moving towards it. The management of Hilti set the framework for a successful change, but it were the individual team members who accepted the change and lived by it. Last but not least, it was a skilled project team which managed the transformation in a focused and professional way, with empathy and respect for their colleagues as well as awareness of the organizational needs of the global corporation.

From that perspective Hilti did many things right and was rewarded by increased economic success as well as a strengthened company culture with everybody taking pride in it. Many of these learnings can be used by other companies to accomplish successful transformations.

17

Enterprise Architecture and Transformation: The Differences and the Synergy Potential of Enterprise Architecture and Business Transformation Management

*Robert Winter (University of St. Gallen),
Simon Townson (SAP), Axel Uhl (SAP), Nils Labusch
(University of St. Gallen), Joerg Noack (SAP)*

Have you ever wondered about the relationship between Enterprise Architecture Management (EAM) and Business Transformation Management (BTM)? Both are management methods with many commonalities, but also with important differences. This article aims at providing insights about the relationship of EAM and BTM, as well as their respective methods.

Abstract

Due to their holistic approach and some common terminology, Enterprise Architecture Management (EAM) and Business Transformation Management (BTM) are two disciplines that need to be investigated in order to better understand their synergies, and to understand where each is best applied. This article aims at clarifying the relationship of EAM and BTM, as well as their respective methods. The article is based not only on the authors' discussion of the "Enterprise Architecture and Business Transformation" question, but on ten interviews with experts from science, consulting and industry practice, and on feedback provided by a sounding board of several SAP experts and managers. It was discussed with the experts who key users and stakeholders are, which problems need to be addressed, which goals are pursued, and the benefits and value added. The authors further investigated capabilities and competencies needed and how EAM and BTM are evolving.

*****

When discussing the subject with practitioners, consultants and academics, we noticed that confusion existed about what the differences and similarities of Enterprise Architecture Management (as a well-established discipline) and Business Transformation Management (as a rather new topic in research and practice) really are. We conducted ten interviews with experts from science, consulting and industry practice in order to base the article on a solid foundation. We discussed the results within the group of authors and integrated further feedback provided by a notable board of several SAP experts and managers.

Since the understanding of Business Transformation Management (BTM) as much as Enterprise Architecture Management (EAM) differs in several available methods or frameworks, we needed to assume a certain mainstream definition for both (see Table 17.1). The key questions we will discuss in this article are: What are the actual differences, and is there any synergy potential? Thus, we will look at who the key stakeholders are, discuss problems that are addressed as much as goals that are pursued. We will further investigate the benefits and value that is added, capabilities and competencies which are needed and how EAM and BTM are evolving.

Who are the Stakeholders?

With regard to the stakeholders of EAM and BTM, one of our interviewees stated: "Enterprise Architecture Management is applied when there is a lack of satisfaction with IT, when the CEO is telling the CIO that he is not happy, and when the CIO's job is at stake; whereas BTM is applied when the CEO needs to react to external markets, change the operating model, and save the business as the CEO's job is at stake."

Table 17.1   Definition of Enterprise Architecture and Business Transformation (Management)

Enterprise Architecture (EA)	Business Transformation (BT)
EA models the fundamental (i.e. no details) structure of an organization concerning: • the business (strategy & organization) • information systems (IS) • information technology (IT). In addition to modeling the components and dependencies of that structure, EA also deals with guidelines and principles that govern the structure's design process and evolution.	A BT is a fundamental change of the way a company operates, be it e.g. by moving into a new market or by overhauling its internal processes. This fundamental change aims to meet long-term objectives. BT affects many functional areas of a company, including organization, human resources, IT or financials. BT is closely related to a company's strategy, its value, and its risks. In order to be effective, BT needs to align changes in people, processes, and technology.
Enterprise Architecture Management (EAM) EAM provides support for decisions regarding the design and further development of EA and involves a wide set of stakeholders in business and IT. Examples of EAM goals are: enhancing the transparency, consistency, simplification, flexibility, or agility of the organization. In many practice settings, EAM is designated "EA governance". In addition to offering decision support, EAM always needs to have a holistic perspective, i.e. it not only covers the entire business-to-IT relation, but also spans a complete business unit, company or corporation. This positioning distinguishes EA from functional architecture management disciplines (IT architecture, business architecture) as well as partial architectures (project view, department view).	**Business Transformation Management (BTM)** BTM encompasses the planning, implementation, and control of BT as well as the support for decisions related to the design and development of business transformations. BTM involves a wide set of stakeholders in business and IT. Examples of BTM goals are: strategy change (e.g. re-focus, diversification), technology-driven innovation, increased agility, or cultural change (e.g. customer orientation). BTM should always follow a holistic and interdisciplinary perspective, i.e. not only focus on financials or IT, but also consider skills, strategy, value, risk, or project management. BTM is applied to large transformation projects or transformation programs that usually affect significant parts of a company.
One of the well-known EA frameworks is "The Open Group Architecture Framework" (TOGAF) (The Open Group 2011). Further summarized reading about EAM is also available in Aier et al. (2009).	Theoretical foundation for business transformations is available in e.g. Rouse (2005). An example for a BTM framework is BTM^2 (Uhl and Gollenia, eds., 2012).

Although Enterprise Architecture (EA) includes many business aspects, its key stakeholders are always somehow involved in IT – be it directly (supply side) or indirectly (demand side). Thus, the people who benefit most from EA are typically the CIO and the CIO's subordinate level. In comparison to BTM, EA is a more technical, engineered approach. Further stakeholders from the demand side of IT are enterprise and solution architects, portfolio managers, service managers, line or business heads. In contrast, the typical key Business Transformation (BT) stakeholders are board members, the C-level management, business unit managers, program and project managers, including many of the EA stakeholders. In other words, BTM focuses on the business side, with rather limited consideration of IT issues.Although stakeholder management is a formal part of EA frameworks such as TOGAF (The Open Group Architecture Framework; cf. The Open Group 2011), the stakeholders are often not involved directly in EAM, but instead collaborate with enterprise architects to define and review the main enterprise components and roadmap. In contrast, in BTM it is essential that stakeholders are involved on all hierarchical levels as part of the transformation. As a consequence, active stakeholder management is a fundamental pillar of the Meta Management layer of BTM (Stiles and Uhl 2012).

Which Problems are Addressed?

EAM addresses huge and small changes – whether in business processes, IT systems, or data. Despite ongoing efforts to further develop its business focus, the main value proposition of EAM is to better align IT solutions with business needs. As a consequence, EAM would not be used to assess how much transformation an organization needs due to external market changes, or whether political powers in an organization support or inhibit a certain transformation, just to name two examples.

In contrast, BTM is intended to support the business in defining and implementing significant business transformation. Thus, BTM would not be used to manage small, incremental changes. Furthermore, BTM is based on the business strategy and might challenge it, while EAM rather tends to adopt the strategy without being in the position to change it.

Another differentiator is the focal object of interest: While EAM's primary objects are states – more precisely "to-be" and "as-is" states – also plans and roadmaps are developed and maintained.

On the other side, BTM's primary objects are improvement and innovation processes, while the implied (input and output) states are objects of secondary interest.

This contrast between an often incremental and "state-focused" view versus a mostly fundamental "transition-focused" perspective explains differences, but also reveals potential synergies between EAM and BTM:

First, EAM might create important inputs for BTM, in particular in the context of complex, enterprise wide transformation programs. Examples typically found in organizations are:

- EAM deals with key technology risks at an enterprise level and provides the associated insights to the Strategy Management process in BTM.
- EAM deals with existing pain points, solution gaps as well as enablers; these are key inputs to the Value management process in BTM.
- EAM also deals with high level solution architecture, gap analysis, and IT roadmaps; these are key inputs to the IT Transformation process in BTM.

Second, BTM results might create important inputs for EAM, in particular for understanding business needs and for decomposing fundamental changes into incremental changes. Typical examples are:

- Previous unsuccessful or failed transformation initiatives provide strong guidance to future roadmap decisions.
- BTM (Process and Organization Change Management) provides key inputs to the "to-be" state of business, application and technology architecture phases in EAM to ensure that lessons from the past are taken into consideration.
- BTM (Strategy Management) provides key input to the "to-be" Business Model used in the development of "to-be" states in EAM.

Figure 17.1 shows that both EAM and BTM consist of a permanent process part (dark long arrows) and of temporary activities which they provide within single transformation programs or incremental changes (bright small arrows). For EAM, the permanent process is of larger importance because it includes the maintenance of "as-is" and "to-be" EA models and principles as the main focus of enterprise architects. For BTM, the permanent task is the maintenance of sustainable transformation capabilities, which is regarded to be more lightweight, while the dominant part is the support of actual transformation programs and projects.

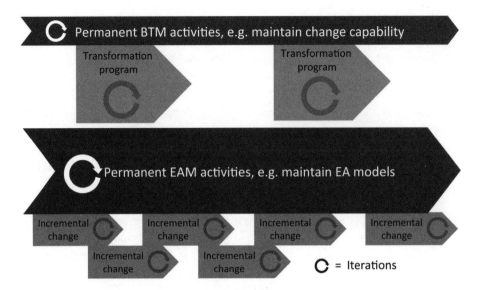

Figure 17.1   Major Processes and Iterations

But even with the best plans, in reality it is impossible to get everything right from the beginning and in one go. Experience shows that both methods ought to be applied by means of fulfilling small packages and following iterative cycles (illustrated by the round arrows in Figure 17.1). More precisely, there are three major reasons for these iterations:

1.   Stakeholders might lose focus or might be hard to convince that the far-away transformation success will be achieved. Showing early benefits from fulfilling small packages and the first iterations helps to convince and motivate the stakeholders and to keep the transformation running.
2.   Since many changes happen simultaneously, long-range planning needs to be flexible in order to adapt to a changing context like new legislation or customer demands.
3.   Occurring problems during the implementation of the transformation can be handled at short notice and the solutions can be used as input for the following iterations, improving organizational learning.

From the comparison of focus areas, problems, and processes we move on to examining the goals of EAM and BTM.

What Goals are Pursued?

EAM helps IT management to better understand the business in order to create better alignment and to build suitable IT solutions, avoiding overlap or duplication.

To illustrate, one of our interviewees provided the following metaphor to explain EAM's purpose and goal: "EAM is about the team lineup and the associated tactics that a football trainer instructs his team with in the locker room before the match starts, i.e. the master plan. In other words, EAM provides the necessary, specific information that belongs to that match. For example: 'We need to attack deep down the left, and the objective is to score two goals before half time'."

In contrast to EAM, BTM helps business management to better plan and implement business change in terms of acceptance, alignment, and sustainability. As a consequence, it targets at developing capabilities that keep the company flexible and agile as a social system. In terms of the football match metaphor: "BTM is about making sure the football team is able to adapt and change the tactics during the game if necessary. For example, when the rival team plays in a different way from what the trainer had expected and the team needs to react in the heat of battle, or when certain players in your own team are not performing."

Figure 17.2 shows how the two disciplines inter-relate. It is common for EAM to define an enterprise roadmap, i.e. known transformation programs, planned projects, known capability gaps, and how they change the business-application-technology landscape. In contrast, BTM will focus on how the organization can best be transformed. Thus, BTM helps organizations to achieve the best possible Return on Investment (ROI) in the "to-be" state by focusing on how the transformation program is implemented in practice; primarily taking into account the business stakeholders, organizational readiness, and openness for change. Different possible routes towards the same "end state" are then evaluated and the best way forward followed.

What are Benefits and Value Added?

Due to its more incremental nature, the added value of EAM activities can be precisely defined in dimensions like speed or quality and measured by KPIs

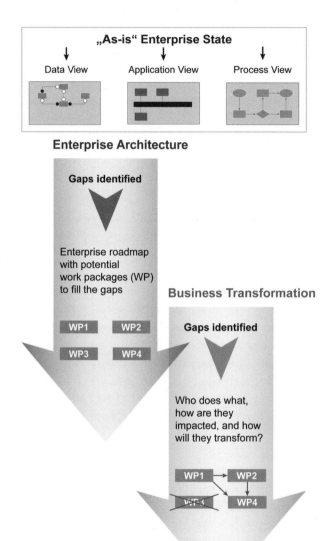

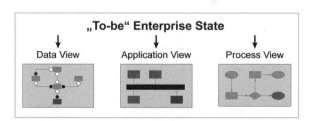

Figure 17.2   Enterprise Architecture Roadmap States versus
Transformation Projects

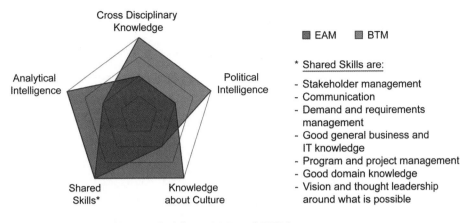

Figure 17.3   Skills Needed for EAM and BTM

like created synergies, reduced redundancies, better alignment, or increased transparency in the organization. Value is created "bottom-up" and focused on business efficiency (doing things right). Efficiency matrices or special balanced scorecards can be used to measure the benefits. Even if monetary measuring and business case definition for EAM is difficult, tangible measures for EA exist, e.g. increased project success, reduced number of applications and interfaces, as well as a reduced diversity and complexity of the information systems landscape (Townson 2008).

In contrast, added value of BTM is created "top-down", long-term, and is focused on business effectiveness (doing the right things). Value is created by successfully achieving a fundamental change and by then operating in this new way. As a consequence, transformation seems to be easier to measure by aggregate quantitative measures (economic value added, ROI, market capitalization). Further examples could be faster hiring cycles or shorter process change cycles. Since changes are fundamental, effects and measures cannot be matched with single projects easily.

Nevertheless, both concepts are dependent on projects that deliver the actual benefits. The reason for this is that benefits are always achieved within operative projects and not on the strategic level.

What Capabilities and Competencies are Needed?

There is a huge overlap in terms of skills required for both BTM and EAM. Yet, there are differences regarding which ones need to be prioritized.

In communication, many enterprise architects use a language that is close to that used by IT experts. BT experts, whilst, use business language in order to explain their concerns.

On top of a solid basis of IT and analytical skills as well as cross-departmental knowledge, enterprise architects need strong social skills in order to undertake their holistic analysis, offer transformation support, and fulfill their communication role. Political and emotional intelligence help to excel when architects reach the most senior levels.

For BT experts, IT know-how, analytical skills, and knowledge of various domains are less essential. What counts is a solid basis of "soft" know-how about leadership and culture, competencies like strategic thinking, as well as emotional and political intelligence. IT knowledge and analytical skills are a beneficial additional qualification for senior levels. Figure 17.3 compares the skill profiles needed in EAM and BTM.

How are EAM and BTM Evolving?

Due to its character as a holistic support for business transformation, BTM needs to deal with a large set of disciplines (for example, value management, process management, project management). As a consequence, BTM operates at a high aggregation level – because otherwise the diversity of the subject-matter could not be handled effectively anymore.

In contrast, EAM covers all business aspects that are important to understand in order to provide appropriate IT support. All non-IT related business matters as well as most non-tangible aspects of an organization do not necessarily need to be covered. Due to the fact that EAM is "narrower" in this regard, all aspects can be addressed on a more detailed level. However, when examining the topics presented at recent EAM Conferences (e.g. Aier et al. 2011), in Research Agendas, and in EAM Communities, one discovers that the scope of EAM may broaden towards the coverage of more business-related aspects (value management, business process management) while remaining restricted to rather stable aspects (e.g. stakeholder management).

A detailed task list (or step-by-step method) is usually only helpful in a stable environment (thus one that is not undergoing a fundamental change). This is possible with EAM, as the approaches are well understood and defined by using common meta-models and processes such as modeling and gap analysis. Thus, EAM frameworks like TOGAF provide well-specified extensions that can be added or removed as needed.

However, during a business transformation such a stable environment is usually not a given – this is already implied by the definition of transformation as fundamental change. Since every transformation is different, e.g. in terms of industry, project portfolio, or people involved, a lot depends on the interests of stakeholders – there are not necessarily suitable best practices for BTM available. A framework is therefore better suited for BTM as it gives enough flexibility for adaption and still provides sufficient consistency and guidance.

Several discussions occurred in our interviews about the future development of BTM as such, and especially of BTM^2 as an example for a concrete framework (Uhl and Gollenia, eds., 2012). Some experts in the interviews and professionals who are working with it on a day-to-day basis raise the question whether it should be expanded in order to incorporate detailed techniques from the covered disciplines (e.g. business process management, value management). Based on the statements of our interviewees, we however believe that BTM^2 is intended to be an umbrella framework that amalgamates existing methods which all focus on a specific sub-aspect of business transformation – and not a "mega methodology" that is bound to fail when trying to be broad and deep at the same time. Therefore, we understand BTM^2 as a framework rather than a method.

Conclusion

As mentioned above, there are some opinions present which propose to combine EAM with BTM characteristics. Why is that the case?

EAM and BTM have much in common. Enterprise Architects and BT experts share many important skills, deal with many similar matters, use many comparable techniques and tools, have some common stakeholders, are both concerned with transformation, and are both involved in change projects.

Both approaches need continuous investment – for EAM the continuous effort of maintaining the architecture landscape is comparably high, for BTM the investments in the single transformation programs are necessary. Current developments in EAM (e.g. positioning it as a more business-oriented approach and focusing less on the IT side) might reinforce their commonalities.

While the goals, outputs, organization, processes, tools, and management of both approaches might be somewhat different, interfaces and shared activities need to be created and preserved. As a consequence, this article should not be misunderstood as an attempt to position two approaches against each other that instead should work hand-in-hand. While the transparency and analyses created by EAM are an invaluable input for BTM, and the "to-be" designs and change project roadmaps of EAM need to be seen as an integrated implementation component of BT, BTM outputs constitute the most important inputs for EAM.

Due to the illustrated differences in stakeholders, goals, value creation logic, control, width, depth, mandatory skills, and organization, EAM and BTM should be regarded as different management approaches. That would help to foster a clear further development and focus of both approaches: Be it the support of business and IT alignment in case of EAM, or the focused support of transformations in the case of BTM. Being able to successfully handle both, EAM and BTM, from our point of view is the key to long-term success of a company.

Key Learnings

- EAM and BTM should be regarded as different management approaches, and should not be merged into one approach.
- Being able to successfully handle both EAM and BTM is the key to long-term success.
- The skills that are needed for EAM and BTM are very similar, but their prioritization is different.
- Both approaches differ in their primary focal objects. EAM's primary objects are "to-be" and "as-is" states. While the "state" views dominate, also plans and roadmaps are developed and maintained. BTM's primary objects are improvement and innovation processes of business transformation.

- The "to-be" designs and change project roadmaps of EAM need to be seen as an integrated implementation component of business transformation, and the transparency and analyses created by EAM are an invaluable input for BTM. BTM outputs constitute important inputs for EAM.

Bibliography

Aier, S., Gleichauf, B., Winter, R. (2011). *Understanding Enterprise Architecture Management Design – An Empirical Analysis*. In: Bernstein, A., Schwabe, G. (eds.). The 10th International Conference on Wirtschaftsinformatik WI 2011, 16.02.2011. Zurich. 645–654.

Aier, S., Kurpjuweit, S., Saat, J., Winter, R. (2009). Business Engineering Navigator – A "Business to IT" Approach to Enterprise Architecture Management. In: Bernard, S., Doucet, G., Gøtze, J., Saha, P. (eds.). *Coherency Management – Architecting the Enterprise for Alignment, Agility, and Assurance*. Bloomington: Author House.

Rouse, W.B. (2005). A Theory of Enterprise Transformation. *Systems Engineering*, 8, 279–295.

Stiles, P., Uhl, A. (2012). Meta Management: Connecting the Parts of Business Transformation. *360° – the Business Transformation Journal*, issue no. 3, February 2012, 24–29.

The Open Group (2011). The Open Group Architecture Framework (TOGAF) Version 9.1, The Open Group.

Townson, S. (2008). *Why does Enterprise Architecture Matter?* San Francisco, The Open Group.

Uhl, A., Gollenia, L.A. (eds.) (2012). *A Handbook of Business Transformation Management Methodology*. Farnham, UK: Gower Publishing.

18

BTM² and ASAP:
SAP's Perfect Match

*Axel Uhl (SAP), Jan Musil (SAP), Tammy Johnson
(SAP), Lisa Kouch (SAP)*

**The Business Transformation Management Methodology and the ASAP
Methodology for Implementation are two prominent methodologies
introduced by SAP AG in order to react to ever changing environments.
However, the scope of application is different for both cases. In fact, there
exists a huge synergy potential between both methodologies, which are
discussed in this article.**

Transformation is a common challenge and procedure for most, if not all,
organizations. On the one hand, external changes such as sustainability,
technological innovations, globalization, economic conditions, and the changing
nature of the workforce have a profound impact on the way organizations
execute business. On the other hand, internal changes such as product
innovation, restructuring, and new business model adoption, also potentially
result in large-scale transformation and consequently in a disruption in the
workplace. Organizations require an excellent transformation process in order
to sustain competitive advantages (Uhl 2012).

In business transformation, both Business Transformation Management
Methodology (BTM²) as well as ASAP Methodology for Implementation (referred
to as "ASAP") describe methodologies to realize and implement changes in
the business environment. Some may wonder: "Are both methodologies
interchangeable? If not, what are the key differences and synergies between
them?" This article answers this question and provides insights into the

relationship of BTM^2 and ASAP by analyzing them from different perspectives and finally illustrating recommendations in four use cases.

The key objective of BTM^2 is to support the management of large scale transformation initiatives, like e.g. business model changes, post-merger integration, shared service center implementations, and large ERP implementations. This means that IT can, but does not necessarily need to play an important role when using BTM^2. In a nutshell, BTM^2 helps to manage the transformation – the path how to get from A to B.

In contrast, the key objective of ASAP is to better implement IT solutions such as ERP systems. Therefore, IT always plays an important role when using ASAP.

Clearly said, BTM^2 and ASAP are two methodologies that provide a perfect match to each other and at the same time benefit from significant synergies in the context of IT implementation programs. In the process of transformation, BTM^2 focuses on the strategic to tactical levels, whereas ASAP concentrates on tactical to operational levels. The appropriate methodology to choose depends on the complexity, scale, and implications of the change.

An Overview of BTM^2 and ASAP

Successful projects – be they in large, medium or small scale – depend on well-defined, proven, and adaptable methodologies. Both BTM^2 and ASAP were developed based on thousands of executed transformation programs.

BTM^2 provides a holistic and integrative view on the organization and the complexity of its ecosystem. The framework manages extensive and complex changes on which an organization's future success strongly depends. The framework is based on a meta management discipline focusing on rather soft cultural factors like values and behaviors, leadership, conflict resolution, and meta-communication, as well as on established management disciplines, including strategy management, value management, process management, risk management, IT transformation, competence and training management, and program management (see Figure 18.1). Each individual discipline is well developed, with a large body of knowledge, and targets a specific group of professional people. Although, of course, each group is very valuable for the organization, there is still a strong tendency for separation and a lack of integration between different

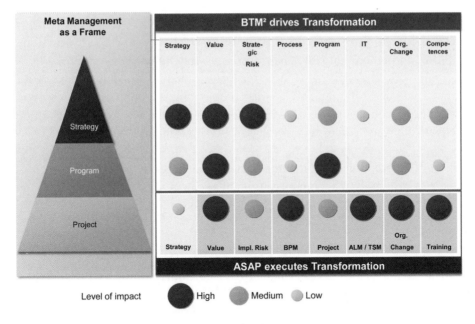

Figure 18.1   Focus Areas of BTM² and ASAP

departments. Therefore BTM² provides powerful coordination mechanisms to coordinate and align between those different management disciplines (Uhl 2012).

BTM² delivers sufficient consistency and guidance and ensures that the business understands the transformation need and its impacts. At the same time, BTM² is flexible enough to be adopted by all kinds of transformation projects, which are by nature extremely diverse, e.g. in terms of industry, project portfolio, or people involved.

The ASAP Methodology is SAP's prescriptive methodology for implementing and upgrading SAP software. It leverages the insights that SAP and its partners have gained through years of hands-on experience with projects in many different customer environments and industries. ASAP provides accelerators, tools, and best practices from thousands of successful implementations. Its prescriptive approach helps reduce project time, cost, and risk. The latest release of ASAP methodology (version 8) extends the solid foundation of ASAP – built around Business Process Management, Project Management, Organizational Change Management, Technical Solution Management, and Application Lifecycle Management – with prescriptive guidance and strong governance to ensure project success.

The ASAP methodology is structured into six phases that support clients throughout the life cycle of a SAP solution – when you plan it, when you build it, and when you run it in your day-to-day operations. ASAP provides a framework for aligning IT and business strategies, quickly getting your software up and running, and keeping it operating smoothly at peak levels. In addition, it includes process checks to ensure that the implemented solution delivers the value you expect from your SAP investment.

Both methodologies include several management disciplines, like business process management, value management, or organizational change management (see the columns in Figure 18.1). The difference between BTM^2 and ASAP is the level of detail.

BTM^2 focuses on the strategy and program level, where the coordination of transformation activities plays a key role. One aim is to leverage the synergies of the different stakeholder interests. Furthermore, BTM^2 reveals the possible value and the corresponding risks from an enterprise-wide perspective.

The business transformation activities are then broken down into several smaller projects, some of which are executed using ASAP. Typically, these projects are characterized by limited complexity, dependencies, and stakeholder groups and have well-defined individual project goals. On this level a pressure to deliver exists.

Again, each project has to be planned considering different viewpoints, and only the combination from all relevant disciplines can lead to success.

In summary, ASAP ensures that each individual project is a success, whereas BTM^2 ensures that the coordination and interplay of the individual projects and the overall transformation are a success.

From Strategy to Execution

The ability to manage business transformation is crucial for companies to stay competitive. One success factor is to adapt quickly to an ever changing environment. Major changes, such as technology shifts, changes in customer behavior, competitive moves, and mergers and acquisitions, might have an impact, either negative or positive, on the ability of a company to achieve its strategic objective. A major transformation might be required in order to align the strategic vision and keep the organization profitable.

In this context, BTM² intends to support the business in defining and implementing a significant business transformation. It focuses on fundamental business changes which have a strong impact on the organization's strategic focus. BTM²'s primary object is "doing the right things" and it focuses on the organization's capabilities to ensure the best execution and situational adoption of this plan (e.g. in terms of Return on Investment). The framework describes all relevant aspects which need to be considered along the transformation process. It helps to coordinate and align all efforts necessary to reach the final transformation target and specifies the direction, roles, and responsibilities of all key stakeholders involved in the transformation process. The actual execution of the transformation process is then moved into the project and service delivery framework ASAP (see Figure 18.2).

ASAP focuses on the more tactical changes and provides clear guidance, time frames, and deliverables for IT projects. It supports traditional as well as agile projects and provides a framework for the design of industrialized services. ASAP is concerned with "doing things right" and specifies a detailed process in order to reach certain project goals. Typical scenarios where ASAP is applied are when pure data migration or technical upgrades need to be managed, i.e. where no business change is involved. It is also applied to manage small, incremental change even if the business side is affected.

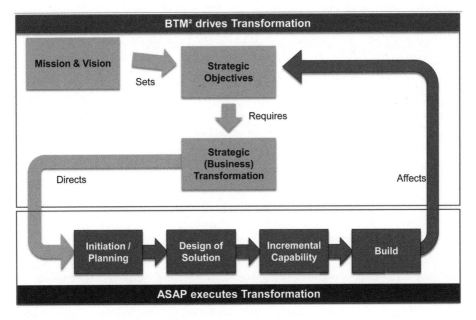

Figure 18.2   From Strategy to Execution

To summarize, BTM^2 considers the strategic and tactical perspective of a transformation and describes the necessary steps and paths to take. ASAP complements these activities on the tactical level and drives them to execution.

BTM^2 will only be used where the transformation is large, ASAP can also be used in projects without large organizational changes.

Major Stakeholders

Considering the characteristics of the two frameworks, we can differentiate between various stakeholder groups. As we highlighted in the previous section, BTM^2 focuses on the strategic and tactical level and supports the business in defining and implementing significant business changes. Therefore, in BTM^2 it is essential to involve stakeholders on all hierarchical levels as part of the transformation. As a consequence, active stakeholder management is a fundamental pillar of the meta management layer of BTM^2 (Stiles and Uhl 2012). Typical key stakeholders in BTM^2 are board members, C-level management including the CIO, business unit managers, program and project managers, and transformation managers, as well as the entire middle management. Other, more IT-related stakeholders are involved as well, but the key part is to observe the business strategy and introduce possible changes.

Since ASAP is a more technical and engineered approach, its key stakeholders are usually somehow involved in IT. The typical stakeholder groups are CIOs and CIO subordinate levels, as well as enterprise and solution architects, project stakeholders, IT consultants, service managers, and SAP key users.

In a nutshell, BTM^2 is applied when the enterprise needs to react to external markets, change the operating model, and make important business changes. ASAP is applied in order to introduce or enhance IT-related concepts.

Skills and Competences

As BTM^2 and ASAP complement each other, the skills required for the individual methodologies are of different nature. BTM^2 experts are more generalists than specialists and need strong cross-departmental thinking. Therefore, they require a solid basis of "soft-skills" on leadership and culture, and competencies like strategic thinking, as well as emotional and political intelligence. Analytical skills and in-depth domain knowledge are less essential.

In contrary, ASAP experts are more specialized in certain domains and topics. Besides strong analytical skills and excellent social skills for holistic analysis, they also offer transformation support and fulfill a communication role. In addition, cross-departmental knowledge is also important, yet ASAP experts use a language that is closer to the one used by IT experts. BTM² experts instead speak a business language in order to explain their concerns.

In the following sections, we will introduce four use cases to illustrate the different business scenarios and scopes where either BTM², ASAP, or both are applied. In each use case, we will first describe the situation of the organization and its objectives, before giving reasons for the choice of a method and summarizing the associated outcome.

1. TECHNICAL UPGRADE OF AN SAP HCM SCENARIO

Imagine an organization running SAP for their entire process landscape including its human resource processes. After a certain period, the technology vendor SAP releases a new version of the SAP Human Capital Management (HCM) scenario, which contains some major technical upgrades, like changes in the data handling and data constraints, modifications in the graphical user interface, und updates to external interfaces. In general, this scenario has no significant influence on the way the business is operated today.

Changes which have no significant influence on the business operation are implemented using ASAP (see Figure 18.3). The methodology provides clear and practical guidelines for the implementation. As the project does not influence the overall business strategy, BTM² would not be the appropriate methodology in this case.

The result of the project is an updated version of the existing IT system.

Figure 18.3   ASAP Phases

2. GLOBAL PROCESS STANDARDIZATION

An organization is running SAP in all locations in Germany. Outside of Germany, they have other IT systems and processes in place. In order to stay competitive and to ensure a consistent IT landscape, the organization wants to align the core business processes and avoid regional differences as much as possible. Part of this initiative is standardizing the HCM scenario and the corresponding business processes across all countries.

This transformation scenario has a significant impact on the way the business operates, therefore BTM^2 is the appropriate methodology to support it (see Figure 18.4). The change has major influence on several different management functions, and several BTM^2 disciplines need to be taken into consideration. For example, the change requires a strategic alignment of all countries and does not only focus on changing IT systems. Coordination and communication with all stakeholder groups are key to success. Usually, standardizing such processes also involves big changes in responsibilities and in the organizational structure. One possible achievement during such a long term project might be the introduction of a completely new IT strategy.

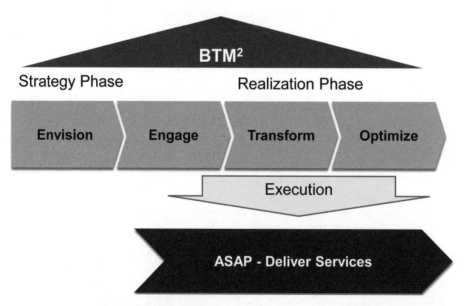

Figure 18.4   Top-down Approach

BTM² provides the relevant methodology to make complex changes a success and to make sure all relevant aspects are considered right from the beginning. After an extensive planning phase and a redefinition of the strategy, ASAP is applied to implement the required changes on the project level.

The long-term results of this scenario are a coherent process landscape, a smoother execution, an alignment of the required IT systems and standardized training efforts. The overall benefit is cost savings.

3. PROCESS STANDARDIZATION USING SAP RAPID DEPLOYMENT SOLUTIONS

The third use case is a slight variation of the second use case and explains how transformation projects can be executed in an agile environment. Again, we assume that an organization is running SAP in all locations in Germany, and outside other IT systems and processes are in place. The transformation requires a strategic alignment of all locations and does not only focus on changing IT systems. One part of this initiative is to standardize the HCM scenario and the corresponding business processes across all countries.

As highlighted in the previous scenario, since the business is driving the change, BTM² is used to realize the transformation. However, on the tactical level the transformation is executed using SAP's Rapid Deployment Solutions (RDS) methodology, which is based on ASAP. An RDS can be generically referred to as a "packaged solution" with a clearly delineated scope, quick to implement and offered at a fixed price. It includes a comprehensive and integrated offering that addresses specific business challenges, enabling companies to go live with new software to address these challenges (Winter 2011). One advantage of RDS is that it enables implementing smaller packages which clearly target specific business scenarios. The implementation is done in an agile manner, and the overall transformation is achieved in smaller iterative projects (see Figure 18.5). After each iteration, the overall system is in a stable mode and can be run productively. This allows continuous improvement of the environment to reach the final transformation goal.

The final goals again are achieving a coherent process landscape and shorter execution life-cycle. However, this scenario frequently involves smaller sub-goals. For example, processes can be aligned step by step, and each iteration improves the solution.

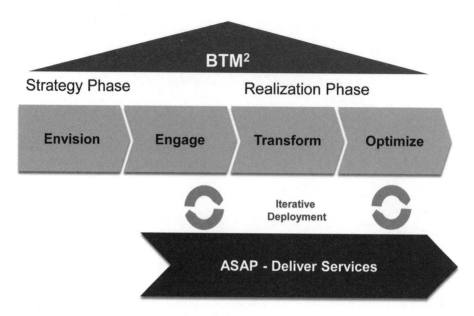

Figure 18.5   Top-down Agile Approach

4. SMALL CHANGE RESULTING IN A STRATEGIC TRANSFORMATION

An organization running SAP plans to implement a new feature of the SAP Sales and Distribution scenario. As explained in the first use case, such feature updates usually have no major influence on the overall business.

Such transformation projects are a tactical issue and typically executed using the ASAP methodology (see Figure 18.6). During the implementation of the project, the organization is consulted about the new possibilities offered by the feature set, including a new e-commerce sales channel. The organization feels that there is benefit potential in selling its services and products via internet. The decision of adding an e-commerce channel changes the original business strategy, influencing different management functions as well. In addition, new roles and responsibilities need to be defined to make this sales channel a success.

With this development, the scenario becomes more strategy-oriented and the transformation is growing in complexity. Consequently, the initially rather tactical project is shifted into a major transformation effort, which needs to carefully consider all facets of business transformation. In order to support the new transformation target, BTM² is used to facilitate the entire process and to coordinate between the different disciplines and stakeholders. Eventually, the

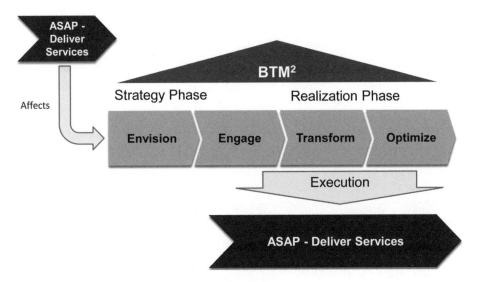

Figure 18.6   From Bottom-up to Top-down

strategic change also leads to a number of tactical changes. On this level, ASAP is utilized again in order to execute the individual projects.

The original goal of making a technical upgrade turned into a major shift in the strategic positioning of the sales efforts. At the end of the transformation project, the organization has a new e-commerce sales channel in place and a new set of roles and responsibilities installed. Overall, the company could increase their total sales thanks to this strategic change.

Conclusion

In this article, we highlighted the interaction of the two methodologies BTM² and ASAP. Both methodologies, individually used, provide great instruments to plan, realize, and implement changes in a business environment. Yet, together they benefit from synergies and create a huge value addition.

As learned from the use cases, on the one hand BTM² is a methodology that focuses on the strategic level. It concentrates on "doing the right things" and considers all relevant activities necessary to make a business transformation successful. On the other hand, ASAP is a methodology to execute the actual changes. It focuses on "doing things right". The appropriate methodology to choose depends on the complexity, scale, and implications of the change project.

Key Learnings

- BTM^2 is used primarily by business functions, and ASAP is used primarily by IT functions.
- BTM^2 focuses on the strategic level, whereas ASAP concentrates on the operational level. BTM^2 concentrates on "doing the right things" and ASAP focuses on "doing things right".
- BTM^2 describes the necessary steps and paths to take. ASAP complements these activities on the tactical level and drives them to execution.
- The appropriate methodology to choose depends on the complexity, scale and implications of the business transformation.

Bibliography

Stiles, P., Uhl, A. (2012). Meta Management: Connecting the Parts of Business Transformation. *360° – The Business Transformation Journal*, issue no. 3, February 2012, 24–29.

Uhl, A. (2012). "Introduction". In: Uhl, A., Gollenia, L.A. (eds.). *A Handbook of Business Transformation Management Methodology*. Farnham, UK: Gower Publishing, 1–12.

Winter, J. (2011). "SAP Rapid Deployment Solutions – The Basics", SAP Services Blog, 3 October 2011. Available from: http://blogs.sap.com/services/2011/10/03/sap-rapid-deployment-solutions-%E2%80%93-the-basics/ [accessed 21.11.2012].

Index

Bold page numbers indicate figures, *italic* numbers indicate tables.